MODERN

lager

BEER

TECHNIQUES, PROCESSES, AND RECIPES

JACK HENDLER & JOE CONNOLLY

BREWERS PUBLICATIONS.

Brewers Publications®
A Division of the Brewers Association
PO Box 1679, Boulder, Colorado 80306-1679
BrewersAssociation.org
BrewersPublications.com

Proudly Printed in the United States of America.
10 9 8 7 6 5 4 3 2 1
ISBN-13: 978-1-938469-82-4
ISBN-10: 1-938469-82-8
EISBN: 978-1-938469-83-1

Library of Congress Cataloging-in-Publication Data

Names: Hendler, Jack, 1982- author. | Conolly, Joe, 1985- author.
Title: Modern lager beer : techniques, processes and recipes / Jack Hendler & Joe Conolly.
Description: Boulder, Colorado : Brewers Publications, [2024] | Includes
   bibliographical references and index.
Identifiers: LCCN 2023049713 (print) | LCCN 2023049714 (ebook) | ISBN
   9781938469831 (ebook) | ISBN 9781938469824 (paperback) | ISBN 1938469828
   (paperback)
Subjects: LCSH: Lager beer. | Brewing. | Home brewing.
Classification: LCC TP577 (ebook) | LCC TP577 .H456 2024 (print) | DDC
   641.87/3 23/eng/20231--dc19
LC record available at https://lccn.loc.gov/2023049713
LC ebook record available at https://lccn.loc.gov/2023049714

Publisher: Kristi Switzer
Technical Editor: Ashleigh Carter, Bierstadt Lagerhaus
Copyediting: Iain Cox
Indexing: Doug Easton
Art Direction, Cover and Interior Design, Production: Jason Smith
Cover and Interior Photos: Jason Sinn Photography

*In memory of Herb Lindtveit, a lager fanatic, a friend,
and a mentor to all at Jack's Abby.
"In Herb We Trust"*

TABLE OF CONTENTS

FOREWORD

BACK IN 2010 I DIDN'T HAVE A CLUE WHAT I WANTED TO DO
WITH MY LIFE. Thinking I might make more of my beer drinking hobby, I
bought my first brewing book, *How to Brew* by John Palmer. I made my own
lauter tun from copper piping, carried around a notebook detailing wild (by
2010's standards anyway) ingredients I wanted to use in my next batches,
and eventually found myself working at a homebrew shop. I would gather
with my friends to imbibe every style of beer I could get my hands on, taking
part in "slaughter my cellar" parties to sample beer lugged back from foreign
countries or limited domestic releases from states near and far; I wanted to
try everything.

It wasn't long before I decided that I wanted to turn my beer making hobby
into a career, so I volunteered in a brewery graining out to try and pick up
any practical knowledge that I could (I discovered I didn't know the inlet side
of a pump after all.) Like so many other fledgling brewers out there, I was
trying to be "different" and "unique," guided by barleywines, double IPAs, and
Flemish sours. I genuinely thought I wanted to be some sort of experimental
flavor genius, one of the cool kids constantly coming up with new beers. But,
as it turns out, that wasn't me at all. It became apparent early on that it was the
beer-making process that excited me the most.

At the time I became serious about making brewing a career, I was working
at a small brewery where we made all kinds of styles of beer. I was learning
the practical aspects of working in a brewery, for sure, but I had no formal
education; so, I went diving into books. I tried to consume as much knowledge
as I could—books like *Yeast*, *Malt*, and *For the Love of Hops* came to occupy

my shelves. In the head brewer, I also had a mentor who loved making lagers. I remember precisely the afternoon he told me he was going to Germany for a couple of weeks and needed someone to take care of the fermentation schedule of our Märzen; despite being the youngest brewer there, I was put in charge of it. Taking care of lager and how it changes so subtly over time, slowly and deliberately—this is when I fell in love with the process even harder. When the head brewer returned, we sat down as a team with beers he brought back. I had my first taste of an Andechser Doppelbock Dunkel, an Augustiner Lagerbier Hell, and a Spezial Rauchbier. I was hooked.

A new job at a brewery focused on German styles drove me further down a narrowing path, that of brewing traditional German ales and lagers. My free time was spent drinking beer off the tank in the basement of the Sandlot Brewery, which was known for its Hefeweizen and German-style lagers. I continued to find new books to read, most notably Greg Noonan's *New Brewing Lager Beer*; I begged my dad to help me buy Jean de Clerck's two-volume *A Textbook of Brewing*, and I was gifted a copy of Stephen Holle's *A Handbook of Basic Brewing Calculations*.

I was armed and ready with all the knowledge and practical experience I needed, but the final piece of the puzzle didn't come until 2014 when I was in Germany looking for a brewhouse to build what would eventually become Bierstadt Lagerhaus in Denver. I finally got to have my first beers in Munich at the Hirschgarten—an Augustiner Pils served *vom Fass* followed by an Augustiner Lagerbier Hell "from the wood." That was endgame. After that trip, my partner Bill Eye and I knew that we were going to narrow our focus even more and stop making ales altogether. Our brewery would be an homage to European lager, anchored by tradition and history, focused on repeatability and consistency. We poured our first beers at Bierstadt in 2016, with Slow Pour Pils, Helles, and Dunkel on the menu. This lineup and those recipes remain the same today. Making lager has now become as natural as walking for me, an instinctual cadence. Despite this level of comfort, I still know there is so much more to learn.

The first time I spoke with brewer/owner Jack Hendler (you can now add author to that list of credentials) was via Zoom as part of a random podcast. I remember I was super excited to be on a recording with him because I admired what Jack's Abby was doing over on the East Coast and, more importantly, what that was doing for lager brewing in the US generally. We had a good vibe riffing off of each other during the podcast, agreeing in most aspects and disagreeing in others, and from that moment I knew he was a kindred lager spirit. (The guest the following week on that same podcast had some other things to say about it, but Jack or I can tell you that story over a beer when you see one of us next.)

That internet meeting with Jack was the impetus that brought us together for a collaboration beer shortly after. It was one for the lager nerds, an export-style lager, employing decoction, cold fermentation, lagering, and two different strains of lager yeast (one for primary fermentation and one for krausening). The facility, care, and dedication of everyone at Jack's Abby is impressive. What makes Jack's Abby special in the industry is the brewery's commitment to pushing the language of lager into the craft mainstream while holding the door open for other brewers to join them. When you talk to Jack and Joe Connolly their pure enthusiasm for beer and lager brewing is readily apparent; why else would they go to all the trouble to coauthor a book for the masses?

As the technical editor of *Modern Lager Beer*, I got to read it before almost anyone else. I was struck by how much I learned and also by how many experiences I have shared with the authors, even though I have not taken any trips with them. Although I've taken many beer-focused trips of my own, they have inspired me to continue to connect with the people who share this passion for lager beer; to go experience those beers in their natural habitat and speak to the people who made them. Such is the impact of the knowledge imparted and experiences shared by Jack and Joe in this important book.

Modern Lager Beer is filled with revelations regarding how we brew and drink lager today, built around the stories of people who care about the future of lager brewing so much they would tell you everything they know about it. These stories are diverse and this book touches on the myriad ways lager can be made and the brewers old and new who make it. This book will not only teach you something, no matter how much you think you know, but also inspire you to seek out these drinking experiences yourself. It is one thing to read a style guideline but it's an entirely different thing to try these beers and develop an emotional connection to them.

I can see this book shaping the next generation of lager brewers and providing much-needed guidance for any brewer looking to improve and expand their lager program. I look forward to reading this book again for pleasure. It will be sat with the other must-reads on my shelf, ready to be referenced and thumbed through again and again.

Congratulations to Jack and Joe. It was an honor to be a part of this book, and I hope you, the reader, enjoy it as much as I did.

Lagerhard!

Ashleigh Carter
Head Brewer/Co-owner, Bierstadt Lagerhaus, Denver, Colorado

ACKNOWLEDGMENTS

OVER THE COURSE OF TWO YEARS, WE SPOKE WITH MORE THAN SEVENTY BREWERIES AND BEER PROFESSIONALS. All gave us valuable insight and motivation to continue this project. Many thanks to all for their generosity and hospitality.

Our colleagues at Jack's Abby Craft Lagers provided us with resources and encouragement to focus on this book. Thanks for the coverage and for rolling with all the inspiration we brought back from each trip.

Thanks to Kristi Switzer and Brewers Publications for their trust and guidance.

We couldn't have done this without our family's support and help. Thank you, Abby and Rebecca, for always holding it down.

INTRODUCTION

LAGER HAS BEEN A GLOBAL PHENOMENON SINCE ITS INTERNATIONAL EMERGENCE IN THE MIDDLE OF THE NINETEENTH CENTURY. In the 1970s, lager's mainstream dominance and reputation for blandness helped launch the American homebrew movement and, by extension, the American craft beer movement. Craft beer in the US is still dominated by the small-scale production of flavorful, interesting ales, yet a new generation of craft brewers has emerged who wish to reclaim and reframe *Lagerbier*, or "lager beer." While American craft ale continues to receive the lion's share of attention and resources, demand for well-made lager continues to grow.

American brewers can and should hone their lager brewing skills to meet this demand. In today's beer scene, with its obsessing over recipes and raw materials, lagers offer an alternative where the focus is on process and technique. In a crowded market, brewing great lager can be a point of differentiation for a brewery. For brewers brought up in an ale-obsessed industry, brewing lager can require investing more in equipment and time, and necessitates acquiring new brewing know-how, but this is less expensive and more easily achievable than one might think.

Our goal with this book is to provide practical techniques that a brewery of any size can perform to elevate the quality of its lager. We've sifted through centuries of brewing tradition with master German and American brewers to highlight the methods that make a lager world class. Along the way we spend time unpacking basic definitions and potential misconceptions about lager. (Sure, it's slowly fermented while cold, but must a lager always be crisper and cleaner than an ale?) We aim to provide context for a broader discussion about lager attributes and the processes that help shape them.

There is a nearly unlimited number of books, scientific research papers, and industry-focused publications that describe, in great detail, the science and engineering behind brewing great lager. What's often missing in this information is the real-world application of the methods described and the myriad ways that they can be applied in practically any brewery setup. We've drawn from the practical experience of generations of lager brewers to show you how to brew world-class lager in your brewery and at home.

There is an aphorism that goes, if you ask a hundred German brewers how to make a *Pilsner*, you'll get one answer: Pilsner malt and noble hops. What then differentiates these beers if the recipe is a forgone conclusion? This book will help you shape these raw ingredients and simple recipes into a beautiful whole.

When we set out to write this book, it was from two very different perspectives and backgrounds. While we use plural pronouns throughout the book, we think it's valuable to talk here about our individual perspectives to understand how we have structured it. Consider these our own personal love letters to lager.

Jack's Journey

My first memorable lager experience was a *Dunkel* at the Hofbräuhaus in Munich with my mother. Her eyes nearly popped out of her head at the size of the liter glass—a *Masskrug*—when it arrived. Mine nearly did the same at the first sip. Underneath that fluffy foam cap was a beautiful, crystal-clear, amber liquid with a depth of flavor I had never experienced before. I was hooked.

It is no surprise that the first professional recipe I wrote was for a *dunkel* lager. I carefully sourced the raw materials and obsessed over that recipe, down to stressing over the artwork and name. And while we did produce a tasty dark beer, that first attempt missed the mark of a truly great Dunkel.

My quest for that perfect Dunkel brought me to brewing school in Germany, where I was immediately drawn to the science and engineering of the brewing trade. However, when it came to the theory and practice of brewing great beer, my fellow craft brewing classmates and I struggled with our professors' rigid interpretation of "greatness" and how it could be achieved. One professor in particular used to punctuate his statements simply: "This is fact." I'll admit this mentality got me into more than one heated argument. There was a clear cultural clash between the rebellious craft contingent and the strict, structured view of our European counterparts. Here was a repository of years of technique and tradition being brashly challenged by some young American know-it-alls. Since our very existence was a challenge to "corporate" beer in the US, we were used to challenging conventional wisdom.

Eventually my brothers and I would use that same Dunkel recipe for the first ever batch of Jack's Abby Craft Lagers beer, which we called Red Tape. Brewed on our original two-vessel infusion system, it was much improved on my first attempt; brewing school hadn't been a waste of time. Yet hindsight shows that it too failed to live up to the original.

It's taken a decade to even come close to replicating that first memorable lager with what is now our winter seasonal release. Thinking back to my brewing professor's insistence that some techniques were simply required for the production of traditional-style lager beer, I have gradually come to better appreciate his perspective. In fact, we brewed better beer once we relied upon his experience and interpretation of brewing. Though our recipes and raw materials have not changed, our understanding of German lager tradition and its methods has grown tenfold.

While brewing school laid a solid foundation, much of what I learned came while traveling and visiting breweries. Most of the brewers that I have met in my travels to Germany have been cautiously willing to answer my questions about their methods. At first I thought their reserved nature might be due to my status as an outsider, or some fear of industrial espionage. In reality, the concepts and processes that fascinate me as an American brewer are simply elementary to most German brewers.

Brewers in Germany train for years at brewing school, followed by years of apprenticeship in breweries that have operated for generations. While the technology has certainly improved, the objectives and philosophy of brewing has changed very little. These concepts have been ingrained in the psyche of these brewers and have become second nature. As a father of curious children I can now empathize with how my German hosts probably felt answering a series of seemingly elementary questions from an American brewer.

As an independent American lager brewery, Jack's Abby is uniquely positioned to observe the natural tension between the freewheeling craft beer spirit and the strict rules and laws from which it habitually rebels. Lost somewhere in between is an understanding of the processes and traditions that have contributed to the evolution and resilience of German lager beer culture and production.

Joe's Journey

My path to lager is much different than Jack's, probably being more like the journey taken by many other American beer enthusiasts. In fact, my first Hofbräuhaus Dunkel was likely consumed during research for this book. My first loves were those loud, huge American and Belgian artisanal beers that shocked my palate into submission. A wave of West Coast IPA crested next, pinning my palate with lovely bitterness. And I do pity anyone who hasn't gotten lost in a beautifully complex barrel-aged beer once or twice. These beers got me homebrewing, however amateurly.

Of course, the palate is a weird and wonderful instrument, and I almost wore mine out. The humble lager was there waiting on the other side. Yes, the same lager that they warned me about, the same style sold in bulk that had bored me into seeking out all those wild flavors. I'm not sure when it clicked, but when I realized the herculean effort that goes into creating these simple beers—these hardest to make, easiest to drink beers—the story and the beer hooked me for good.

Throughout the writing process, as we've shared beers with fellow brewers across the globe, I've had an awakening to the culture of lager: how and where it's served, who's drinking it, and why it is worth obsessing over. The story of lager is one of devotion and belief. If it were a religious experience, one of our hymns would certainly be "the future is lager."

Yet, to paraphrase one great lager brewer, great conversations are not *about* beer, great conversations happen *over* beer. Alongside the technical material we present in the pages that follow, we endeavor to relate some of these conversations. What emerges are vignettes of a culture that welcomes lager brewers and their craft, from breweries packed into city blocks to those perched on the edge of cornfields.

Why We Wrote This Book

For the average consumer in the US, years of brilliant advertising has positioned lager as a light-colored, low-flavored, highly carbonated mass-market beverage. Even for knowledgeable craft consumers, lagers are often seen as less "crafty," perhaps something to enjoy between other, higher-strength beers. Well-executed lager usually fails to incite the same hype as the next great American craft ale trend.

Even if American consumers aren't (yet) lining up for Dunkels or Dortmunders, there is still reason to be optimistic about the future of craft lager in the US. Indeed, more and more attention is being paid to this once overlooked category, as brewers try their hands at brewing *Kellerbiers* and dry-hopped Pilsners. Consumers seem increasingly willing to reward this choice.

And yet when American craft brewers create lagers, they often do so without changing any of the processes or brewing techniques they use for their ales. They may take time to source European malts and hops, but less attention is paid to the technicalities of brewing and conditioning. As a result, while American craft ale fermentation is at the absolute cutting edge of quality, American craft lager is lagging woefully behind. Part of the issue stems from the costs associated with brewing in more traditional ways, but much of the disconnect stems simply from a lack of education and experience. Considering the pipeline between homebrewing and future professional brewing in the US, the significant challenges that come with brewing great lager at home likely also contributes to this disconnect.

Most brewers will state that their aim is to make great beer. But consider that greatness can often come at the expense of quality. While unique, bespoke products with interesting provenance can captivate a consumer in a specific moment, it is quality and consistency over time that defines the truly great lagers of the world. The techniques and traditions used to create these world-class beers can be applied to breweries of any size, with the right knowledge and experience.

In this book we try to answer the question, what makes a great lager beer? One of the most general answers, and one that guides our approach to this book, is process. Over and over again, lager brewers emphasized to us the importance of their process to the finished quality of their beer. We explore the many techniques and processes used in the oldest and greatest lager breweries in the world, and how a new generation of American craft lager producers are applying those techniques in their brewhouses. We do our best to unpack which of these techniques is tradition for tradition's sake, and which can have a measurable impact on beer quality.

We also explore raw materials and their impact on lager. In a market dominated by hop varietals, the impacts of malt, yeast, and water are often overlooked. In these most "naked" of beers, the world's best lager brewers keep a constant eye on the agronomic side of the industry and how the techniques of maltsters, hop growers, and yeast scientists can manifest in a finished beer. This is an area of particular interest to us American craft brewers as we experiment with North American-grown raw materials and see their impact on classic Continental lager styles.

Perhaps it is the sum of all these considerations that makes a truly great lager beer. We aim to suss out which techniques, processes, and ingredients can best improve any brewer's lager. We also explore the many boundary-pushing ideas being applied to traditional lager production in modern brewhouses, from adding spices and unmalted grains, to fermenting and conditioning in oak.

There are many ways to make a world-class lager. Join us with a pint as we explore that world and ponder what the future might bring to the humble lager beer.

A Word to the Homebrewers

For the homebrewer, the challenges presented by brewing lager will be similar to those faced by the earliest lager brewers. Temperature control, refrigeration, oxidation, and handling pressurized vessels can be vexing to even the most experienced brewer.

Some of the technologies we will cover in later chapters have easy adaptations for use in the home, while others may be overly complex, complicated, and expensive. We'll discuss workarounds where applicable and provide guidelines for the risks involved.

It's important to note that many of the techniques we discuss provide the opportunity for incremental improvement. For every example of a lager brewery using one of these techniques to brew world-class beer, you can find brewers making world-class beer a different way. Understanding these techniques and how to employ them will help you brew to a specific goal, but there are often many paths to that single destination. We hope to provide you with the opportunity to choose a path that is right for you.

1

WHAT EXACTLY IS A LAGER?

Defining Lager Beer

LAGER, OR LAGER BEER, IS THE WORLD'S MOST CONSUMED TYPE OF BEER AND IS AVAILABLE ON EVERY CONTINENT AND IN NEARLY EVERY COUNTRY IN THE WORLD. Many of its consumers would define the lager that fills most bottles and cans as fizzy, pale-yellow beer. To professionals and enthusiasts alike, lager is understood as beer that is cold fermented with a lager yeast strain and matured for a relatively lengthy period.

Myths, misunderstandings, and mass-marketing have all combined to cloud the reality of lager, even among professionals. Our collective image of lager as crisp, bright, dry, and refreshing is the direct result of the ubiquity of industrial "Pilsner-style" beers in the United States. The range of styles found within the lager pantheon is actually quite broad, ranging from the pale and bitter to the dark and sweet.

Lager yeast's close association with pale lagers has led to the widely held belief that lager yeast fermentations are always clean and neutral. The beers they produce are often held up as "naked," perfect canvases upon which any flaws are immediately evident. While fermentations carried out with lager yeasts are known to produce beers with lower levels of esters (fruity flavors), fusel alcohols, phenols, or other notable ale yeast fermentation characteristics, it is a mistake to believe that lager yeast will always process raw materials while leaving no trace of its existence.

The nuances of lager fermentation are abundant. In many classic lagers from around the world, yeast-derived "off-flavors" are today defining elements of their flavor profiles. The best lager fermentations create complex, balanced beers with unique, often overlooked, fermentation characteristics. The balance of sulfur compounds, esters, carbonation, and the base raw materials all work in tandem to create a compelling and characterful beer.

Steve Holle of Missouri's Kansas City Bier Company believes that the "clean" categorization of lager is a particular misnomer in the modern brewhouse. While it may have once been true that lager's colder fermentation temperatures reduced contamination, today a brewery has a higher probability of brewing a "clean" beer with a neutral ale yeast than a lager yeast. One study group, having sequenced the DNA of 157 industrial beers sold as lager, found that at least ten *Saccharomyces cerevisiae* (ale) yeast strains were currently being used for their production (Gallone et al. 2016).

Yeast fermentation is only the beginning of what defines the production of great lager. How lager is processed has evolved over centuries. Unique brew-house procedures and cellaring steps combine with raw materials in ways that may surprise ale brewers. Examples of characterful historic styles that have inspired many mass-marketed lagers can still be enjoyed across central Europe and, increasingly, in American craft breweries and drinking establishments. Indeed, while adjunct lager continues to make up the lion's share of global beer consumption—that is, industrially mass-produced beers brewed using barley alongside corn, rice, or simple sugar sources—craft lagers that take inspiration from those central European classics continue to gain ground.

When we set out to write this book, we set out with our own biases unknowingly intact. Our appreciation and love for the rustic lagers of Franconia and the sparkling *Helles* of Bavaria was built into our business at Jack's Abby Craft Lagers; in our minds those styles represented the pinnacle of quality and authenticity for lager. The Bavarians, who are widely credited with inventing *Lagerbier*, certainly seemed to support our bias. Yet, in some ways, this perspective is only slightly less reductive than the idea that all lager beer is industrial Pilsner.

Bavarians' pride in beer is justified both by their prodigious consumption and their brewers' outsized influence on modern lager beer. Brewing beer to be consumed in massive quantities surely influenced these brewers to approach the flavor profile of their golden lagers with drinkability in mind. The fact that the first brewmaster at Pilsner Urquell was a Bavarian is used by some to subtly suggest that the world-famous Pilsner (literally "of Pilsen," which is a Czech city) is itself a derivative of German beer culture.

Czech beer culture and consumption may superficially resemble that of the Bavarians, but the lager in Czech glasses is completely unique. Brewed with Czech malt and hops, usually open fermented, and always decocted, Czech pale lager has a distinctly high extract and pronounced bitterness. This balancing act between sweet and bitter is meant to encourage repeat consumption. These full-flavored lagers have next to nothing in common with adjunct pale lager beers.

In the US, beer brewing was first imported by European settlers as a domestic activity. The first generations of industrialized brewers in America were German and Czech immigrants in the late nineteenth century. These brewers famously used central European family names and places of origin to market their products to rapidly expanding immigrant communities, adapting their traditional techniques to new raw materials along the way. They formed the first trade association for brewers in their new homeland, at first conducting their business entirely in German. These brewers gradually overcame the xenophobia of their fellow Americans, introducing them to new interpretations of Pilsner and *Bock* (Ogle 2006, 25–34; Benbow 2018, under "Saloon Culture").

From a handful of common origins, each discreet lager tradition has grown into its own unique branch of the lager beer family. Comparing all these styles today is revealing. No matter their historic origins, they have evolved into distinct and delicious styles. A full glass of fresh lager can be appreciated as a harmony between the history of the style and the craftsmanship of brewers and tapsters alike. Each part informs and is informed by the other.

Our research has yielded an appreciation for the many traditions and techniques that make up the mosaic of modern lager styles. The twists and turns these styles have taken throughout history to arrive where they are today are particularly interesting, though by necessity some imagination is required to consider what lager would have been like in centuries past.

Lager is no longer uniquely Bavarian, Czech, or American. Nor is it always crisp, clean, and refined. By sheer quantity, most of it consumed in the world is adjunct lager. But with a brewer's care and attention a lager becomes an elegant, captivating glass of beer.

Whither Lager?

Beer's industrialization fostered a special relationship between the brewer and the customer, wherein the brewer became beholden to their audience's expectations of consistency. As these audiences grew, so too did the pressure on breweries to tame beer's agrarian origins in a bid to sustain commercial success. And it has done so with an ever-expanding marketing and advertising budget that has only confused lager's origins more thoroughly.

Marketing has positioned lager beer as traditional, wholesome, and pure, even as these beers have changed drastically over time. The reality of modern industrial brewing contrasts sharply with the "traditional" methods marketed by the world's biggest lager producers. That the terms used in these marketing campaigns are interchangeable with those used by traditional producers further confuses lager's origins. Can a Pilsner truly be called such if it is triple-hopped and brewed in Milwaukee?

The Major Lager Traditions: A Quick Tour

There are many fine works that cover lager's illustrious history in greater detail. For our purposes, it is important to acknowledge the historical context of lager and the many techniques that evolved alongside it.

For all the centuries of tradition flaunted by lager breweries, it's useful to remember that lager is one of the youngest traditional styles of beer. The single strains we know today were only isolated in the late nineteenth century by scientists at Carlsberg. And the ubiquity of pale lager only truly came to fruition over the second half of the twentieth century. In lager's relatively short history, this remarkable beverage has grown and changed considerably alongside the processes and raw materials used to make it.

Time is the single ingredient that unites lager beers throughout history: the word *Lager* is descended from the German word for storehouse. Long, cold fermentation and maturation has been understood as a positive for beer quality for centuries. For Bavarians in particular, two sixteenth-century laws laid the foundation for methods that continue to shape lager today.

The *Reinheitsgebot*, or beer purity law, has remained in the beer drinker's consciousness for centuries. The purity law famously limits the ingredients of beer to malt, hops, water, and (in later iterations) yeast and has lived on in part as a marketing tool used by breweries globally. Economic impact was at the heart of the Reinheitsgebot, as it limited the production of beer to specific taxable raw materials, set prices for specific types of beer, and protected local agriculture and industry. It also protected a royal monopoly on brewing beer with wheat.

For modern German brewers, the Reinheitsgebot poses some significant unintended consequences, complicating otherwise standard brewing practices such as mashing programs, fermentation plans, beer carbonation, and mash pH adjustment. These limitations have significantly shaped how German brewers process beer, and have turned seemingly simple brewing require-ments into complicated, sometimes convoluted, workarounds. While it serves as a handy example of the regulated and regimented nature of German beer philosophy, the Reinheitsgebot was arguably less important for the develop-ment of Lagerbier than the *Brauordnung*.

Enacted in 1539, the Brauordnung required brewers to produce beer only between September and April, borrowing an idea that had already been enacted by some Bavarian cities. It was understood that beer brewed during these periods was less likely to sour, and so a correlation between cooler tem-peratures and better-quality beer was thus recognized and codified. Significant resources were required for beer storage and cooling during the warmer sum-mer months, including extensive cave systems and ice harvesting operations. These pressures limited the size of operations, encouraging the proliferation of smaller breweries.

The Brauordnung marked a turning point from ale brewing toward lager beer production. In those cool cellars, something new was growing. Yeast strains that could survive the cold temperatures won out over time, shaping lager yeast into its modern form along the way. While its primordial origins are still being researched, modern lager yeast emerged from these cold Bavarian cellars. The various challenges associated with brewing beer for extended maturation also laid the foundations for a variety of techniques still used in modern lager production, from decoction mashing to krausening.

Though these techniques have survived, the lagers produced in the mid-sixteenth century have not. These early lagers would have been dark, sweet, likely smokey, and meant for local consumption in opaque stoneware. The majority of lager from this period would have shared much more in common with a Bamberg-style *Rauchbier* than a dry, golden Helles. Over time, these early lagers evolved into the ancestors of styles still recognizable today. For example, the popularity and reputation of the strong, dark beer from Einbeck was such that a copycat lager called *Bock* became a Bavarian specialty.

TO THE PALE

While the modern perspective on lager holds Bavaria in high esteem, in medieval times this landlocked nation was a bit of a backwater. Trading leagues, the Church, and various royal families competed for influence and power until the formation of a unified German state in the nineteenth century. The brewing industry was a local one that built itself to serve its constituents with the raw materials at hand.

By the seventeenth century, Britain was a global powerhouse by comparison. Industrializing British breweries were serving an increasingly far-flung population by shipping their beer around the world. The introduction of coke-fired maltings was an early key development: the lighter colored, less smoky malt allowed for the descriptor "pale" to be applied to a new style of beer.

In the mid-nineteenth century, Austrian and German brewers took British malting technology back home to create new pale malts. These lighter-colored base malts were used to develop Vienna lagers and amber-colored styles that would have held novel visual appeal to consumers drinking in newly affordable translucent glassware. These styles may have been seen as revolutionary to consumers used to drinking dark, murky lager, but they would soon be outdone.

Pilsner's explosion onto the beer scene is well-documented, as it is the founding story of Plzeňský Prazdroj, a.k.a. Pilsner Urquell. Josef Groll, a famously cantankerous Bavarian brewer, introduced his Pilsner beer to the world in 1842, almost instantaneously changing the beer landscape of the world. Pale, hoppy, and snappy, Pilsner-style beer was the immediate envy of Bavarian brewers, who would pridefully develop the golden Helles in response. Brewers around the world would follow suit, eventually leading to the present-day hegemony of pale lager.

Another fine example of this shift can be found in the US. Spirits, ciders, and English-style ales were the drinks most consumed by Americans until the middle of the nineteenth century, when lager was first introduced from central Europe. Immigrants brought with them the knowledge, experience, and taste for lager beer, yet they found difficulty producing them with the raw materials at hand. Bridging the gap between traditional brewing methods and the bountiful harvest of rice and corn available at their disposal, they paved the way for a new style of American adjunct lager. Today, it remains the majority of the beer sold in the US.

Breweries like August Schell Brewing Company in New Ulm, Minnesota, were situated near rivers for easy access to ice and built with ample underground storage for extended cold maturation. The techniques of old-world lager brewing were adapted for use with North American barley, corn, and rice. From the 1870s to the 1910s, a campaign for an "American Reinheitsgebot" was waged by maltsters and barley growers looking to keep a monopoly on American beer grain, protesting the "adulteration" of beer in various Congressional hearings (Greg Casey, pers. comm.). Luckily for the story of American lager beer, adjunct lager won the day.

There is no single source of an "authentic" or "true" lager style; rather, traditions that have shaped lager continue to do so today. While many of the ideas and processes that we'll talk about in this book hark back to centuries-old practices, modern lager has little in common with the lager of a hundred years ago, and nearly nothing in common with lager from two centuries ago. Modern lager production is state of the art; while it may pull inspiration from the past, it bears little resemblance to its antecedents.

BAVARIAN LAGERS TODAY

Like in most countries today, in Germany pale lager beers dominate the market. Though there are upward of 5,000 beer brands produced in Germany, there are only approximately 1,500 breweries, about half of which are located in the state of Bavaria.

As the capital of Bavaria and home of the world-famous Oktoberfest, Munich looms large in the mind of modern lager enthusiasts. Yet Munich is dominated by only six large breweries, four of which are owned by two global corporations. All of them brew the pale golden lager, Helles, though the relative quality of each is a subject of debate. Southern Bavarian beer today is dominated by Helles, which easily outsells the darker Munich Dunkel. The style is so popular in Bavaria that at least two Munich-area breweries, Giesinger Bräu and the Bayerische Staatsbrauerei Weihenstephan, each have two distinct Helles in their portfolios. Likewise, the state-owned Hofbräuhaus and the independent Augustiner-Bräu both serve incredible amounts of delicious, bright Helles in their expansive beer halls and gardens.

New-generation "craft" breweries have begun to open in the past few years, and they too are producing fine Helles.

Modern Helles is a study of restraint—a bright, soft, airy beer that earns the descriptor "naked," where any flaws are immediately evident. This reflects a progression toward the drier end of the flavor spectrum, representing shifting consumer expectations and an effort on the part of breweries to compete with industrial lager. Some versions open with a snappy, attention-grabbing note of yeast-derived sulfur that is prized by some lager brewers and drinkers.

Though it has been going out of fashion for generations, the delightful Munich Dunkel is a challenge to the "crispy" lager stereotype. With pronounced malt character and depth and an amber to red-brown hue, Dunkel offers both malt complexity and drinkability. It is easy to imagine that this drinkability has increased over time as tastes have favored lighter, drier beers. Stronger, darker, and more complex lager styles are still to be found, of course. Among these "special beers" is the *Doppelbock*, famous for being a fine substitute for bread during Lenten fasts. History has seen these beers grow lighter and drier as higher quality raw materials are used along with better control of mashing parameters to affect attenuation.

Travel a little outside of Munich, however, and the beer landscape changes considerably. To the north, the land of Franconia is officially still part of the Bavarian state, though its residents often bristle at being called "Bavarian." Indeed, the Franconians are a culturally distinct people, with their own dialect and a rich and complicated history. As outsiders, it's difficult to understand the cultural and linguistic distinctions between the two groups, so we'll confine ourselves to comment only on Franconian beer. Luckily, the beer speaks for itself.

The breadth of beer styles in Franconia is staggering. This is perhaps unsurprising for a region once served by communal village breweries, each of which would have produced its own distinct beer. While the communal brewhouse tradition lives on to the east as *Zoiglbier* (or simply *Zoigl*), there is an incredible density of breweries large and small in Franconia today. The Franconian village of Aufseß in the Bayreuth District holds the Guinness World Record for most breweries per capita, with its 1,200 residents able to choose between the town's four breweries.

While there is no single style that dominates Franconian lagers, they are commonly more rustic, yeasty, full-bodied, and darker in color than Helles lagers. Though they may defy easy definition, these varied and interesting lagers generally display an unrefined, less polished character than many mass-marketed beer brands. Many are sold simply as lager or *Vollbier* ("full beer," which, unhelpfully, actually means a beer of standard strength), though other breweries use terms like *Kellerbier*, *ungespundet*, and *Landbier*. Some are deeply smoky and intense, while others are simple, medium-bodied, gold- to amber-colored lagers.

Many of the breweries in the region are hundreds of years old, and so use a complicated variety of older technology and equipment. Some breweries that have modernized will still intentionally use a hybrid of older technologies to preserve the rustic character of their beers. Ben Neidhart of OEC Brewing in Connecticut shared his personal philosophy about beer: "All great products have flaws that make them interesting." In the case of Franconia this certainly holds true.

ČESKÉ PIVO (CZECH BEER)

What holds true for the varied lagers of Franconia may also be equally applicable to the lagers of Bohemia in what is now the Czech Republic, or Czechia. The Czech beer market today is dominated by three large breweries and their associated brands: Pilsner Urquell, Budweiser Budvar,[1] and Staropramen. Before Pilsner Urquell's introduction in 1842, 90% of the beer brewed in the Kingdom of Bohemia was ale. Within a few decades, 90% of the beer brewed was lager. Today, ordering a Pilsner, "*prazdroj*," or "P-U" in Czechia means only Pilsner Urquell, uniformly served in a dimpled goblet with a two-inch cap of fine, dense foam.

Plenty of Czech pale lagers rather famously display the trait of diacetyl. This buttery, tongue-coating sensation is considered a part of the flavor profile of these beers, and ranges in intensity from the subtle to the overwhelming. But there are many, many interesting Czech lagers besides the few world-famous brands, and not all of them feature diacetyl. They are often named and ordered by degrees Plato, as is the case at Únětický Pivovar: the brewery's year-round offerings are 10°, 10.7°, and 12°, all pale lagers around or below 5% ABV. Darker lagers can be ordered by color, like a dark *cerne* (black) or an amber-colored *polotmavý* (half-dark). In certain specialty draft locations, lager can be ordered with a specific amount of foam ranging from the all-foam *mlíko* to the half-foam *šnyt*.

---

[1]   Budweiser Budvar is a Czech brewing company that first gave the world Budweiser. It is unrelated to the American Budweiser brewed by Anheuser-Busch. Due to ongoing trademark disputes, Budvar's Budweiser brand is sold in the US as Czechvar.

České pivo is a geographic appellation that protects the cultural significance of Czech beer. Beers that bear this mark are double decocted, brewed with at least 80% Czech ingredients, and fermented in two stages, with a primary fermentation often in an open vessel and a longer secondary fermentation in a closed pressurized vessel. Beer produced this way generally has a higher proportion of unfermented extract, which is balanced by firm hop bitterness. Higher levels of extract also make this style of beer susceptible to spoilage, necessitating pasteurization by those Czech breweries that serve global markets. Unpasteurized Pilsner Urquell is only sold at tank pubs, where the beer is kept cold throughout the supply chain all the way to bag-lined vessels at the pub.

The story of České pivo is thus inextricably intertwined with the raw materials of this resource-rich land and its politically fraught history. Moravian two-row spring barley is prized by brewers for its flavor and performance. This historically authentic ingredient remains a part of Czechia's modern beer scene through its use by the Pilsner Urquell brewery, where it is still malted on site today. Where current international quality guidelines give preference to more highly modified malts, the lower levels of modification in these classic Czech malts encourages decoction mashing and results in higher residual extract.

Hops are required to balance the higher extract. In the eyes of many, Czech hops are the finest in the world. The Czech hop-growing region of Žatec gives its name to the Saaz varietal (*Saaz* being the German name for Žatec), known for its fine and delicate bitterness. Though other varietals are grown in the three main hop-growing regions of Czechia, Saaz is the most renowned. It has played prominent roles in the advertising campaigns of breweries like Anheuser-Busch, who at one point claimed to use only "the finest Bohemian Saaz hops" in their American-brewed Budweiser lager. Bohemians have long protected this crop, in the Middle Ages going so far as to threaten death for those caught smuggling roots out of the region.

Czechia's relatively recent period of isolation from the Western world plays a part in the uniquely idiosyncratic nature of modern Czech beer. The insular Czech beer industry adapted locally-grown and processed raw materials specifically for the styles being produced by Czech brewers. Methods and means of production were built around using these raw materials. Czech beer was still being fermented in pitch-lined wooden vessels until relatively recently, when modernization and investment brought stainless steel vessels within reach of brewers. Other advancements were not welcomed as warmly, however.

Czech brewing legend Jan Šuráň, now of Břevnovský klášterní pivovar, recounted how, after the Velvet Revolution, many breweries started to experiment with newer brewing techniques like infusion mashing and steam kettles. Beers with lighter color and less bitterness were quickly introduced to the Czech market and were met just as quickly with angry opposition. The sudden changes had left consumers behind and most brewers quickly reverted back to the old ways of multistep decoctions, direct-fire kettles, high IBUs, and high extract. A sampling experiment performed since has found that over 90% of Czech consumers prefer double-decocted beers to single-decocted or infusion mashed beers (Jan Šuráň, pers. comm.). Whether this trend continues over future generations remains to be seen.

Beer's deep integration into Czech society has left its mark on the language and culture. Czech beer drinkers consume more beer per capita than anyone else in the world, by a factor of around 30% (sorry, Austrians). At some pubs, the establishment's tapster may be noted on the menu alongside its chef. Writer and resident Evan Rail believes that this appreciation for the labor of the beer industry is due in part to the population's close relationship with it: many current residents of Prague once participated in "hop brigades" during hop harvests in their university days. The Czech language itself is casually littered with idioms and couplets about beer and its role in society, for example, "Kde se pivo pije, tam se dobře žije" (Where beer is drunk, life is good).

A modern appreciation for beer's role in Czech culture can be gained simply by observation. In most places, you can witness beer being served carefully, uniformly, and constantly. A dimpled glass of pale lager topped with the same two fingers of wet foam seems to be the most popular beverage wherever you go in Prague, from breweries and pubs to Indian restaurants. Pale lager has even made inroads at the famed U Fleků pub and brewery, which for hundreds of years only served a single dark lager. Its (somewhat controversial) new pale lager is, by some accounts, an attempt to win back a local audience it has ceded to tourists over the years.

Even in a beer culture as rooted in tradition as Czechia's, progressive lagers are on the rise. Small breweries are exploring the boundaries of *světlý ležák* (pale lager) in particular, with an eye toward an even more hop-forward take on the style. Some that we sampled in 2022 approached IPA territory by strength and bitterness. But more importantly, what makes these beers still unique, still so inherently Czech, is the adherence to brewing practices that many other breweries might regard as outdated and time-consuming.

AMERICAN LAGER: THE OLD GUARD AND THE NEW

Beer in the US is a tale of two very different industries. A few large companies produce adjunct lager brands in huge breweries, which represent most of the beer sold in the country. While these beers are remarkably consistent, it is a consistency of unremarkable character. The thousands of craft breweries that make up the remaining share of beer sold in the US are best known for ale fermentations, though an increasing minority are brewing lager as well. Some of these smaller breweries brew all-malt lager of extremely high quality.

Prohibition had and still has a lasting and profound impact on the American brewing industry. The more bitter, fuller-flavored beers that were popular before Prohibition mostly disappeared when the law took effect. The breweries that survived Prohibition had to market their products to a generation weaned on sweet soda, and they adjusted their products accordingly to fit shifting consumer palates. Consolidation, mergers, and acquisitions reduced the overall number of breweries in America to its lowest level in the 1980s. Some historical labels once produced by other breweries were kept alive after this consolidation, nostalgia still accessible today via brands like National Bohemian and Hamm's.

Large industrial lager breweries are not the focus of our book, so we will not spend much time analyzing their processes. We won't address high-gravity brewing, dilution water practices, pasteurization, or any of the other ways these breweries chase efficiencies. The small handful of lager breweries that survived Prohibition and remained independent do offer glimpses into US lager's historic past, and so attract our attention. We will address using corn and rice with an eye toward pre-Prohibition American beer styles. Schell's, Spoetzl Brewery (Shiner Beer), and F.X. Matt are examples of such breweries.

The American lagers we will spend the most time on are those being produced by craft breweries across the country. Many of these breweries produce world-class examples of traditional styles, some of which have come to eclipse their inspiration. Such is the case with Dortmunder Export, a style whose popularity in Germany peaked in the 1970s but lives on in fine form in American examples brewed by Washington's Chuckanut Brewery and Ohio's Great Lakes Brewing Company.

Of course, true to the craft beer spirit, American craft lager brewers continue to create styles of their own. Hoppy lager, *foeder*-fermented Pilsner, and novel adjuncts and additives are some of the more obvious ways lager brewers are pushing the envelope. But by judiciously applying traditional techniques and methodology in the modern brewhouse, American craft lager producers are also using elements from lager's past to shepherd it into the future.

Figure 1.1. Ted Marti in front of the historic brewhouse at Schell's in Ulm, Minnesota.

Drinkability in Lager

Lager brewers around the world aspire to create lagers that are not only delicious, but also *drinkable*. While not every lager is designed to earn this description, it is remarkable how much consideration lager brewers give this seemingly subjective concept.

Drinkability has been studied and debated throughout lager's written history. A 1937 American brewing "handybook" by the father-and-son team of Robert and Arnold Spencer Wahl presents an amusing anecdote regarding the German word *Süffigkeit* (roughly, "tastiness" or drinkability). In the anecdote, town leaders don ceremonial pants and sit on a bench soaked in beer and proceed to drink five steins. The beer is pronounced to be *süffig* if the bench sticks to their bottoms upon standing up. Those wishing to determine Süffigkeit while remaining dry are advised to finish a glass of beer and see if they want another (Wahl and Wahl [1937] 2014, 133–136).

The idea that one glass leads to another is an important, if less than scientific, aim of lager brewers. Dusan Kwiatkowski of Live Oak Brewing Company in Austin, Texas, regularly assesses his beers with what he calls a "six-pack test," taking home a box of one of their lagers and seeing if one beer leads to the next. And while the ceremonial pants stay dry today, German brewers do spend time and effort working on the Süffigkeit of their beers. Yet, if the test of Süffigkeit is simply whether one glass leads to another, what gives a beer this quality is indeed subjective. Some brewers believe bitterness or sulfur help accentuate the drinkability of their lagers. For others, a lean body and a snappy finish are what drive Süffigkeit.

For Czech brewers, *pitelnost* (drinkability) seems to be a balancing act between the body of the beer and its bitterness. More than a few Czech brewers have derided German lagers as naked and empty; ironically describing the same "crispness" some Germans might associate with Süffigkeit. For the Czech palate, pitelnost seems to be achieved by a balance of a full-bodied sweetness with a firm, assertive bitterness.

Drinkability is part of the story of American light (or "lite") beer, albeit with less nuance. By stripping beer of body, flavor, and character, brewers of light beer chased the widest possible audience. This approach conflates the concept of drinkability with flavor impact—meaning that if a beer has more flavor impact, it is inherently less drinkable. The fact that these beers are also low in alcohol also drives how many are required to have the same effect as full-strength beers. This is, cynically, a type of drinkability forced upon the consumer, and a reason that these beers are sold by the case.

Lager as Process-Driven Beer

Brewing lager is an art driven by processes, particularly the processes of fermentation and maturation. This is one reason why lager brewers spend so much of their time talking about time and temperature, two of lager brewing's most impactful variables. World-class lager brewers like Lisa Allen from Heater Allen Brewing and Gold Dot Beer in McMinnville, Oregon, often cite time as the single most important ingredient for their beers.

Well-resourced industrial breweries have found ways to quickly and efficiently brew lager in timeframes that resemble ale fermentations. While this streamlining may come at the cost of flavor, character, and complexity, the resulting gains in efficiency can be incentive enough. Most craft brewers we have talked to aspire to brew complex, characterful lagers that have more in common with classic European styles than modern adjunct lager. The time and resources needed for this can often be intimidating or seemingly impossible to achieve for smaller craft brewers more familiar with brewing ales.

Learning the specific techniques associated with brewing lager, like decoction mashing, is inherent in the education and training of many Bavarian and Czech brewers. It's reasonable to point out that traditional and delicious lagers and ales are created all over the world using simple single-infusion mashes. Brewers that have success with these methods may balk at the idea of introducing more complicated and expensive techniques into their processes. Why overthink it, after all?

Many of the traditional processes associated with lager production have a substantial sensory impact. Understanding these processes and their individual effects is what sets apart many of the best craft lager producers in the world. While it may be second nature for German and Czech brewers, it requires creative thinking to cherry-pick these processes for use in breweries not designed for their implementation. Progressive lager brewers choose to implement these traditional techniques to take advantage of their sensory impact. This is sometimes presented as historical curiosity, or as an effort to be traditional or authentic—it is an acknowledgement that lager has changed considerably, even within our lifetimes. These processes were developed with different raw materials in mind and work differently with modern ingredients. By combining old-world methods with modern raw materials, brewers are creating something new altogether.

Raw materials are certainly linked to the processes that create lager, even if comparatively little time is spent talking about them. Modern malt quality has had a huge impact on the mashing process. A worldwide marketplace for hops opens the door to endless experimentation with first wort hopping, cool pool hopping,[2] and dry hopping. A growing industry of lager yeast providers offers a multitude of fermentation options. All combine to increase the opportunity to create unique and flavorful lagers.

Some brewers feel that a focus on raw materials is the domain of ale brewers, while lager brewers are more focused on traditional methods and time spent in tank. For ale brewers, bringing lager yeast into their breweries is itself a form of experimentation. Craft brewers free from a "traditional" mindset are brewing complex, characterful lagers with atypical and interesting raw materials like fruit, spices, and lactose. Modern lager brewers are also experimenting with fermenting, maturing, and serving their beers using oak, albeit with a nod to the significant historical roots of these methods.

We have seen lager breweries begin to be more assertive and proactive about communicating their efforts to the consumer. At Goldfinger Brewing Company in Illinois, where owner and brewer Tom Beckmann brews traditional and progressive Czech- and Polish-style beers, the mash regimen for each beer is listed on the menu alongside the style and strength. Slow pours and the proliferation of side-pull faucets also help communicate that these seemingly simple beers can be premium products requiring considerable effort to brew and serve correctly.

Rather than dogmatically applying methods from the world's classic lager traditions in search of authenticity, we believe that modern lager brewers can thoughtfully use traditional methods in search of flavor and character. We will explore the costs, benefits, risks, and rewards offered by these methods. By interviewing brewers from around the world, we aim to provide real-world applications for these methods in any type of brewery.

One of the pioneers of American craft lager production, Will Kemper of Chuckanut Brewery in Washington, sums lager up this way: "It is the sum of subtle considerations. If you add all these slight things up, you make better beer."

---

2   Cool pool hopping refers to adding hops into the whirlpool after the wort has been cooled to below 180°F (82°C). This allows for hot side extraction of hop aroma and flavor without the associated bitterness.

The Old and the New

Tucked into a neat, tree-lined college campus outside of Munich in the town of Freising, one of the world's famous breweries is built into the side of a small hill. Old breweries were typically built this way to use gravity for moving beer and for cold storage using caves dug into the hill. And this is an old brewery. Being able to trace the origins of brewing on the site to 1040 AD, Bayerische Staatsbrauerei Weihenstephan lays claim to being the oldest existing brewery in the world.

Today, the state-owned Weihenstephan is world-renowned for the quality of its beer, perhaps most notably the Original Helles and vibrant Hefeweißbier. There is some irony in considering these beers "old-school" because, under the veneer of its historic origins, Weihenstephan is today one of the most technically advanced breweries in the world.

In the arch-ceilinged quarters where monks once resided, the Technical University of Munich (TUM) now operates a state-of-the-art food and beverage laboratory. Brewers from around the world send samples here to identify infections and other brewhouse issues. The brewery itself is able to take samples of its beer from around the globe and use genetic testing to determine the origins of any beer spoilage organisms. A huge freezer keeps samples of pure strains of the world's brewing and distilling yeasts, including the origins of the "34/70" strain used by many of the world's lager brewers.

The Weihenstephaner brewery bridges its historical origins with its present-day progressive practices and modernization. The large cellar of fully modern stainless steel vessels occupies a portion of a vast, old underground cave system long used to cellar beer. Samples taken off the tank reveal wonderful, thoughtful beer with character and depth.

In Prague, the Břevnovský klášterní pivovar sv. Vojtěcha (Břevnov Monastery Brewery of St. Vojtěcha) boasts a brewery, as it once did in the tenth century. The new brewery, which was founded in 2011, has been built into the ancient stone building of the monastery, a dramatic juxtaposition between gleaming steel vessels and stout stone arches. The brewery is so tucked into the space that malt delivery is a manual operation, bags being unloaded one at a time from the delivery truck.

In this ancient space, Jan Šuráň and his brewers are brewing everything from open-fermented traditional Czech beers to Russian Imperial Stouts, IPAs, and sour ales. The brewery serves a few pubs with a veritable cornucopia of beers, its specialty being draft pale Czech lager. Using modern technology and Czech brewing methods, the Břevnov brewery balances its output between the traditional and the trendy.

It's tempting to believe that beers like the ones made by the breweries at Břevnov and Weihenstephan are a window back in time. This temptation is surely stoked by the not infrequent practice of marketing beers as "authentic" or "original." But that view discounts the work of many generations of brewers and tradespeople who have made the beer what it is today. These modern brewers performing their work, striving to incrementally improve their beers every day, are leaving their mark as much as their predecessors did centuries before. And modernity continues to make its mark on lager. Recipes, raw materials, and resources have surely changed lager's characteristics considerably, even within our lifetimes. If the walls of these German and Czech breweries could talk, they'd have over a thousand years of recipe and process changes to reveal.

2

RAW MATERIALS

LAGER BEERS ARE FAMOUSLY CREATURES OF PROCESS. After all, lager takes its name from the German word *lagern*, "to store," and the specifics of that storage process are essential in its production. One of lager's most endearing qualities, and perhaps a reason for its continued dominance, is its ability to balance delicate flavors derived from the raw materials used in its production. The character and origins of these raw materials can be made to shine through in the finished beer. Lagers can also be the perfect medium to highlight interesting and unique raw materials.

Many great lager brewers are quick to point to the simplicity of their recipes—after all, pale malt, continental hops, and lager yeast can make a mighty fine beer. The lager brewing traditions of Germany and Czechia in particular are intertwined enough that lager recipes from both countries can seem more or less the same, if you discount the specific regional provenance of the ingredients. In many ways, these traditions have been built around access to raw materials; as those materials have changed over time, so too have the beers brewed with them. The impact of locally grown raw materials on these brewing traditions accounts for much of the recognizable process and sensory differences between these styles today.

One of the realities for modern brewers is that raw materials from any corner of the globe are always at our disposal. It is possible to create and combine raw materials in myriad ways that would have been historically impossible. With modern technique and vision, lager can be an expression of terroir, a glimpse into the past, or something altogether new. With the breadth of raw materials available to today's craft lager brewer, really any flavor imaginable is possible in a modern lager. The raw materials chosen can help differentiate craft lager from its industrial counterparts, but they must be chosen thoughtfully. While choosing raw materials traditionally associated with a style is a start, even that is no guarantee of success.

Most modern commercially available malt, hops, and yeast strains have been designed and shaped with efficiency and ease of use in mind. Modern raw materials are the culmination of generations of choices made by brewers and their suppliers, choices which have had a major impact on the character of lager. Some choices made in the name of efficiency have bent the trajectories of lager's sensory qualities toward a common center. This has resulted in a slow march toward uniformity, especially for pale lagers. This can be observed in the ubiquity and consistency of industrially produced lager.

With a solid understanding of the brewing process and good technique, it's difficult to make truly bad beer with these ingredients. It is also, perhaps paradoxically, difficult to make truly exceptional lager beer. How these raw materials are used needs to be considered to ensure that the process matches the ingredients. The details are fundamental when composing yeast strains, malts, hops, and water profiles to brew a great beer of any style. This is especially true when trying to coax out the finest balance between flavor, drinkability, and attenuation in a lager. Brewing within these fine margins remains difficult to excel at, even with a modern scientific understanding, and requires intimate knowledge of raw materials. The agronomic nature and design parameters of malt and hops in particular, combined with the brewer's goals, philosophies, and technologies, makes for a complex decision matrix.

Smaller-scale lager brewers generally choose to emphasize the unique sensory qualities, drinkability, and tradition of their beers. These small brewers are coming to rely more and more upon small growers in their search for interesting and unique raw materials. Some are focused on traditional production methods and styles, while others are using raw materials unique to their local environment. As a result, many craft lager brewers are creating interesting new pathways for lager beer along the way.

Tradition has certainly been kept alive in many German and Czech breweries. Though many of these breweries have held onto traditional brewing processes, these processes have had to evolve to some degree alongside changes in raw materials between the past and present. These adaptations are not always apparent or advertised but they are necessary for most modern raw materials. When traditional methods and materials are used in modern breweries, intentional adjustments need to be made.

Understanding the evolution of your raw materials through history will allow you to better appreciate their current realities and how those affect lager brewing in the present day. Modern craft lager brewers are combining technologies, processes, and raw materials in endless ways, many of which we will explore in this chapter. We'll also examine the philosophy behind many of these decisions, as well as how new developments continue to push lager brewing forward. We'll provide lager-specific insight into yeast, malt, adjuncts, water, and hops in order to help brewers determine how to match their raw materials to their processes.

Yeast

By the modern definition, the difference between an ale and a lager is the type of yeast used to produce them. Lager yeast, *Saccharomyces pastorianus*, is a hybrid yeast that contains DNA from two parental yeast species. One parent, *S. cerevisiae* (otherwise known as ale yeast, or "brewer's yeast"), provides lager yeast with its ability to highly attenuate wort, while its other parent, *S. eubayanus*, provides lager yeast with cold tolerance. The combination of these two important traits changed the course of brewing history.

Lager yeast's ability to highly ferment wort at cold temperatures gave it an advantage over ale yeast. Before sanitary brewing conditions were standard, the cold temperatures at which lager yeast excelled at fermenting limited the metabolism of other yeast and bacteria that would have otherwise enjoyed fermenting at warmer temperatures. The cold temperatures, which limited extraneous fermenters, certainly must have created beers that were less contaminated and led to flavors that could be better controlled.

Beer brewed with a *S. pastorianus* strain is often described as "clean" or "neutral" in comparison to beer made with ale yeast, but this can be misleading. These descriptors have similar meanings, but they are not synonymous.

"Clean" fermentations refer to the off-flavors, or lack thereof, produced during fermentation, while "neutral" refers to the amount of nonvolatile flavor compounds that remain in the finished beer. These definitions made more sense in a world where sanitary fermentations were not the norm.

Lager yeast is certainly not cleaner than ale yeast. Lager fermentations frequently produce more off-flavors, particularly sulfur compounds. This is one of the main reasons that traditional lager fermentations still require a long time to condition. So, while many lager fermentations may be typified by clean flavor profiles, it is by no means a guarantee.

From the perspective of having a neutral character, the reality of modern lager fermentations is far more nuanced. While lager yeasts generally produce fewer esters and fusel alcohols than ale yeasts, this is not a hard and fast rule. In fact, lager yeast includes many strains with subtleties that lager brewers can use to their advantage. Many flavor compounds are produced by lager and ale yeasts at levels near the threshold where they are perceived by the drinker, and small differences can change which side of the threshold these compounds end up on in the finished beer.

ORIGINS OF LAGER YEAST

Originally, lager was referred to as *bayerisches Lagerbier* because of its Bavarian origins. While modern exploration for a genetic ancestor to lager yeast has spanned the globe, it's clear that modern lager yeasts all share a blue-and-white-checkered Bavarian past. For modern brewers, it's helpful to understand the working conditions of the last few centuries that have shaped modern lager yeast strains.

Many believe that the evolution of modern lager yeast comes from the specific fermentation processes codified by the *Reinheitsgebot* of 1516 and the lesser-known *Brauordnung* of 1539. While brewers were "lagering" beer for generations before the enactment of these laws, it is unclear what yeast strains were actually fermenting these early beers. By following these new laws, Bavarian brewers unintentionally created an environment perfect for a hybridization event, which created new strains of yeast that were well adapted to these brewing conditions. Scientists estimate that the common ancestor of present-day lager strains dates back to the mid-sixteenth century and the lager clade is most closely related to *Hefeweizen* (Gallone et al. 2019).

While the science is still out on the exact origins of lager yeast, there are compelling theories. One such theory belongs to Dr. Mathias Hutzler, a yeast scientist at the Technical University of Munich (TUM). There was one clause of the Reinheitsgebot that made lager and ale fermentations almost impossible to brew in the same location. The Reinheitsgebot dictated that wheat beer (i.e., ale) brewing was the exclusive right of the nobility, while civilian society was only allowed to brew lager beer. According to Dr. Hutzler, the only facility known to have been brewing both ale and lager beer in Bavaria at this time would have been the state-owned Hofbräuhaus in Munich, which held a license to brew both royal and common beer. He theorizes that this might be the location of the hybridization event that created the ancestor of the modern lager yeast (Hutzler et al. 2023, 5–8). Liters of both styles consumed at the Hofbräuhaus during the research of this book were delicious but inconclusive.

Even though lager yeast probably first appeared in the sixteenth century, it wasn't until the nineteenth century that Emil Christian Hansen famously isolated the first single strain of lager yeast. Until this point, lager fermentations were a mix of lager, ale, and wild yeast strains along with bacterial cultures. Following their isolation, these pure single-strain yeasts were gradually dispersed to breweries around the world, though it still took many decades for them to become commonplace in many smaller breweries. It wasn't until the 1950s that the vast majority of breweries had truly transitioned to using single-strain yeast cultures.

The most popular lager yeast strain in Germany during the 1950s was TUM 35, a yeast strain that was noted for its neutral and pleasant fermentation profile. However, this yeast was poorly suited for the problematic malts that were grown during this time, leading to both premature yeast flocculation and significant repitching issues (Hutzler et al. 2019, 74). The German brewing industry was forced to find a new lager strain that was better suited to these challenges.

This is where the story of TUM 34 begins, now commonly referred to as 34/70, and officially called Frisinga - TUM 34/70®. Due to the troubles associated with TUM 35, a new more reliable yeast strain needed to be identified. By the end of the 1950s most German brewers had switched to using TUM 34 because it showed the most promise for both flavor profile and industrial use applications. In 1970, this strain was "reselected," resulting in its /70 moniker. This process was repeated in 1978, leading to the strain now known as 34/78. While all these yeasts are essentially the same yeast strain, small variations through continual brewing have occurred. Many lager brewers are particular about the source of their strain. The yeast strain that is sold as "3470 German Lager" from the yeast bank of the Brewing Science Institute (BSI) is, theoretically, an original 34/70 yeast and was specifically selected from the Schönramer

Brewery in Germany. Many claim that the BSI yeast is marginally more attenu-ative than the original TUM 34/70 and prefer to use it to ensure the highest possible attenuation in their beers.

Various lager yeast strains have their origins in specific breweries or regions, having adapted to their respective environments over generations. One such famous yeast, the "Urquell" H-strain, has its origins in Czechia. The H-strain lends its unique characteristics to Czech lagers of various strengths and colors, and is preferred by many Czech brewers for its authentically "Czech" fermenta-tion characteristics. Many of the brewers we spoke to in Czechia would never brew a traditional Czech lager with 34/70, lamenting its fermentation profile as boring and thin.

There are two yeast providers, Wyeast Laboratories and Omega Yeast, who mention the H-strain specifically in relation to their available Czech yeast strains. In both cases these yeasts strains are described as high attenuators, which is in contrast to how many of the beers that are brewed with this yeast taste. We'll go into how mashing affects the fermentation profile and attenua-tion level, particularly of Czech fermentations, in chapter 4.

While the hybridization event that created modern lager yeast is under-stood to have occurred in Bavaria, the search for the non-*S. cerevisiae* parent is ongoing. In 2011, it was announced that the most likely parent of lager yeast was a strain of *S. eubayanus* found in Patagonia. This yeast had a 99.56% match for lager yeast's DNA. It was theorized that somehow this yeast migrated from Patagonia to Europe and was hybridized with ale yeast to create this new lager yeast. Since 2011, a more closely related strain from a Tibetan source was found with a 99.82% DNA match (Wendland 2014, 1257). The Tibetan yeast strain seems more likely than a Patagonian source given the land connection between Tibet and Europe via the Silk Road. In 2022, yet another close relative was found, this time in Ireland—the first such relative to be found in Europe (Bergin et al. 2022). The search continues!

There may be an even simpler explanation, according to yeast scientist Dr. Greg Casey. Dr. Casey's career has involved working for a veritable who's who of large American breweries and he is spending his retirement writing a forth-coming history of American lager beer. Dr. Casey believes that, since wood is a known habitat for *S. eubayanus* and early brewing vessels were almost all made of wood, it is more realistic that the hybridization event occurred with local *S. eubayanus* strains that already existed in these vessels. Centuries of selection pressure imposed by brewers storing their alcoholic beverages for months at low temperatures favored the descendant hybrid strains to the point where they constituted the major part of the brewing yeast population. Until another potential ancestral strain is found in closer proximity to the historical lager brewing areas of Europe, we can't say for sure.

TYPES OF LAGER YEAST

Lager yeasts scientists have grouped lager strains into two main categories, Saaz and Frohberg. These two lines of yeast emerged around the same time and it is still not fully understood if there were two unique hybridization incidents that created the Saaz- and Frohberg-type strains or if they split from the same lineage at some point. The Saaz and Frohberg classifications are not commonplace descriptions assigned to lager yeasts in the US. We searched all the American yeast providers we knew of and couldn't find much information regarding the terms *Saaz* or *Frohberg* when describing their yeast. This may be because the vast majority of commercial lager yeasts are of the Frohberg type; we haven't found any advertised Saaz types in the US. While the brewers at Live Oak in Austin, Texas, have had success sourcing Saaz-type yeasts from a few vendors, these are not readily available.

Frohberg yeast strains take a higher percentage of DNA from their *S. cerevisiae* parent and are noted for being highly attenuative, more flocculating, more stable, less susceptible to contamination, and for fermenting maltotriose. Saaz yeast strains (referred to sometimes as "dusty" yeasts), share more *S. eubayanus* DNA. They tend to be less flocculant, less attenuative, produce more sulfur, are more cold-tolerant, are unable to ferment maltotriose, and produce fewer esters (Gibson et al. 2013). Most commercially available single-strain cultures come from the Frohberg line, the famous 34/70 strain being the most common.

The lager lineage story gets a little more complicated when looking at American lager strains. Dr. Casey studied hundreds of American lager yeast strains during his time at Anheuser-Busch and at Coors. His research on the DNA sequences of these strains showed two clearly distinct groups, which he personally classified as "Carlsberg-type" and "Tuborg-type." The Carlsberg-types were known for their consistency, reliability, and high flocculation, albeit with a rougher aroma profile and higher sulfur content. Tuborg-types were divas, preferring specific brewing parameters to work well; however, their flavor profile was more refined, offering subtle ester characteristics and limited sulfur production. Anecdotally, the number of brewers in the US who used Tuborg-types eventually overtook the number who used Carlsberg-type yeasts (Greg Casey, pers. comm.). Maybe surprisingly, it was the more estery yeasts strains that beat out their more neutral-flavored counterparts. This can be seen through the apple and banana aromas of two of the bestselling American lager brands. Dr. Casey did not determine how the Tuborg- and Carlsberg-type yeast strains compare to the Saaz and Frohberg classifications, although he is inclined to believe that they both may be of Frohberg lineage.

An interesting case study exists today at the Schell's brewery in New Ulm, Minnesota, run by the Marti family. The brewery's classic Deer Brand, a pre-Prohibition-style lager, still features a Carlsberg-type strain. When Schell's acquired the Grain Belt brand in 2016, Ted Marti and his son Jace faithfully recreated the brand's classic American lager using a Tuborg-type yeast for a rounder, more estery profile. Jace has plenty of experience shepherding generations of both yeast types and has a liking for the sulfur created by the Carlsberg-type, which can also be relied upon to repropagate for dozens of generations. The more delicate Tuborg-type, however, is usually only reliable for about ten generations at the Schell's brewery.

Blending both Frohberg- and Saaz-type yeast could potentially balance the pros and cons of each strain. Mixing of strains could happen in one of two ways. First, multiple yeast strains would be pitched to complete fermentation together. Alternatively, one yeast strain could be used for primary fermentation (usually a Frohberg type) while a different strain (typically a Saaz type) would be used to complete the secondary/maturation fermentation. Pilsner Urquell was famous for using three different yeast strains. Today, only one strain is used, the famous Urquell H-strain. The late Professor Ludwig Narziß, the architect of single-strain brewing in Germany, lamented the homogeneity of lagers brewed this way, suggesting that multistrain fermentations would be worthwhile to revisit (Mathias Hutzler, pers. comm.).

Genetic and phenotypic variation between lager yeast strains is significantly less than that found between ale yeast strains. The period of the nineteenth century covering the rise of lager brewing coincided with the invention of mechanical refrigeration and the isolation of single yeast strains, which narrowed the environmental pressures applied to lager yeast strains and their subsequent diversity as a result (Gallone et al. 2019, 1570–71). Lager yeasts in brewing have simply had less time to evolve compared to their ale counterparts. While we now refer to these unique lager strains by where they significantly diverged (e.g., Mexican, Danish, American), all these strains are of Bavarian origin. Another key factor that limits the diversity of lager yeast is the fact that it is a hybrid yeast strain, which makes it effectively sterile. *S. pastorianus* either can't sporulate or has low spore viability (de la Cerda Garcia-Caro et al. 2022, 4).

While there is less variety between lager yeast strains than is found between ale yeast strains, there are some notable differences even within lager strains bearing the same 34/70 moniker (Müller-Auffermann et al. 2015, 56). Steve Holle from KC Bier Company and Bill Eye from Bierstadt Lagerhaus traveled around Bavaria helping source yeast directly from breweries to assist BSI in mapping out some of these variations. The samples they selected displayed differences in maltotriose fermentation, attenuation, sulfur production, acetaldehyde production, diacetyl removal, and ester production. This is perhaps evidence for the adaptability and versatility of lager strains, many of which have been working in the same Bavarian breweries for generations. Lager yeast strains have an amazing ability to adapt to their environments. In tests performed by Dr. Casey, it was possible to identify chromosomal variations between the original strains within a dozen generations (Casey 1996, 1–10).

CHARACTERISTICS OF LAGER YEAST FERMENTATION

While lager fermentations may often be described as "clean" and "neutral" compared to ale fermentations, it does not mean they are without significant sensory impact. Indeed, lager yeast will lend a defining character to the beer it ferments; the complexity and variety of flavors created by lager strains offer both opportunities and challenges for brewers. Controlling for the positive and negative flavor attributes of lager yeast is one of the lager brewer's main responsibilities.

Yeast metabolism during fermentation is responsible for around 80% of the aroma-active compounds in beer (Meier-Dörnberg et al. 2017, 1). Lager and ale yeast produce nearly all the same flavor compounds, albeit in different quantities. Ale fermentations may contain esters at levels up to 80 milligrams per liter (mg/L), while lager fermentations contain up to 60 mg/L (Kunze 1999, 330).

Lager yeast has an additional gene compared to ale yeast that, when expressed, results in enhanced acetate ester production, which could lead to increased banana, rose, apple, and solvent-like characteristics (Pires et al. 2014, 1941). Expression of this gene is highly sensitive to temperature and is a factor to consider when deciding at what temperature lager beer should ferment.

Even though there are comparatively few variances between all the different available lager yeast strains on the market, there are some important distinctions that do differentiate them. Depending on the goals of the brewery, each of these strains may offer an advantage in terms of fermentation performance and aroma impression. One study has attempted to characterize the variations

Table 2.1

Fermentation characteristics of lager yeast strains compared to 34/70

Fermentation characteristic	34/78	193	194	66/70	44	69
— = no difference, ↓ = reduction (each approx. 5%), ↑ = increase (each approx. 5%)						
Extract consumption	↓	—	↓↓	↑	↓↓	↓
Rate of CO_2 production	↓	↑	↑	—	—	↓
Amount of CO_2 production	↓	↓	↓	↑	↓	↓
Initial rate of fermentation	↓	—	—	↓	—	↓
Total sugar utilization	↓↓	↓	↓↓↓	↑↑	↓↓↓	↓
Maltotriose utilization	↓	↓↓	↓↓	↑	↓↓↓	↓
pH reduction						
pH reduction	—	↓	↑	—	↑↑	↑
Capacity for acid production	↑	—	↑	—	↑↑	↑
Physical behavior of the yeast cells						
Cells in suspension	↑	—	↓	↑↑	—	↑
Sedimentation in Imhoff cone	—	—	—	—	↑	—
Turbidity	↑↑	—	↑↑↑	—	—	↑
Fermentation by-products						
Diacetyl	↓	—	—	↓↓	↓	↓
SO_2	↓↓	↑↑↑	↓↓	↑	—	—
Acetaldehyde	↓	↑	↓↓	—	—	↑
Esters	↓	↑	↓	↓	—	↓
Fusel alcohols	↓	↑	↓	↓	↑	—
Aroma impression						
Sulfury	—	↓↓	—	—	↑	↓
Floral	↓	↑↑↑	↓↓	↑	↑	—
Apple (green)	↑	—	↓	↑	↑	↓
Apple (ripe)	↑	↓↓↓	↓	↓↓↓	↓	—
Yeasty	↑↑	↓	—	↑↑	↑	—
Malty	↑	↑	↑	—	↑	—
Marzipan	↑↑↑	—	—	—	—	—
Worty	↑	—	—	—	—	↓

Müller-Auffermann et al., BrewingScience, vol. 68 (March/April 2015), p. 56.

in fermentation between six commercial lager yeast strains using 34/70 as a "standard" reference strain (Müller-Auffermann et al. 2015, 56). Table 2.1 maps these behaviors of the six yeast strains assessed.

HOW TO SELECT A LAGER YEAST STRAIN

Careful consideration of subtle flavor and process changes is necessary when selecting lager yeast. Each potential benefit offered by a particular strain often has a corresponding drawback. Attenuation, flocculation, fermentation by-products, pH reductions, and aroma characteristics must all be balanced to achieve a brewery's desired fermentation performance for its lager.

Understanding these variations is helpful for selecting a yeast that will meet a brewer's goals. Depending on the style of beer and other raw materials being used, determining which lager yeast strain will be helpful. What follows here are some examples of how other brewers go about yeast selection.

Victory Brewing Company in Parkesburg, Pennsylvania, uses a Munich yeast of unknown origin that provides a more noticeable ester profile and unique fermentation character. This character is on display in Victory's classic Prima Pils, a rather hoppy Pilsner that supports its hop profile with mild ester character. Consumers have been drawn to the fruiter, softer character of these fermentations, even though many craft brewers seem to prioritize cleaner, more neutral fermentations. Could Victory's yeast potentially be a Saaz- or Tuborg-type yeast? Maybe: Dr. Casey believes that the Tuborg type yeast found by Anheuser-Busch and Coors were from a Munich brewery as well.

The brewers at Schilling Beer Co. in Littleton, New Hampshire, manage up to six different lager strains. Even though it's a large time and resource commitment, the brewers feel that each strain is unique and best suited to the different styles they produce. Because they believe that fermentation is the key to the unique character of their beers, they commit to designing fermentation profiles, pitch rates, and other related aspects that are tailored to each strain. Schilling's lagers showcase a variety of fermentation characters that is perhaps unrivaled by modern craft lager brewers.

At Halfway Crooks Beer in Atlanta, Georgia, the bulk of its in-house lagers are split between two lager strains. One yeast accentuates hops and has a drier finish, while the other yeast has lower attenuation and is used for maltier beers like Halfway Crooks' Reset Helles. Choosing which strain to use when is one of the ways owner and brewer Shawn Bainbridge highlights differences in the brewery's impressive lager portfolio.

Malt

Malt is the name given to grain that has been modified to allow it to be used for brewing. Malted barley is the primary source of fermentable extract in most lager beer. The malting process is a significant variable that affects both the flavor and how the malt will need to be processed in the brewhouse. The variety and specifications of malt used will determine the type of mashing process required in the brewhouse. Over the years, changes in barley cultivars grown and advances in malting technology have combined to alter how brewers process malt in their breweries.

Helpful Malting Definitions

Extract. The total amount of soluble components including sugars, starches, proteins, and other compounds extracted from grain regardless of its fermentability.

Apparent Attenuation (AA). The calculated difference between the original extract of wort and the observed extract of beer to determine the amount of extract that has been fermented. It does not account for the density of alcohol present, hence apparent.

Modification. The degree to which cell wall, protein, and starch modification has proceeded and, consequently, the ability of the malt to perform in the mash.

Cell Wall Modification (Cytolysis). The breakdown of cell walls to release starch granules and aid in the run-off. Generally, a fine/coarse extract difference of 1.5% is considered well modified. A friability over 90% for non-Pilsner-type malts and over 85% for Pilsner-type malts is considered fully modified.

Protein Modification (Proteolysis). The breakdown of proteins to release free amino acids (a source of nitrogen) that can be assimilated by the yeast. Generally, a Kolbach index from 37% to 45% and free amino nitrogen (FAN) level above 120 mg/L indicate well-modified malt.

Starch Modification (Amylolysis). The breakdown of starches into fermentable extract, generally by the enzymes α-amylase and β-amylase. Most of these reactions will happen in the mash.

MALT ANALYSIS PARAMETERS

Today's brewers can easily access statistical analyses for every bag of malt they procure (table 2.2), but this was not always the case. The first known American malting barley report can be found in *Chemical Studies of American Barleys and Malts* by J.A. Le Clerc and Robert Wahl, published in 1909. In this book, most of the common analyses used to assess modern malt are missing: no Kolbach index, fine/coarse extract difference, diastatic power, or free amino nitrogen (FAN) to be found. It wasn't until the 1930s that these tests became possible, and it took until the 1950s for them to become industry standards.

Table 2.2
Parameters found on a typical malt certificate of analysis

Free amino nitrogen (FAN)	Amount of assimilable nitrogen released into wort for yeast metabolism
Diastatic power (DP)	Enzymatic potential to convert starch to sugar via amylolysis
Kolbach index (KI), or soluble nitrogen over total nitrogen (S/T)	Measure of protein modification; a ratio expressed as a percentage
Fine/coarse extract difference (F/C difference)	Measure of cell wall modification; the difference between extract obtained mashing with fine-milled malt versus coarse milled
Friability	Measure of cell wall modification; the percentage of malt that is easily crushable

Modern malt analysis ought to be considered critically, however. The numbers on a modern malt specification sheet are mostly derived from Congress mash experiments, which mimic a decoction mash in a laboratory setting. Malt scientist and author Evan Evans believes that brewers and maltsters should reevaluate this process, as it provides statistics from a decoction mash when most breweries primarily use an infusion mash (Evans 2021, 7–8). Many of the malt variables given in a certificate of analysis may be subject to change depending on the brewhouse mash program.

MALT MODIFICATION

Malt modification can be broken down into three main areas: cell wall modification (cytolysis), protein modification (proteolysis), and starch modification (amylolysis).

Cell wall modification. Cell wall modification allows enzymes in the mash access to the protein and starches within the malt kernel. Poor cell wall modification can result in stuck mashes or inhibit a brewer's ability to extract and modify the protein and starch within the kernel. A fine/coarse extract difference (F/C difference) of 1.5% or less indicates a high degree of cell wall modification. The reasoning is that the more extract it is possible to obtain from a coarser grind compared to very finely ground malt (which brewers wouldn't typically employ), the greater the degree of modification; hence the smaller the value for F/C difference, the more modified the malt. Friability is another measure of cell wall modification. The value indicates the percentage of non-steely kernels and gives an understanding of how malt will crush through a mill. Depending on malt varieties and region, values between 80% and 90% are considered well modified. Mechanical modifications are also important for cell wall modification. The physical process of boiling helps to break down cell walls and expose more extract. This is one advantage of decoction mashing.

Protein modification. Protein modification provides crucial nutrients for yeast health by the way of free amino nitrogen (FAN), as well as soluble proteins needed for foam in the final beer. FAN values over 120 mg/L are generally considered sufficient, the majority of which will be produced during malting (Kunze 2014, 186). The Kolbach index (KI), or the ratio of soluble nitrogen over total nitrogen (S/T), identifies the degree to which proteinaceous material has been broken down. Protein breakdown results in the release of soluble protein fragments into wort; the higher the KI or S/T value, the more protein modification has occurred. A KI value over 45% indicates modification is too high, while below 37% is considered undermodified.

Starch modification. Starch modification is the conversion of starch into fermentable sugars that yeast eventually turns into alcohol. This occurs almost entirely during the mash and, therefore, starch modification is brought about by the brewer. However, malts have differing levels of diastatic power (DP) depending on their degree of kilning. For all-malt beers, a DP of 200°WK is considered sufficient for starch conversion (Back et al. 2020, 21). There are two main enzymes responsible for breaking down starches, alpha(α)-amylase and beta(β)-amylase.

Modern brewing science tells us that there are temperature ranges that are beneficial to different groups of modifying enzymes. The three enzyme groups for mash modification—glucanases, proteases, and amylases—work at continuously warmer temperatures, and the process of decoction generally works well to hit all these different temperature ranges. There is also the phytase rest, or acid rest, which affects mash pH and is discussed in chapter 4.

β-Glucanase activity	104–113°F (40–45°C)
Protease activity	122–131°F (50–55°C)
Amylase activity (optimal)	143–162°F (62–72°C)

In the past, brewers working with undermodified malts needed a way to overcome this issue to brew successfully. Modern malt is consistent and highly modified in a way that smaller, less modern facilities would find difficult to match. Before specialization and industrialization, when many breweries produced their own malt, brewers were beholden to their supply of raw grain and were occasionally forced to malt a poor harvest and make do with the results. Large modern maltsters can adjust for poor crop years by blending with grain from other years and from different growing areas. As the malt business has industrialized, the way brewers interact with malt has changed and their specifications have become more exacting.

Specialization has allowed modern maltsters to hone their craft and chase efficiencies. Robert Spitzl of IREKS Malting in Kulmbach notes that, quite recently, malts have further increased in diastatic power, modification, and extract. At the same time, protein levels, dimethyl sulfide (DMS) precursors, astringency, and husk character have all decreased. Large maltsters work closely with farmers, private research companies, and universities on barley breeding programs that continue to drive efficiencies in the brewhouse to historic highs.

This efficiency also puts modern maltsters in an interesting situation when advising brewers on how to use their malt. Highly refined modern malts certainly don't require a decoction step for brewers to gain their full extract. Representatives from IREKS told us that, while they could theoretically create an undermodified malt, they believed that even their least modified malt would be more modified than any historical example. Modernizing malting processes is only one part of the equation, as decades of barley breeding has meant taking a step back in time is almost impossible for large maltsters, even if they wanted to. All of this has opened up a lane for small-batch, artisan maltsters to source heritage grains and malt them to unique specifications.

Figure 2.1. Overlooking a Saladin box at the IREKS malting facility in Kulmbach, Germany.

MODIFICATION AND OTHER FACTORS AFFECTING MALT QUALITY

The biggest flavor impact comes from changes wrought by the malting process itself. Dr. Patrick Hayes, a professor and barley researcher at Oregon State University, believes that malting is the single largest contributor to the flavor profile of grain used by breweries. But terroir and the cultivation of specific barley varieties will impart unique qualities to the malt and resulting beer (Patrick Hayes, pers. comm.).

When it comes to developing new barley varieties, farmers, maltsters, and breweries all have competing interests. Farmers need varieties that grow well, maltsters need varieties that will malt properly, and breweries need varieties suited for the beer they sell. Smaller breweries are, unfortunately, often the least influential of these three groups when it comes to making decisions about new varieties. As a result, sensory impact is generally not prioritized by malt breeders (Herb et al. 2017). Priority is often given to finding better-yielding and more disease-resistant characteristics. One of the biggest challenges to breeding malt for sensory reasons is that the malting and brewing processes massively change the flavor profile of the original barley. Breeding programs take years, and many malting and brewing tests have to be performed in order to truly measure the flavor impact of different varieties.

Thus, the methods and objectives of breeding programs contribute significantly to the differences between US and European barley varieties. Two-row barley isn't native to North America; early brewers used native six-row barley. A key reason for early North American brewers deciding to use corn (maize) and rice as adjuncts was six-row barley's notable husky character and rough flavor profile. Ashton Lewis of Rahr Malting Co. believes these issues have contributed to an industry-wide switch to two-row malt that has been ongoing for decades. For farmers and maltsters, the fact that six-row is more prone to disease due to bunching of the kernels on the head of the stalk made the switch attractive as well.

Even with the US brewing industry's shift to two-row barley, there are still clear differences between two-row cultivars grown in North America and those grown in Europe (table 2.3). β-Glucan levels are a key differentiator. Fully modified infusion-capable malts from Europe still have higher average β-glucan levels, which protects against coloring reactions and allows for extra kilning time and higher temperatures without excessively darkening the malt. Thus, more toasted malt flavors can be developed in European malts than in US malts of comparable color. This manifests in what Ashton Lewis calls the "almond-like" flavor profile of German Pilsner malt, which is distinct from the rounder and sweeter flavor profile of US-grown two-row malt. Growing conditions also create notable differences. The US two-row crop has less disease pressure due to the drier and hotter environment but is less plump as a consequence, while European barley is plumper due to wetter growing conditions.

Table 2.3

**Modern malting differences between
US "adjunct" two-row and German two-row**

Parameter	US "adjunct" two-row guidelines (AMBA 2023)	German two-row guidelines (Kunze 2014, 187)	"České pivo" malt guidelines (Olšovská et al. 2014, 312)
Diastatic power (°WK)	>470 approx. (>140° ASBC)	>200	>218
Total protein, dry weight	≤12.8%	9%–11%	9.5%–11.7%
Free amino nitrogen (FAN) (mg/L)	>210	130–160	210–230
Kolbach index (S/T)	40%–47%	38%–42%	36%–42%
β-Glucan (ppm)	<100	<200	<250
Friability	>90%	80%–86%	>75%

Other natural properties of the grain being malted will certainly have an impact. Lower S/T ratios and FAN levels will lead to fewer Maillard reactions during malting; Maillard reactions are responsible for many complex malt flavors in finished beers. A malt of high diastatic power is more likely to result in crisp and dry beers. Lower modified malts may lead to grassier flavored malts (Windes et al. 2021).

The malting process and resulting level of modification is the largest factor in determining malt flavor. However, there is a tendency to conflate increased modification with higher quality, but increased modification creates its own set of challenges for brewers. Here are a few to consider:

1. **Less flavor development during malting.** Highly modified malts require lower kilning temperatures, resulting in less flavor development than in lower modified malts of similar color.

2. **Increased DMS potential.** The lower kilning temperature and higher degree of malt modification increases the potential for DMS in the wort.

3. **Lower foam potential.** Newer barley varieties have been bred to have lower protein content, and with increased modification, fewer foam-stabilizing proteins end up in the finished beer.

4. **Thinner beers produced.** Highly modified malts can result in worts with less body and mouthfeel that may require the addition of specialty malts to mitigate.

5. **High enzymatic activity.** All-malt beers made with US malts tend to have too much enzymatic activity and FAN. This leads to less control of mashing and residual FAN causing pH increases after fermentation and increased diacetyl.

There are, of course, other barley cultivars coveted for their special sensory contributions. In the UK, Maris Otter and Golden Promise are two examples that don't meet modern standards for extract and modification levels yet continue to be demanded by brewers. In Germany, Steffi is one heritage barley variety with the cachet to demand higher pricing and specific requests from brewers who want malt-driven styles.

Understanding the modification level of the malt you receive will help you determine how to process it in the brewhouse. Many brewers do not wish to change their brewhouse mash programs and instead try to source malts that match their process. Large malting operations have considerably reduced the impact of seasonality on the consistency of their finished product. This makes for easy shopping for brewers looking for specific and easily repeatable malt characteristics.

One interesting program that gives breweries the opportunity to obtain modification specifications to match their intended brewing process comes from Bamberger Malt. The maltsters at Bamberger have taken what can only be described as a holistic approach to malting, where they allow the grains they intend to malt to determine the finished modification level. Instead of homogenizing malts, they keep lots separate, understanding that it will result in different finished products. Each batch is then stored separately and brewers are given finished specifications for up to a dozen batches. The brewer can select a single-batch malt or order a blend of malts to suit the needs of their brewhouse.

HISTORICAL REGIONAL TRENDS IN BARLEY MALT

Lager brewing traditions in the US, Germany, and Czechia all have unique barley growing and malting characteristics and histories. Many of these characteristics have shaped—and continue to shape—how brewers employ mashing programs to prepare wort. The differences in mashing techniques contribute to the character of the final beer. How barley variety selection and malting operations have variously modernized and changed, particularly advances made over the past century, have helped to further differentiate lager brewing traditions in each of these countries.

Arguably, malted barley has changed more than any other brewing ingredient over the last century (table 2.4). The entire malting process has grown out of brewhouse attics into a highly specialized industry of its own, becoming more efficient in the process. New varieties of barley have been bred that optimize yield and malting quality, with trials for the next generation of malting barley continuously ongoing. Farmers and maltsters have worked together to develop disease-resistant varieties that maximize potential extract for their brewing customers. Climate change, shifting consumer preferences, and changing technologies have influenced and will continue to influence how this global industry grows and malts barley. Many of the technological advancements of this industry have been made in service of creating consistent, highly modified malts out of naturally inconsistent barley and other cereal grains. These advances have had significant impacts on brewing processes and the sensory aspects of the finished beers.

Table 2.4
How important malt parameters have changed over the last 70 years

Year	Source	Diastatic power (°WK)	F/C difference	FAN (mg/L)	Kolbach Index, or S/T
1957	de Clerck	200–250	Up to 2.2%	...	...
1966	Narziß	...	1.5%–2.0%	...	37–40
1974	Narziss	315	1.3%–2.9%	...	35.8–40.1
1981	Briggs et al.	307	1.8%	150	39.4
1999	Kunze	240–260	1.2%–1.8%	120–160	38–42
2006b	Ockert	369–491.5	0.8%–1.2%	175–220	40–46
2021	Evans	344–412	0.7%–1.1%	150	39.4–47.6

Note: For many variables, it is a challenge to apply perfect comparisons as the testing methods and key metrics have varied over the years.

°WK, degrees Windisch-Kolbach; FAN, free amino nitrogen; F/C difference, fine-coarse extract difference; S/T, soluble nitrogen over total nitrogen

Understanding the origins of malt from a lager brewer's perspective will help to illustrate some of the unique mashing protocols undertaken in lager breweries. Historically, malted barley would have been of variable quality and highly undermodified compared to modern malt. Large industrial malthouses that can better monitor and control the malting process didn't start until the Industrial Revolution had taken hold in Europe and the US. Despite the ubiquity and technological proficiency of such malting operations today, agronomic and process factors discussed earlier in this chapter combine to create differing characteristics between malts from various growing regions. These differences continue to affect how lager brewers use specific regional malts in the brewhouse.

North American and European malt breeding programs have had drastically divergent goals for generations. Brewers in the US have a long history of brewing lager beer with adjuncts, which has necessitated the development of barley malts with high enzymatic power to help convert rice and corn. European brewers have continued their tradition of all-malt lager beers, which require malts with less enzymatic power.

Interestingly, it is the American brewers who are uniquely positioned to compare North American and Continental malts, as Bavarian malts have been imported to the US since the early days of the craft beer movement. American brewers have been able to brew side-by-side with both sets of ingredients for decades. By contrast, when asking German brewers (and maltsters) about American malt, their knowledge is mostly limited to their experience drinking American beer.

German Barley and Maltings

The barley grown in Germany, particularly Bavaria, was intended for brewing all-malt beer. Historically, the malt of Bavaria was considered inferior to other regions and best-suited for dark lagers and intensive mashing protocols.

In Germany, malt production generally remained the responsibility of brewers until the 1960s and 1970s. At that time, needing an influx of capital, German brewers divested from their malting operations and a specialized malting industry took its place. In Bavaria alone, approximately 220 brewery-operated malthouses were in operation just after WWII; only a handful remain today. This specialization has also resulted in rapid advancements in malt modification levels and efficiencies in the last few decades.

Figure 2.2. Ancient malting shoes in the rafters of the former malthouse at the Schönramer brewery.

A few examples of this history can be seen throughout German breweries. At the Schönramer brewery in Germany, the upper floors of the building still contain relics from its previous incarnation as a malthouse, including "malting shoes" once worn to rake malted barley by shuffling across the floor. One German brewery malting operation that survives and still operates is the wood-fired maltings at Brauerei Heller-Trum, brewers of the famed Schlenkerla smoked beers of Bamberg. While the oak and beechwood smoked malts are still produced at the family-owned brewery today, the brewery purchases its base malt from a local maltster.

This separation and specialization is key to understanding modern lager malt, production of which began in earnest just as the first craft brewers were getting started in the late 1970s. Hans-Ludwig "Halu" Straub of Drei Kronen in Memmelsdorf believes that German malt truly modernized when malting operations transitioned from an artistic approach reliant on maltsters to "know" when malt was ready, to a modern, data-driven approach. With this malting modernization, Drei Kronen stopped using a double decoction process in the mid-1980s in favor of a less arduous single decoction process, eliminating the need for a protein rest and streamlining brewhouse operations. This is an example of the kind of operational change modern lager brewers can consider with the modern, highly modified malts readily available today.

Czech Barley and Maltings
Over the last two centuries the quality of Czech malt has been held in high regard. The most famous malts came from the Haná region in Moravia in the eastern part of the country. Czech malt offers interesting insights into older barley growing and malting traditions. Limited changes to the malting industry occurred during communism, but since the Velvet Revolution the development of more modern varieties and technologies has accelerated.

Although half of the barley grown in Czechia today consists of varieties bred outside the country, traditional barley varieties continue to be grown to ensure the survival of *České pivo*. The varieties recommended for this type of beer have a lower level of proteolytic and cytolytic modification; beers brewed with these malts tend to have lower levels of attenuation and a higher presence of residual extract (Mikyška et al. 2022, 663). Adherence to older-style flavor profiles are preferred over newer ones by Czech consumers.

Even so, within the various Czech malt varieties that have been used for the two last centuries there have been dramatic increases in efficiency and modification levels. In studies of Czech malting varieties that were bred between 1902 and 1926, compared to those bred in the twenty-first century, it is obvious that key malt characteristics have changed to reflect modern trends (table 2.5).

Table 2.5
Comparison of malt produced from Czech barley varieties, 1902–1926 versus 21st century

Malt property	Typical values for period	
	1902–1926	21st c.
Protein content (% dry wt.)	13.4–14.9	10.7–12.9
Friability (%)	46.2–57.7	77.1–91.2
β-Glucan (mg/L)	291–522	109–197
Proportion unmodified grains (%)	9–28	<2 (but closer to 0)

Source: Mikyška et al. (2022)

It's tough to imagine how challenging it must have been to brew with a malt that had 28% of its kernels completely unmodified. In a 100 lb. batch of malt, only 72 lb. would have provided enzymatic potential, have undergone cell wall and protein modification, and be processable with an infusion mash. This offers a glimpse into why boiling grains during a decoction mash would have offered a real advantage (chap. 4). By triple decocting beers, brewers at least ensured many of the dead kernels were gelatinized through boiling. This would have been their only hope to gain any extract from these unmodified kernels.

In some ways, using these poorly modified malts may very well have been similar to brewing with corn or rice for early American lager brewers. These adjuncts provided no enzymatic power, just potential extract. Rice and corn need to be heated to gelatinization temperatures to expose the starches in the grains to make them accessible for conversion when added back to the barley mash.

All the deficiencies in these malts specifically cause challenges for the mashing process, potentially explaining the need for double or triple decoctions. Yet other key analyses like diastatic power, extract, and FAN were right in line with what brewers would expect from modern malt today (Mikyška et al. 2022, 666). Clearly the ability to boil grains to deal with poor cell wall modification would have been useful, as was having a protein rest to help break down the large quantities of protein. With these processes in place, saccharification and fermentation may not have been very problematic at all.

The relative recency of the Velvet Revolution has meant the malting industry in Czechia has undergone modernization in a very short space of time. In the last few decades, consolidation between large multinational companies has put significant pressure on the price of malt, and only a handful of malthouses, such as the one run by the Klusáček family, still practice less cost-efficient traditional floor malting. These floor malts offer yet another option for brewers, especially those looking to recreate authentic Czech lager styles.

Sladovna Klusáček

Visiting Sladovna Klusáček in Kounice outside of Prague is like stepping back in time. The ornate facade of the building faces a huge castle estate now in disrepair, its wild grounds being grazed by a herd of irregularly shaped livestock. In their sprawling complex under a traditional malthouse flue, 91-year-old Karel Klusáček and his son operate one of Czechia's five remaining independent floor maltings.

The malting facility can trace its history back nearly 500 years, though it came into the Klusáček family in 1883. It was nationalized during the Communist era and restituted back to the family in 1992, though it had fallen to ruin in that period. Today, Mr. Klusáček and his son use their malting floors to create highly sought after pale malts. The facility is a blend of different vintages of technology, from brand-new palletizing robots to floor raking machinery from the 1950s. The family installed a pilot brewery to brew with their malts, packaging it in plastic screw-top bottles—it is some of the freshest and most delicious beer these authors have ever had.

Sladovna Klusáček still exclusively uses Czech-grown spring barley. All of the barley malted at the facility is floor malted. The malthouse considers their malt to be "fully modified," although the specifications reveal it is not as highly modified as its US or German counterparts. "Fully modified" as it is, Sladovna Klusáček malt is meant to be decocted in the production of Czech lager. The combination of Czech barley varieties and the methods used by Sladovna Klusáček create malts best suited for this type of brewing.

Floor malting creates challenges that modern malting operations don't need to worry about. The Klusáček malthouse can only malt barley ten months of the year, as the temperature during the height of the summer is too hot to produce consistent malt. The entire malting process also takes nine days and uses techniques that have fallen out of fashion. For example, the moisture content during germination gets as high as 45%, compared to the 36%–37% typical for most modern maltings. The drying process is done very slowly in order to avoid shrinking of the grains and to ensure friability of the finished malt. The malt also has higher protein content, with up to 13% during tough harvest years.

For all these challenges, Sladovna Klusáček sells its malt at a premium and has trouble meeting the current demand for its products. Czech-grown barley malt tends to produce slightly less attenuative extract, which translates to more body in the finished beer.

Figure 2.3. Father and son Karel and Vojtěch Klusáček at their family floor malting outside Prague.

US Barley and Maltings

In the US, the development of barley varieties has focused on malts suitable for adjunct brewing. Historically, six-row barley was the dominant type of barley used by American brewers. North American six-row barley offers both advantages and disadvantages compared with European varieties. Six-row has high enzymatic activity and higher agronomic yields but has more husk material that can lead to astringency issues. The prevalence of six-row barley was a major motivating factor for American brewers to start including adjuncts like corn and rice in their recipes. By adding these adjuncts, wort profiles could be brought closer to those obtained using malts made from European two-row barley varieties.

However, the focus has shifted from six-row varieties to two-row varieties in the last century. Breeding programs tailored to American brewing methods helped create two-row barley malts that had similar specifications to malts from six-row barley, such as retaining six-row's high enzymatic activity. This enzymatic power allowed for the continued use of adjuncts and other cereal grains in relatively high proportions. European breeding programs continued to be influenced by all-malt brewing, with less emphasis on enzymatic power than in US malthouses. Consequently, standard US malts differ sharply from those produced in Europe in several respects (table 2.3). German and Czech malts have lower protein levels, fractional amounts of diastatic power, yield noticeably lower FAN, and contain double the β-glucan content of that recommended by American malting standards.

The characteristics of American malt make it more suited to brewing with corn, rice, and other non-malted ingredients. Mashing with adjunct levels hovering near fifty percent of the total grist do not pose a problem when using American malts but would be challenging if performed with German or Czech malts. At the same time, brewing all-malt beers with American two-row can lead to problems, with excessive DP and FAN causing unwanted pH increases and reduced diacetyl uptake.

In 2022, the switch from six-row to two-row is almost complete. Dr. Patrick Hayes laments this change, noting that it would be relatively easy to breed six-row to overcome disease resistance and astringency concerns. The yields and climate adaptations could make six-row an appealing grain as climate issues continue to wreak havoc on the barley crop (Patrick Hayes, pers. comm.).

There is evidence of growing interest in six-row barley from US craft lager brewers. As brewers look to America's brewing past for inspiration, the use of six-row is compelling. Suarez Family Brewery in New York's Hudson

Valley has begun using local six-row grown in-state. Besides the local connection, owner and brewer Dan Suarez appreciates the flavor profile that the barley provides, describing it as giving his light lagers a flavor reminiscent of malted milk balls.

TRADITIONAL SPECIALTY MALTS

Lager beer can be brewed with any malt, but what follows are some of the more traditional specialty malts associated with lager production.

Munich malt. The original malt of lager beer, sometimes referred to as dark malt. Munich malts are darker due to higher kilning temperatures and longer kilning times, typically 4–5 hours at 212–221°F (100–105°C). Due to this high kilning temperature, much of the diastatic and enzymatic power of the malt is destroyed. The DP of Munich malts tends to be less than half of that found in Pilsner malts (de Clerck 1957, 236). Today, Munich malts are closer in modification level to Pilsner-type malts; historically, this would not have been the case. There is a loss of up to 40% of the nitrogen content of Munich malt, which is indicative of active melanoidin formation. For this reason, barley with a higher protein content or barley with other deficiencies might be used for this type of malt instead of being used to create paler malts.

Vienna malt. Emerging slightly ahead of its time, Vienna malt was quickly overshadowed by Pilsner malt. Vienna malt is cured at 194–203°F (90–95°C), which is midway between the 176°F (80°C) typical for Pilsner malt and the 212–221°F (100–105°C) typical for Munich. Not surprisingly, this creates a malt with a color somewhere between that of Pilsner and Munich malts. Kunze (2014, 189) notes that Vienna malt may be used for 100% of the grist for *Märzen*, festival beers, and export lagers to add malt character without adding too much color.

Foam/chit malt. These types of malts are essentially just very poorly modified malts. Mike Schroth of Stone Path Malt in Wareham, Massachusetts, explains that the foam malt they produce might be close in specification to historical malts. To create foam malt, Stone Path reduces germination times to ensure minimal modification to the proteins in the barley. General specifications for this malt are β-glucan in the 600 ppm range, an F/C difference of 3.6%, and α-amylases at 30%–50% the level found in standard malt, indicating poor modification. This highlights the fact that poorly modified malts can have more foam potential than highly modified malts.

Melanoidin malt. Melanoidin malt is a special type of malt used to create intense malt character that, arguably, mimics the flavors developed during decoction. These flavors differ from typical crystal and caramel malts. Strong malt characteristics of biscuit, honey, and toast are common. The type of extract that this malt provides tends to be unfermentable and therefore adds body and sweetness to beer by decreasing attenuation. Melanoidin malt is generally not used in traditional German breweries as a substitute for decoction in pale lagers.

Acid malt. Acid malt helps manage mash pH. Acid malt typically has a lactic acid concentration of 2%–4% (Kunze 2014, 191), meaning for every one percent it makes up of the grist the pH will drop by 0.1. For example, if a mash needs to drop from pH 5.8 to 5.5, then 3% of the grist should be acid malt to ensure this change. The production of acid malt is important for small breweries in Germany where additions of pure lactic acid are not allowed under the beer purity laws. Only lactic acid formed by the four ingredients permitted under the Reinheitsgebot can be used, which means the lactic acid must be produced on the malt by naturally occurring bacteria.

Adjuncts

Adjuncts are any non-barley sugar source that contribute fermentables to wort, with rice and corn (maize) being the most common. They get a bad rap from craft brewers, as they have long been associated with products of questionable integrity. While craft brewers often use adjuncts to increase flavor contributions to their beers, the substitution of rice and corn for a portion of malt is typically regarded as being the domain of industrial brewers of American light lager. After all, these adjuncts are often used to smooth and lighten the character of beers rather than to add flavor.

Early American brewers used a plethora of non-malt ingredients to produce beer, not just rice and corn but persimmon, peapods, and glucose too. Immigrant brewers from Bavaria brought with them disdain for anything other than all-malt beers, inciting a complicated national debate about lager beer's supposed "purity." In the end, American brewers fought for and won the right to use adjuncts in beer (Alberts 2021). One of the complications stemming from this fight was that ingredients other than malt were seen as inferior. Yet these ingredients, corn and rice in particular, were considered necessary to make the light tasting, crystal-clear lagers that were increasing in popularity at the time.

While rice and corn are currently used to help dry out and lighten beer, they were originally marketed as a means to reduce attenuation. Jan Brücklmeier, author of *Bier Brauen*, explains that the high enzymatic activity of six-row barley compared to the European two-row barleys created beer too highly attenuated for the brewers' expectations. Additionally, the strong husky and astringent character that was accentuated by decoction brewing was diluted by these adjuncts. Corn and rice reduced the enzymatic activity of the mashes, lowering the fermentability of the wort and reducing attenuation and problematic flavor components. The results were beers that better compared to their German counterparts.

Quickly, the original purpose for corn and rice use in US breweries changed as the types of beer being brewed became lighter and drier. Now the addition of rice and corn was intended to increase attenuation while also lightening a beer's color and reducing issues with DMS formation (table 2.6). This helped brewers create the sparkling clear, mild lager beer that was increasingly becoming the expectation of consumers.

Table 2.6

Properties of worts and their respective beers (after maturation) comparing all-malt (0%) and corn adjunct grists (adjunct added at 10% and 20%)

Properties		Unit	0%	10%	20%
Wort					
	FAN	mg/L	240±10.9 a	233±8.0 a	223±8.5 b
	Color	°EBC	12.2±0.1 a	11.1±0.1 b	10.5±0.2 c
	DMS	µg/L	109.7±5.0 a	81.2±3.5 b	74.9±2.9 c
	Fermentability	%	80.7±1.2 a	84.7±0.9 b	84.0±1.0 b
Beer					
	Ethanol	% v/v	6.7±0.16 a	7.13±0.02 b	7.14±0.01 b
	Apparent attenuation	%	80.9±1.26 a	84.9±0.87 b	85.8±0.91 b

Reproduced, with permission, from Poreda A., Czarnik A., Zdaniewicz M., Jakubowski M., and Antkiewicz P., "Corn grist adjunct – application and influence on the brewing process and beer quality," *Journal of the Institute of Brewing* 120, no. 1 (2014): 77-81, DOI 10.1002/jib.115, © 2014 Institute of Brewing & Distilling.

Notes: n ≥3; mean±standard deviation. Means within the same property followed by a different letter are significantly different at $\alpha = 0.05$.

Today, the importance of corn and rice for brewing American lagers stems partially from their affordability and availability. They are particularly useful for brewing pale lagers due to their ability to provide plenty of carbohydrate but also lighten body. Neither grain has any diastatic power or provides FAN, and brewing with them requires the enzymatic potential of barley malt; consequently, North American barley malt has been designed with these adjuncts in mind.

When using unmalted grains, both corn and rice need to be gelatinized in order to access the starch within. Gelatinization is the heating of starch granules in the presence of water until the starch becomes hydrated and loses its crystallinity, causing the granules to burst and the starch to become liquified. Both corn and rice can be purchased pre-gelatinized in either torrefied or flaked versions, which are more expensive but eliminate the need for cooking the grains, thus simplifying the brewing process. Even after gelatinization and the solubilization of starches into the mash, the protein in rice and corn will not be soluble and the result will be reduced levels of FAN in the wort.

German-trained brewers were comfortable with the cooking processes required to gelatinize raw corn and rice due to their experience with decoction brewing. The standard mashing program for corn and rice came to be known as a "double mash." In this system, corn and rice are cooked, typically with up to 10% of the barley grist contribution, until all starch has been solubilized. It is then added to the remaining barley mash to raise the temperature of the combined mash. This type of cereal processing is still used at F.X. Matt Brewing Co. in Utica, New York; we go into this process in more detail in the decoction chapter (chap. 4).

Table 2.7
Comparing corn (maize) and rice as brewing adjuncts

Property of adjunct	Corn (maize)	Rice
Carbohydrates (% dry wt.)	76%–80%	85%–90%
Protein (% dry wt.)	9%–12%	5%–8%
Oil (% dry wt.)	1.0%–1.5% (post degerming)	0.2%–0.4%
Gelatinization temp.	140–158°F (60–70°C)	158–185°F (70–85°C)

Most corn varieties have a significant oil content, up to 8% by dry weight, which is detrimental to beer and foam stability. Corn mills deal with this by degerming the corn, which removes the portion of each kernel with the most oil content. But there are some corn varieties with low oil content, and one such variety is grown by the Riggs Beer Company in Urbana, Illinois. This special low-oil white corn variety is the key to Riggs American Lager, one of the most unique American lagers we've encountered (see "Riggs Beer Company" sidebar). The variety was developed at the University of Illinois as part of the world's longest ongoing directional selection program in plants. Until the Riggs brothers began using it, no commercial use had been found for this low-oil variety.

Brewers at Riggs crush the whole grain corn and then add it to their mash kettle/cereal cooker for gelatinizing. Around 10% of the malt grist is added to the cereal cooker to ensure the gelatinized mixture doesn't thicken. (Many first-time adjunct brewers have had the misfortune of finding out what happens to a corn mash when barley is not added—the corn will congeal into large balls, wreaking havoc in the brewhouse.) Riggs finds that processing corn in this way gives a desirable nuttiness instead of the more common "tortilla flavor" that often comes from standard degermed corn. The most surprising feature of Riggs American Lager is the strong, sturdy foam, something not typically associated with this style.

There are emerging modern applications for adjunct lager beers beyond just recreating historic styles. Progressive lager brewers like Kevin Davey, formerly of Wayfinder Beer in Portland, now at Gold Dot Beer in McMinnville, Oregon, took to using adjuncts in his hop-forward lager beers to lighten the body and color and allow the hops to take center stage.

Riggs Beer Company

"People who come here, want to drink a beer." — Matt Riggs

Two and a half hours south of Chicago, the city of Urbana is best known as one half of Urbana–Champaign, a metropolitan area formed by dual (and dueling) college towns surrounded by horizons of corn and soy fields. It's now also home to the Riggs Beer Company, a family brewery whose reputation has even sparked the interest of some German hop farmers we spoke to.

We ate lunch with Matt Riggs at a local hangout, where workers coming off late shifts at the Solo Cup factory next door gather over beers and platters of fries. Matt took us through his family's history over a plastic pitcher of Riggs American Lager. Amidst the slot machines and various tchotchkes of dive-bar-dom, a three-foot-tall "R" logo advertises the two Riggs Beer Company beers on draft.

Matt and Darin Riggs grew up a dozen miles south of Urbana on their fourth-generation family farm. Early on, their parents warned them that the farm, which had been tilled by their ancestors since the late nineteenth century, would not be enough on its own to support the next generation. Matt and Darin would need to forge a different path. Scholarships with the Reserve Officers' Training Corps and careers in the US Navy and the Marine Corps ensued.

The armed forces have long played a role in the romance of the American craft beer movement. The first generation of (legal) American homebrewers handed down tales of fine, frothy European beer consumed en masse while on tour abroad, beers that outshone any of the readily available American lagers of the time. That generation planted the seeds of the American craft beer industry by rebelling against the norm of fizzy, yellow American adjunct lager.

The Riggs brothers, however, took their love of German beer and turned it into a business plan built for fizzy, yellow, *delicious* American adjunct lager. The brothers grow corn, wheat, and barley on their family farm that the brewery buys at a premium price. An elderly local farmer has taken an interest in malting, so the brothers work closely with him to malt their own grain. This close relationship between farm, malthouse, brewery, and taproom takes its cue from the earliest days of brewing in America.

Back in the taproom, the Riggs brothers' German influence is on display, with communal tables and mugs of lager at the ready. The pristine brewing space stands out as particularly unusual for an American craft brewery, as do the handful of production employees in identical Danish overalls. Sat with a beer and looking out over the green fields outside the brewery, you could be forgiven for forgetting you weren't deep in Franconia.

But the folks that drink Riggs American Lager at the local dive bar are the Riggs brothers' customers. These customers aren't necessarily interested in new hop varieties, lagering times, or waiting for slow pours. They are, in Matt's words, there to drink a beer. And Riggs American Lager is just that: a beautiful, idiosyncratic beer that captured the attention of curious lager heads like ourselves. Or you can just drink it, enjoy your company, and not overthink it.

Water

Judging by how some breweries speak to their customers about water, you'd imagine that an ancient water source filtered through lava tubes and underground streams would represent the imaginary ideal for water perfection. But of course, fine lager is created throughout the world using an endless variety of water sources. A water source may matter to some extent, but knowledge on how to calibrate water to compensate for variations in other raw materials is perhaps even more important.

For brewers, knowing the quality and characteristics of their water is essential. For something that seems so simple, water is undeniably complicated when it comes to its effect on finished beer. In fact, water may be the least understood ingredient in beer. Plenty of brewers point to their water as an essential component of their beer's quality but far fewer can define the chemical properties that comprise it. There's much more to water than just hardness and softness.

While regional variations in water's hardness and alkalinity are often credited in the development of beer styles, these are but two data points out of many. Even if the water source seems perfect for the style being brewed, a brewer will need the ability to change their water. Whether by simple filtration, acidification, the addition of brewing salts, or some other process, water treatment is a requirement for brewing quality lager.

Water's most important attribute is generally defined by its ability to achieve a desired mash pH in the brewhouse. Mash pH has a direct correlation to the rate of activity of mash enzymes, which are most active in the fairly narrow range of pH 5.2–5.6. Brewing with lightly kilned malt will almost certainly require mash pH adjustment using brewing salts or acidification. Advancements in brewing technology, shifts in recipes driven by consumer preference, and agricultural changes in raw materials all require some need for water adjustments.

Water treatment is an effective way of smoothing out differences between the acidifying powers of different grists. Without water adjustments, most pale malt mashes will exceed the ideal pH range. Maltsters provide a certificate of analysis (COA) that includes a pH value representing the pH of a mash produced using deionized water (i.e., extremely soft water). A typical pH for pale malt is close to 6.0, significantly higher than the target values for optimal enzyme activity. Brewers will adjust the hardness and alkalinity of their water to help achieve the desired mash pH.

There are varying opinions about pH optima for the mash, wort, and finished beer. Mash pH levels toward the higher end of the target range are likely more traditional since they more closely reflect mashes that, historically, would not have been adjusted. The higher end of the optimum pH range tends to maximize enzymes and maltose creation. Even so, a trend toward lower mash pH values has become standard as there are other benefits offered by lower pH, such as long-term beer stability. Arguably even more important than the pH of the mash is the pH of the finished beer. Most research recommends a pH of 4.4 or lower for finished beer, which could prove problematic for lager brewers since lager fermentations tend to have a higher finishing pH than ale fermentations.

One solution for lager brewers is for a secondary adjustment at the end of the boil to drop the pH. Matt Westfall of Counter Weight Brewing in Cheshire, Connecticut, finds pH is a key factor in creating crisper malt profiles. By lowering the pH at the end of the boil, he can take advantage of the higher wort pH for better hop utilization and flavor profile while also ensuring the proper finishing pH at the end of fermentation.

Water treatment is a bit more complicated for brewers adherent to the Reinheitsgebot (Narziss 1984). Essentially, the rule concerning water is that brewers are allowed to remove anything they want from water but can only add back ingredients that would naturally be found in water. Salts like calcium chloride and calcium sulfate can be added into brewing water, although not into the brewhouse directly. Other additions, such as lactic acid for pH adjustments, are not allowed. These brewers instead rely on biological acidification or they use acid malt in the grist for mash pH adjustment.

HARDNESS AND ALKALINITY

The properties of brewing water that have the greatest impact on mash pH are hardness and alkalinity. Water hardness refers to the total amount of calcium and magnesium in water. Alkalinity describes water's buffering capacity and, for brewing purposes, expresses water's resistance to lowering mash pH. Alkalinity does not describe the pH or how alkaline (i.e., pH >7.0) the water is.

Hardness in water will cause a decrease in mash pH. All things being equal, harder water will create lower mash pH values, and softer water will create higher mash pH values. Calcium and magnesium react with phosphates in malt to lower pH, which is why calcium chloride, calcium sulfate (gypsum), and magnesium sulfate (Epsom salt) are added when mashing to lower mash pH.

Increased alkalinity will result in higher mash pH as increased buffering capacity inhibits a drop in mash pH. Lower alkalinity will result in lower mash pH as the buffering capacity doesn't as strongly inhibit a drop in pH. Alkalinity should not, however, be confused with the pH of a water source. For example, water with a pH of 8 could have higher alkalinity than water with a pH of 9. Even acidic water with a pH below 7 can still have alkalinity. Brewers can also add alkalinity with calcium carbonate. This may be needed when brewing darker beers that include a high percentage of roasted malts that could lower the mash pH too much.

Water's hardness and alkalinity can both be defined within set ranges as low, medium, or high (table 2.8). This is sometimes a source of confusion because these terms can become conflated—natural sources of water tend to have correlated levels of hardness and alkalinity, meaning that water sources with high hardness tend to also have high alkalinity and vice versa. Of course, there are exceptions to every rule.

Table 2.8
Water hardness and alkalinity expressed by mg/L as CaCO$_3$

Hardness as CaCO$_3$	Soft	Medium	Hard
CaCO$_3$ (mg/L)	<60	60-120	>120
Alkalinity as CaCO$_3$	Low	...	High
CaCO$_3$ (mg/L)	<150	...	>150

It's first important to understand the distinction between water's hardness and its alkalinity. The fact that naturally hard water tends to also have high alkalinity causes conflation between these terms. It's generally not the hardness that causes hard water to be problematic for mashing, but rather the high alkalinity that's typically associated with hard water sources.

To make matters even more confusing, hardness and alkalinity in water are each referred to with values "as calcium carbonate," either in milligrams per liter (mg/L as CaCO$_3$) or parts per million (ppm as CaCO$_3$). This means that a single sample of water has two different mg/L (or ppm) CaCO$_3$ values, both of which only paint a limited picture of the water's actual hardness and alkalinity.

Both soft water and hard water offer their own unique challenges for brewers. Naturally soft water that tends to have low alkalinity is described as aggressive and highly corrosive (see sidebar p. 65). As we have seen, naturally hard water tends to have high alkalinity, which means that it tends to have increased buffering capacity that may make it challenging to hit a target mash pH. Water that falls between these extremes of hardness and softness will likely offer a better balance of attributes but will still need adjustment to ensure proper water chemistry for mashing.

Brewers may need to adjust their water profiles by adding various brewing salts to achieve the appropriate water chemistry. But brewing salts alone can only be used to change hardness or alkalinity in this way up to a point. In large quantities these salts reach their flavor threshold, meaning that other adjustments may be required to hit the desired mash pH. In these cases, acidifying the mash may be necessary.

RESIDUAL ALKALINITY

A better way of understanding how a water source will affect mash pH is predicted by determining the residual alkalinity (RA) of mashing water. The RA value effectively explains whether water has more hardness or alkalinity. This value describes the relative values of hardness and alkalinity for a water source, which in turn reveals if the water will result in a lower or higher mash pH. After mashing, all the ions that contribute to water hardness will react within the mash to lower the alkalinity. If more hardness exists than alkalinity, a negative RA value will be the result and the pH of the mash will be lower. If more alkalinity exists compared to hardness, a positive RA value will be the result and the pH of the mash will be higher.

The higher a water's RA value is, the more help will be needed to lower the resulting mash pH to the optimal level. This is why brewing regions with high RA water historically brewed very dark beers, because the acidity of roasted malts helped to lower mash pH. The lower a water's RA value (they can be negative), the lower the mash pH will be. For brewing with all pale base malts, which, as we saw earlier, do not lend much acidity (pH 6.0 is typical for pale malt mashed in deionized water) having a low RA will be best. When brewing a stout, for example, using low RA water can be problematic, resulting in a mash pH value that is too low. In this case alkalinity may need to be added to achieve the correct mash pH.

Based on analysis from John Palmer and Colin Kaminski's book, *Water*, water profiles from the cities of Pilsen (Czechia), Dortmund (Germany), and Burton-on-Trent (UK) all have a similar residual alkalinity value. Based on the average of two estimates, Pilsen has an average of +0.5 RA (−6, +7), Dortmund an average of −8 RA (−36, +20) and Burton an average of −1 RA (−3, +1). With everything else being equal, a mash using any of these water sources should

Insight from the Massachusetts Water Resource Authority

Massachusetts water is generally considered to be of very high quality for drinking. This reputation is earned through the efforts of local organizations that assure its quality and treatment. David Coppes, Chief Operating Officer at the Massachusetts Water Resource Authority (MWRA), is himself a brewer and is familiar with the adjustments required to brew with this area's water. Coppes suggests that most public water authorities are only too happy to talk to their brewing constituents about the chemical composition of their water, including what adjustments might be beneficial to brewing better beer.

The MWRA provides water for the Boston area, sourcing it from a series of surface water reservoirs. This water is quite soft and not so dissimilar from the water of Pilsen, Czechia. The hardness of the water fluctuates around 15 mg/L as $CaCO_3$, with around 4 mg/L calcium ions for both raw input water and processed output water.

The biggest processing change is related to alkalinity and the corresponding pH. Incoming preprocessed water pH is 6.7, with an alkalinity of 6–7 mg/L as $CaCO_3$. This is problematic for the old water system of Boston, which features plenty of lead piping. Water this naturally soft is corrosive to metal pipes, leaching lead into the water and creating a major health concern. To reduce the raw water's corrosiveness, its alkalinity is adjusted higher with the addition of soda ash (Na_2CO_3), which increases the water's pH to 10.5. The addition of carbon dioxide by the MWRA lowers the pH to 9.5, a more acceptable value for drinking water, while at the same time maintaining the total alkalinity around 40 mg/L as $CaCO_3$.

While Coppes considers the overall shift in alkalinity from 6–7 to 40 mg/L a significant change, the water leaving the treatment plant still falls well within the guidelines to be considered soft water with low alkalinity. Yet that high ending pH is a key metric for brewers looking to brew with this water, making regular measurement of water pH key to success in the brewhouse. While some pH adjustments are helped by the addition of brewing salts, mash acidification is often needed to provide regularity and consistency in achieving pH goals.

result in a similar ending mash pH (Palmer and Kaminski 2013, 141–143). Therefore, the soft water of Pilsen was no more likely than the medium-hard water of Dortmund or the extremely hard water of Burton-on-Trent to produce a proper mash pH for the first pale lager.

In fact, the theory that Pilsner was a product of the unique water chemistry of Pilsen is worth reexamining. The soft water of Pilsen was actually a challenge for brewing light lager. Brewing pale beer with this type of water required the use of brewing salts and a lengthy acid rest during the mash (John Palmer, pers. comm.). Any brewer attempting to recreate Pilsen's water in order to brew this style without also including the associated water treatments is likely running a fool's errand.

Two variables that affect RA and are important for lager brewers are the water-to-grist ratio and the crush level. A higher water-to-grist ratio, as is typical of decoction mashes, will result in less buffering capacity. This means that the mash pH will be higher with thinner mashes than with thicker mashes. More finely crushed malt will also lower the RA value of wort.

WATER TREATMENT

Brewers will need to factor in their water's hardness, alkalinity, and pH to best determine which treatments will achieve the desired results. The most common and readily available options for water treatment are filtration, acidification, and the addition of brewing salts. Sophisticated filtration systems like reverse osmosis (RO) can offer a way for brewers to strip away most hardness and alkalinity. The resulting water is not ideal for brewing, so hardness and alkalinity will need to be added back to hit target levels. Blending a portion of raw water with the RO water offers one way to add back hardness and alkalinity in workable ranges.

Other water treatment options are available, including the Reinheitsgebot-compliant slaked lime treatment often used by German brewers. This is a treatment process that was developed in the mid-nineteenth century to help treat brewing water and is generally described as a method to reduce hardness in water. But using slaked lime—which is $Ca(OH)_2$, calcium hydroxide—isn't exactly a water softening process and it will change water in other ways. Slaked lime will cause a reaction between calcium bicarbonate and magnesium bicarbonate, thus reducing hardness and alkalinity in theory until Ca^{2+}/Mg^{2+} or CO_3^{2-} reaches zero. The slaked lime process will also cause a sharp increase in pH.

The other problem with slaked lime is that the reaction leaves 20–30 mg/L slaked lime in solution. Unlike RO water that creates the same finished water regardless of water input, output water treated with slaked lime will vary depending on the input water. American brewers who want to emulate the water profile of a favorite German brewer that uses the slaked lime process will find it difficult without an understanding of the input water.

The amount of hardness in brewing water can play a factor in the sensory and aroma properties of finished beer. Calcium sulfate can add dryness and highlight hop character, while calcium chloride can highlight malt and add body. High concentrations of brewing salts often lend bitter, astringent, salty, and minerally characters to beer. Yet very hard water can still result in fantastic lager. Agostino Arioli of Birrificio Italiano uses the naturally hard water from the brewery's local water source for the hop-forward Tipopils. Arioli says the hardness of the local water is 18 degrees French hardness, which converts to 180 mg/L as $CaCO_3$, falling into the hard to very hard range. Rather than change the character of his water source, Arioli works with the water when designing his beers.

Achieving beer clarity with soft water that has minimal dissolved calcium will be challenging, which is a potential problem for beers like Pilsner and Helles. From a purely practical perspective, adding calcium up to 50 ppm (i.e., 50 mg/L) will both help mashing pH and achieve finished beer clarity (Palmer and Kaminski 2013, 167).

Hops

Lager, particularly in modern brewing history, has been associated with very low hop usage. Pale industrial lager beer is so easily overwhelmed by bitterness that the most popular lagers in the world today have little to no hop character. An obvious trend in worldwide industrial lager has been a steady decrease in bitterness levels; even in Germany bitterness levels have been declining. One study that compared German-made Pilsner styles from a period beginning in 1983 and ending in 2013 saw a statistically significant decrease in IBUs of around 10% (Mayer and Lachenmeier 2015). As a result, and perhaps unfairly, hops don't generally receive very much attention when talking about lager.

Dry hopping was not uncommon in Germany until the 1980s, but was largely abandoned thereafter. Many of the downsides of dry hopping, mainly related to colloidal stability and shelf-life concerns, started to outweigh the benefits. Since lager is aged for many weeks, special consideration needs to be made to combat the high oxygen uptake that often occurs due to adding dry hops to beer (Back et al. 2020, 47).

Historically, while ale brewers relied on the antimicrobial power of hops to prevent beer spoilage, lager brewers relied on extended cold maturation to similar effect. As such, many lager styles, like the beers that transformed into modern Dunkel, used very low levels of hops.

The introduction of Pilsner Urquell in 1842 changed lager. This original Pilsner was highly hopped, with around 40 IBUs being contributed through the use of whole-leaf Saaz hops. Even by modern craft beer standards, that hopping rate is high: hitting 40 IBUs in a 13° Plato (1.053 SG) wort with 3% alpha-acid whole-leaf hops clocks in at an impressive 1.5 lb. per barrel (0.58 kg/hL). With its pale malt base, this would have represented one of the most aggressively hop-forward beers of its time. Many Pilsners that followed were additionally dry hopped, drawing comparisons with English pale ales (de Clerck 1957, 321).

The pale malt base was essential for keeping the character of this new pale lager focused on hop character, where the light color and reduced malt intensity allowed for the hop aromas and flavors to truly star. The assertive bitterness of Pilsner played the foil to the higher residual extract, balancing the beer and increasing its drinkability. The malt character of a similar strength Dunkel and Rauchbier would have overshadowed the hop aroma.

Žatec in northwest Czechia is perhaps the most famous hop growing region in the world, though in English it is usually referred to by its German name, Saaz. The Saazer, or Saaz, hop is inextricably linked with Pilsner, being the original hop used to brew it. Saaz is usually described as having "fine" bitterness, and it has been prized in brewing for centuries. There isn't necessarily anything specific about Saaz that makes it ideal for brewing lagers other than its long association with Pilsner. Today it's nearly impossible to separate the characteristics of Saaz hops from Czech lager. Saaz hops were so key to the identity of Czech beer that they were the only hops allowed to be grown in the country until the 1990s.

Using Saaz for Czech-style lager can throw up some surprises on brew day. The combination of very low–alpha acid hops and a high IBU target requires volumes of kettle hops to rival some craft IPA recipes. Břevnovský klášterní pivovar still uses hops from a historic hop yard in which the bines can be dated back 70–80 years. These hops typically only have an alpha-acid content of 1.9% and deliver a particularly woody character that's evident in the brewery's lagers. A typical whirlpool addition involves approximately 1.3 lb. per barrel (0.5 kg/hL) of hops to help achieve the required bitterness.

What makes Saaz and similar continental hops so remarkable are their particularly high levels of farnesene, a component of hop oil that is often described as herbal, floral, and woody. This trait is notably missing from most English, German, and American hop varieties, but it is found in Tettnang, Spalt (both German), Lubelska (Polish), Styrian Golding (Slovenian), and, as it happens, Sterling (American). Interestingly, most varieties either have high farnesene or almost none at all; there isn't a lot in between (table 2.9).

Table 2.9
Oil composition of common lager hop varieties

Hop variety	Hop oil as proportion of total hop oil content (%)		
	Humulene	Caryophyllene	Farnesene
Saaz	15–30	6–9	14–20
Tettnang	22–32	6–11	16–24
Spalt	10–22	4–10	15–22
Sterling	19–23	5–8	11–17
Lubelska	25–28	6–11	10–14
Cascade	8–13	3–6	3–7
Styrian Golding	34–38	9–11	2–5
Hallertau	45–55	10–15	<1
Tomyski	45	15	<1
Hersbrucker	20–30	8–13	<1
Citra	11–13	6–8	<1
Liberty	35–40	9–12	<1
Golding	35–45	13–16	<1

Exploring Polish Lager

Tom Beckmann of Goldfinger Brewing in Downers Grove, Illinois, has explored his family's brewing roots in Poland. His ancestor was a manufacturer of brewing equipment and one of Beckmann's prize possessions is a faucet produced by his family's firm. A drawing of that faucet features prominently in some of the brewery's branding.

Beckmann has also explored raw materials classically used to produce Polish lager beer, including many unique hop varieties. One of these varieties, Tomyski, has a dramatic history. Narrowly surviving the Nazi occupation, this variety was nearly lost when the Nazis destroyed 98% of the hop fields in Poland. The Tomyski hop was of particular interest to the occupiers since they were deemed to be of equal quality to German varieties and were thus seen as a threat. Only one hop yard, hidden in a forest, survived the war with Tomyski hops. All Tomyski hops today are descended from those bines that remained secret until the end of the war.

The oldest hop varieties of Czechia and Germany are generally described by European brewers as "fine" aroma hops. The hop oil of fine aroma hops is characterized by a low fatty acid ester content, by the presence of a secondary alcohol fraction (2-nonanol), and by a high content of β-farnesene and trans-α-bergamotene (Krofta 2003, 264–265). The noble hops Spalt and Tettnang have been shown through DNA analysis to have descended from the original Saaz cultivar (Alberts 2019). As these hop varieties share a common ancestor, it is apparent that the one-time punishment of death for smuggling Saaz root stock across the border into Germany was not enough of a deterrent!

Climate Change

Climate change will pose severe challenges for European hop growers, where both the hop varieties and how they are farmed will be problematic. Unlike in the US, where most hop fields are irrigated, few hop yards can say the same in Germany and Czechia. Hops without irrigation will suffer as changing weather patterns bring hotter temperatures with less consistent rain. These issues are compounded in very old hop varieties that have not come through more modern breeding programs specifically designed to produce varieties resistant to diseases and selected for their environmental tolerance. The future could be bleak for many of the older landrace varieties so highly desired by lager brewers. Time will tell, but there is likely a near future where Mittelfrüh and Hersbrucker are no longer grown. The race is on to breed new varieties that offer similar sensory profiles but also can grow in what will be the new climate.

Historically, almost all cultivated hops were of low bitterness and those old varieties that are still in use today are what we now refer to as aroma hops. In modern times, hops have been bred to increase the bittering values (mostly in the form of alpha acids) to create categories of hops we now refer to as dual-purpose hops and bittering hops. The definitions that have been found to describe hops over the years are arguably subjective, meaning that the boundaries that separate fine aroma hops from aroma hops and dual-purpose hops from bittering hops is not altogether clear.

When it comes to brewing traditional Continental-style lagers, using Continental hops is considered crucial by many brewers. For all their interesting aromas and flavors, American hops can be overbearing when paired with subtle pale lager styles. This isn't a new phenomenon. Though many are descended from European hops, American hops have always had this association as rather fruity and unsuitable for European beers (de Clerck 1957, 57). Perhaps a fairer description of American hops would be that they are challenging to substitute directly for their European counterparts.

However, American lager brewers are beginning to see the value in American hops, not for their "noble" characteristics but for these fruitier and more robust aromatic characteristics. The fact that the most popular American aroma hop currently, Citra, has a typical alpha-acid range of 10%–15% challenges the conventional wisdom that aroma hops are low in alpha acids. While these hops may not be suited to traditional styles, they can be used for new and interesting lagers.

The American hop scene has changed rapidly over the past few decades, continually ushering in entirely new generations of hops. These hops have predominantly been used for IPA brewing, but modern craft brewers have increasingly brought these varieties into all manner of lager styles. Modern lager brewers can choose from a seemingly infinite variety of hops to brew their lagers. We'll discuss the use of modern hop varieties in lager production when we explore the future of lager in chapter 7.

Seitz Family Farm in the Hallertau Growing Region

When we visited him in the Hallertau region of Upper Bavaria, Florian Seitz was sitting in a hunter's blind at the corner of his family's hop farm, where farmed land gives way to forest. With his two huge dogs, he was waiting for one of the small local deer to emerge from the woods and into his sights. His eventual success meant a few more hours of work cleaning the animal, seasoning the sirloin, and separating the organ meat for the dogs. But, in 2021, after months in a pandemic, this was work Seitz was excited to do to welcome us to his farm.

"I just love great food and beer," Florian said over a half-liter of local favorite, Müllerbräu Hell, pulled from the kegerator into an impeccably clean glass. Florian and his younger brother Georg had converted a portion of the house that was once used to store wood into a *Gasthaus*, or small pub, with a few long tables facing Georg's coaster collection. As some of the first guests to be able to share the space in this fourth-generation homestead with the Seitz family and friends, it was hard not to feel the emotion.

Over venison and farm-grown potatoes, we excitedly emerged from the awkwardness of the long months spent without social contact. The elder Seitz generation joined us for a toast; though they had already retired from the day-to-day business of the hop harvesting operation, they remained on the farm.

Hallertau is synonymous with German hops, but these hops are of course a many-splendored thing. The Seitz family grows five varieties: Hallertau Blanc, Hallertau Mittelfrüh, Hallertau Hersbrucker, Herkules, and Perle. The latter two varietals are bittering hops sold to brokers to make, well, any beer. We had made our visit to check on the year's crops of Blanc, Mittelfrüh, and Hersbrucker that are sold directly to brewers looking for the highest-quality aroma hops.

Seitzfarm is closer in spirit and design to the early American craft beer spirit than any of the other hop harvesters whose names adorn swag throughout the craft beer world. It is no space-age operation—in fact, some of the equipment predates the space age entirely—and there is no marketing sheen to any of it. What is evident is a targeted approach to technology, and the Seitz family's understanding of what's important to their customers.

When we rode around the 70-acre property in their homemade ATV trailer, Florian and Georg pointed out some of the subtle ways they manipulate their environment to ensure the utmost quality of their hops. Unlike most farms in the wet region of Hallertau, the Seitz farm is fully irrigated, allowing the moisture content of the hops to be adjusted every year as needed. One corner of the farm is lined with a stand of fast-growing trees Florian planted as part of his graduate program. These trees provide a natural break between the farm and the forest and can be harvested for fuel every few years.

Figure 2.4. Trust in your hop farmer is essential. Florian Seitz lends his support to one of the authors.

Unlike many of his customers, Florian's drive to innovate is not as simple as creating a new beer or recipe. Introducing new hop varieties is a cumbersome investment, made over multiple growing cycles. Drawing attention away from the classic German varietals has proved difficult.

While American consumers may not be seeking out these Hallertau varietals by name, their impact on the lager market is evident. Many of the world's best examples of Pilsner and other traditional pale lagers rely on these varietals. The subtle impact of these hops in the right brewer's hands is revelatory.

As for the Seitz family, whose bias in the matter is obvious, there is, of course, no question. Said Georg: "You cannot make real German-style beer without German ingredients."

Outside of limited bittering additions, many lager brewers eschew high–alpha acid hops. Still other traditional brewers refuse to use any hops other than low–alpha acid landrace varieties. Using hops that provide a "finer" bitterness is preferred by many brewers to impart nuance to their finished beer.

Andrew Foss of Philadelphia's Human Robot brewery identifies the low–alpha acid hops that lagers are traditionally brewed with as a key differentiating factor. Brewing with hops low in alpha acids instead of hops high in alpha acids will impact the flavor of a beer, even when attempting to hit the same number of IBUs. Utilization tends to be dramatically lower when using hops low in alpha acids, presumably due to needing a significantly larger quantity of hops to achieve a given level of IBUs. For a typical 3% alpha-acid Saaz addition, more than four times the amount of Saaz would be needed to provide the same IBUs as a 12% alpha-acid Citra addition. How much more will depend on brewhouse efficiency, but the added mass of hops will certainly affect the finished beer's aroma and flavor. When thinking about using hops in lager, alpha acids aren't the only important factor. Hop oils and plant materials tend to give a rounder flavor to the finished beer, especially at such high volumes.

FIRST WORT/EARLY KETTLE HOPPING

First wort hopping is when hops are added to the kettle during the transfer of wort from the lauter tun or mash filter to the kettle. First wort hops are in contact with the wort during the runoff, while the kettle gets to a boil, and during the entire boil. This technique was developed for practical reasons. One common problem for breweries is the overfoaming of wort as it comes to a boil. This represents a loss of product as well as a major safety issue. Historically, first wort hops were commonly used in an effort to reduce the surface tension of wort in an attempt to limit kettle foaming.

The early kettle hops designation can be applied to any hop that boils for extended periods of time and produces "kettle hop" aroma, including first wort hops and early boil hop additions. In a modern brewery, 60 minutes is a typical time for an early boil addition. Yet older brewing traditions often had longer boils, with two hours not uncommon.

Classic brewing literature mostly suggests that hops added for extended periods of time in the kettle are only for the purpose of bittering, while late kettle additions highlight aroma and flavor. Contrary to this widely held belief, lager owes a significant portion of its hop aroma to early kettle hop additions. Much of the spicy and herbal hop aroma of Pilsner-style beer is created during wort boiling and not from late hop additions. While it's true that volatile hop oils are boiled away, the boiling process continuously converts nonvolatile hop compounds into aroma-active compounds. Prolonged boiling of hops, which causes humulene and caryophyllene oxidation and hydrolysis products, creates the spicy herbal note in lager beer (Praet et al. 2015). The longer these hops are boiled, up to a maximum of two hours, the higher the values of these components in the finished beer.

This flavor, defined as "early kettle hop aroma" or "noble kettle hop aroma," is a defining characteristic of many traditional Pilsner-style beers. While adding all the hops to the beginning of the boil is the exception, it is also the normal procedure at Pilsner Urquell, where the hops are all boiled for two hours (de Clerck 1957, 322). Ashleigh Carter of Bierstadt Lagerhaus in Denver, Colorado, has long been a proponent of first wort kettle hopping, which she uses as part of her hopping regime for Slow Pour Pils. In particular, Ashleigh appreciates the flavor of the first wort hops that have time to steep in the lower-pH wort at the beginning of the runoff. In addition to first wort hops, a 70-minute early kettle hop addition is added. There are no typical late additions of flavor or aroma hops in Slow Pour Pils. The flavor and aroma of this beer arises from the early boil hops combined with the effect of the first wort hops added before the kettle is even a quarter filled.

Whole-Leaf Hops

At one point in time, only whole-leaf hops were used in the brewhouse. The modernization of breweries has made the use of whole-leaf hops more problematic, increasing the use of pelletized hops in the industry. In historical times, whole-leaf hops would have been separated out in a basket upon entering the coolship. With modern plate and frame heat exchangers, new methods are required to deal with this plant material. In one such modern brewhouse, Germany's Alpirsbacher Klosterbräu, the 420-hectoliter brewhouse still uses all "pressed" whole-leaf hops for hot side operations. Budvar is one of the only Czech breweries to do this as well, believing that the flavor associated with whole hops is key to the flavor profile of its beer. This has required the installation of a sophisticated method for hop removal.

DRY HOPPING LAGER

Dry hopping lager offers some unique challenges, especially when managing spunded lager with its high concentrations of carbon dioxide. Any beer under pressure is at risk of gushing out of tanks, causing safety, cleanliness, and oxidation concerns. The cold maturation temperatures of lager will ensure that, spunded or not, the beer will have more carbon dioxide in solution.

Two options are available to dry hop fully carbonated lagers. The first is to dry hop when transferring beer from a primary to a secondary tank; this is a unique opportunity to take advantage of a traditional fermentation method. A second method is to introduce hops under pressure by using a pressurized hop dosing tank. There are a few commercially available hopping systems that can accomplish this task, but it requires significant time compared to throwing hops into the top of the tank.

Lager's development has clearly been shaped by raw materials. Brewing traditions informed by association with and access to raw materials have given rise to different categories of lager, and many of those brewing traditions continue today. These traditions have carried with them techniques and processes suited to these materials. Whether it is the famous water of Pilsen or the hops of the Hallertau, much of our modern understanding of lager styles is closely tied to the materials that have been historically used to brew them.

The unprecedented control a modern lager brewer has over their beer brings with it extra responsibility. Unfettered global access to raw materials and the ability to selectively implement traditional techniques means that a brewer is limited only by their imagination. With the right amount of care and attention to detail, truly unique, historically informed, and progressive lager can be fashioned from raw materials old and new.

3

FERMENTING WITH LAGER YEAST

FERMENTATION IS WIDELY ACKNOWLEDGED TO BE THE MAIN POINT OF DIFFERENCE BETWEEN LAGERS AND ALES. The common wisdom goes something like this: ale yeasts ferment faster and warmer, are top fermenting, and are more flavorful compared to the slow, cold, bottom-fermenting and neutral-flavored lager yeasts. American industrial lager producers have trained their customers to expect clean, crisp flavors from their "bottom-" or "cold-fermenting" lager beers. There is, as you might expect, more to brewing great lager than simply selecting a lager yeast and providing a cold environment for fermentation.

While low-temperature fermentations are certainly the norm in most traditional lager breweries, those temperatures rarely remain static. For a variety of reasons that we will explore, many lager brewers take care to modify and manipulate the temperature of beer throughout their fermentations. There are, however, other lager brewers who ferment their beer at relatively warm temperatures. But while temperature is an easy choice for brewers who know their yeast well, time is a variable that often eludes the control of even the best breweries.

Longer fermentation times are certainly traditional for lagers, but there is little consensus on exactly how much time is required for a high-quality lager fermentation. The brewer's vision, coupled with their personal desire to adhere to tradition, and the resources available to them make this a particularly difficult variable to pin down between different breweries. At one end of the spectrum, industrial lager breweries have made every effort to reduce the total time required to meet quality guidelines. At the other end, small traditional breweries that can sell a premium product may extoll the virtues of lager that has been given months to condition. Most brewers find themselves between these extremes and are left to consider the potential tradeoffs between time and quality.

Likewise, there is no single agreed upon method for the maturation stage, that is, lagering. The time and temperature of maturation is thoroughly and vigorously debated among lager brewers. With modern refrigeration technology, storing lager at or near freezing temperatures is typical even in otherwise very traditional breweries. Yet, many of the actual stone *Kellers* (cellars) that we visited struggled to stay below 45°F (7°C) in the summer, suggesting that lagering temperatures were once much warmer than we typically see today. One can argue over the exact time and temperature needed to properly lager beer, but for our purposes we'll refer to lagering as the period of time spent in tank after primary fermentation. We'll explore many of the different variables and considerations that come into play when deciding how long and at what temperature to store your beer.

One of the most important variables in determining a fermentation profile is the brewer's philosophy. The many months once standard for conditioning lagers is not necessary in modern breweries. Yet some of the advancements that have shortened lagering times have brought with them unintended consequences. Tradition can be part of a brewer's inspiration, but with modern raw materials and methods some adaptation of traditional methods is advantageous. Even the most traditional breweries operating today have adopted certain modern techniques. And in many otherwise modern breweries, vestiges of traditional techniques are still preserved and practiced.

Understanding the pathways available for lager yeast will help chart a course in the brewer's mind. With all the tools and raw materials available to a modern brewer, lager yeast can be used to produce nearly any sensory profile imaginable. From the stunningly dry and crisp to the intensely malty or hoppy, lager yeast can be shaped to meet the needs of nearly any beer style. Knowing your yeast and what keeps it healthy will allow you as a brewer to cover this spectrum, as will an appreciation of the differences between lager yeast and ale yeast strains.

Much has been written about the neutrality of lager yeast strains. From our experience and research, we find that lager yeast, even with its relatively low production of esters and fusel alcohols, contributes the defining flavor characteristics of the beer it ferments. Rather than relying on raw materials for sensory contributions, lager yeast makes its presence known to the drinker with its distinctive fermentation characteristics. Lager yeast is impactful enough that otherwise forthcoming brewers closely guard information about their yeast strains and fermentation profiles. If lager yeast strains were truly neutral, this secretiveness would not make much sense.

Many claim to use a unique or hybrid version of lager yeast that has adapted genetically to their brewing environments. Brewer Alexander Büch of Müllerbräu in Pfaffenhofen, Germany, has traveled with a single strain of yeast for his entire brewing career. Büch has brought it from brewery to brewery because it performs in a specific way that works for his fermentation program. While he is secretive about the source of the yeast, he notes that even though you could buy this yeast from a lab, a single-strain commercial version would not work the same outside of his brewery. Specifically, it has adapted to extremely cold temperatures, as low as 34°F (1°C), to finish secondary fermentation. This yeast has now gone through decades of generations that have slowly made it unique. Even yeasts descended from the famous and nearly ubiquitous 34/70 strain can adapt and change to exhibit distinct and interesting fermentation characteristics.

While fermentation certainly influences how a beer tastes, it also has a direct impact on how it smells, looks, and feels on the palate. While each style of lager is unique and will require different fermentation processes, the heart and soul of all lager is the fermentation process. In this chapter, we'll explore the fermentation characteristics of lager yeast and the many ways brewers can act to shape it.

In the end, fermentation is at the center of what defines lager. As brewer and owner Brian "Swifty" Peters of Austin Beer Garden Brewing Company (ABGB) puts it, all brewers are "accommodating the needs of a living organism." Yeast pays the bills in good lager breweries, and learning to make it happy should be a brewer's priority. Careful attention to the fermentation process is a theme throughout successful lager breweries.

What to Expect from Traditional Lager Fermentations

Brewing with a modern commercial lager yeast strain is, essentially, fairly straightforward. This is especially so with the most used lager yeast in the world, the 34/70 strain. It has been selected to be a workhorse: reliable, consistent, and repitchable. However, providing the right inputs and the proper environment for healthy yeast can prove challenging for first-time lager brewers and seasoned veterans alike. A normal lager fermentation has several characteristics that may surprise or alarm brewers more familiar with ale fermentations.

Many metrics that are taken for granted when brewing with ale yeast can cause more serious issues for lager fermentation. Cell counts, oxygen supply, temperature, osmotic pressure, autolysis, and repitching volumes are just some of the measures that require specific testing. These variables all have impacts on the performance of lager yeast and, ultimately, the flavor profile of the beer.

Brewing with lager yeast can be shocking for the senses too. While primary fermentations with some ale strains can produce lovely aromas, the same is not usually said for lager. Lager yeasts are notorious sulfur producers, throwing aromas of "struck match" and "rotten eggs." These aromas can carry through fermentation and end up in the finished beer. Many traditional lagers prominently feature sulfur compounds like sulfur dioxide in the finished beer; this is a character prized by some European drinkers but is less tolerated by US consumers.

The time it takes to condition and ferment lager beer is perhaps its most infamous and intimidating feature. Traditional primary lager fermentations are quite slow, taking as long as two weeks. Expect a 1° to 1.5° Plato drop per day for a standard 12° Plato wort (roughly 4°–6° gravity per day from 1.048 OG), with the last Plato degree taking days to drop off before terminal gravity is reached. Thus, primary fermentation with lager takes 7–10 days, nearly double the time it takes to ferment most ales. Jean de Clerck notes the "golden rule" that primary lager fermentations can be conducted in any manner so long as it is regular and active and finishes in 8–10 days without any sharp changes in temperature (de Clerck 1957, 409).

When plotting a graph of changes in gravity for an ale fermentation, the rate of reduction of gravity will often look exponential. By comparison, the same graph for a lager fermentation is typically quite linear through the first 80%–90% of fermentation until that long, slow grind to reach terminal gravity—those final days of fermentation where you patiently wait and hope that you made all the proper choices along the way. Faster lager fermentations are possible, especially for beers with warmer fermentation profiles or a large percentage of simple sugars in the wort. In some cases, a faster fermentation can also be the result of overpitching yeast. While quicker fermentation can provide reassurance and relief, the resulting beer likely won't meet the expected flavor profiles of a traditional lager. Often, quick lager fermentations can result in unintended long-term problems that require adjusting the secondary conditioning schedule.

After primary fermentation, so begins the cold storing and conditioning process that gives lager its name. No conversation about lager fermentation is complete without a discussion over how long beer should be stored before packaging. There are markedly differing philosophies between various lager producers as to how long lager should be aged. Given a beer with the same raw materials and gravity, how primary fermentation is conducted and the brewer's goals will have the largest impact on the amount of time required for conditioning.

Despite its romantic associations with tradition, months of lagering requires a difficult calculation of risk and reward. Even if keeping product for such an extended period is economically feasible for a brewery, extended lagering is not always a net positive. Long lagering times with healthy yeast following a low-temperature primary fermentation with carefully controlled nutrient sources can reward the patient brewer. Long lagering times with unhealthy yeast, or after a warmer primary fermentation, or using extremely low lagering temperatures may prove detrimental to the finished beer due to yeast autolysis.

Very cold and slow fermentations for a beer that will be naturally carbonated will require weeks or months to properly lager. This is the method favored by many of the world's best-regarded German lager breweries, such as Klosterbrauerei Andechs, Weihenstephan, and Schönramer. These well-known traditional breweries have inspired some American lager producers to design their fermentation programs in this way. Historically, it has been assumed that for each degree Plato of original extract, one week of lagering should be employed (de Clerck 1957, 431). So, for a standard 12° Plato (1.048 OG) beer, twelve weeks of lagering are needed.

One of the more dramatic departures from traditional lagering methods is the warmer primary fermentation temperatures favored by modern industrial breweries. Fermentation temperatures near 60°F (15.5°C) allow these breweries to shorten lagering time considerably, mimicking ale fermentations and allowing these force-carbonated beers to be turned around within two weeks.

Lager yeasts generally produce more esters and fusel alcohols at warmer temperatures, leading to a less neutral flavor profile, while simultaneously reducing sulfur and diacetyl faster. This is due to the higher growth rate of lager yeast colonies and resulting vigorous fermentation. This results in beers with fewer off flavors as a vigorous fermentation with healthy yeast will metabolize many common off-flavors. This runs counter to the widely held belief that lower temperatures create "cleaner" beers. We will explore and compare these fermentation techniques shortly.

Some yeast researchers, including Mathias Hutzler of the Technical University of Munich, believe that the target flavor profile of lager fermentation can be best defined by a ratio of fusel alcohols to esters of approximately 1.0:2.5–3.0; however, the lower the overall levels of both the better (Kunze 1999, 330). All things being equal, lower temperatures equate to lower levels of esters and fusel alcohols, the majority of which are produced in the very beginning of primary fermentation. However, the lower temperatures also prolong the reduction of sulfur, diacetyl, acetaldehyde, and other off-flavors. It is only the long lager process that helps to manage these flavors.

In many types of ale fermentation, stress is often a tool to enhance the flavor profile. For example, German wheat beer yeasts tend to create more banana character when they are poorly aerated or underpitched. In contrast, lager fermentation is always best performed by healthy yeast under ideal conditions. We have not found any examples of a stressed lager yeast producing positive fermentation flavor profiles. Process decisions should support the health and vitality of the yeast, which has a direct and measurable impact on beer quality. These qualities are also key to allowing for proper foam retention in the finished beer. The more stressed the yeast, the more off-flavors are created, while at the same time increased autolysis negatively affects beer foam (Bamforth 2012, 34).

Other unique processes for traditional lager fermentations include "spunding" and "krausening." These are two ways that lager is naturally carbonated at the end of fermentation. Both these techniques will be discussed at length in chapter 5.

Spunding and Krausening

Spunding refers to the act of capturing carbon dioxide (CO_2) produced during primary fermentation by bunging a tank.

Krausening involves the addition of fermentable material (usually wort) to induce a secondary or tertiary fermentation from which CO_2 is then captured by bunging.

Historical Fermentation Process

Lager yeast strains adapted to meet the needs of Bavarian brewers, who, to protect beer quality, were prohibited from brewing during warmer months when beer spoilage was more likely. Instead, brewers in Bavaria had to brew during the colder months and then store many months' worth of beer in cold cellars to get them through the summer. Yeast that could thrive in these environments while continuously and slowly fermenting beer were essential to the success of these breweries. The modern ancestors of these yeasts still exhibit some of these characteristics, continuing a marginal yet active fermentation months after brewing. In the cold conditioning room at Schönramer, lagers that have been krausened and left to age in the brewery's cellars still have activity for up to two months, their spunding valves bubbling away while the beer rests close to 32°F (0°C). Traditional lager breweries were built to take advantage of this feature of lager yeasts. At the Budvar brewery in Czechia, we witnessed active fermentation in tanks of lager that had been aging for nearly a year.

Present-day Franconia is famous for its incredible density of breweries, many of which were rebuilt just after World War II. For all that density, there was little diversity in the design of these breweries. Primary fermentation was typically performed in open square vessels, followed by secondary fermentation in unjacketed horizontal tanks in the cellar. Most of these 1950-era setups feature enamel or aluminum tanks that mimic the shape and size of the wooden vessels that would have preceded them. In this setup, the primary fermentation happened in an open tank where yeast could be skimmed from the top of the fermenting beer. At the end of the primary fermentation, the beer was transferred to an unjacketed tank in a temperature-controlled cellar room. The spunding or krausening of the beer would happen at this point. The result of this design is that carbonation and secondary fermentation happened very slowly and at a colder temperature than the primary fermentation. The brewer had little control over how quickly the tank chilled and how fast the end of fermentation was reached. Strong fermentations with healthy yeast would finish before the tank got too cold, while struggling fermentations might show inconsistencies in carbonation levels as well as exhibiting diacetyl and other off-aromas.

For traditional breweries that still follow this setup, krausening is a very important part of the conditioning and carbonation process. Since the temperature can't be controlled well, it's very important that there is healthy yeast that can survive very cold conditions. Krausening will help eliminate off-flavors like diacetyl and acetaldehyde while ensuring full attenuation and carbonation. Weeks or months may be spent waiting for the beer to be ready.

Mittenwald and Schell's

At the Brauerei Mittenwald high in the German Alps near the Austrian border, a lively *Gasthaus* allows patrons to look through glass walls at the gleaming brewhouse installed in 2016. Yet under that modern brewhouse another story unfolds. Fifth-generation brewer-owner Christoph Neuner still uses a *Keller* (cellar) cut deep into the bedrock beneath the brewery more than one hundred years before.

Mittenwald's beers undergo a week-long primary fermentation in large square enamel fermentors. Cooling pipes, clearly added to the fermentors at a later date, poke through the walls and run through the middle of the tanks to keep the beer cool while fermenting. At the end of fermentation, the beer is racked or moved into non-jacketed aluminum tanks in a room kept near freezing temperatures. Bubbles in the aluminum mark spots where overpressurization tested, but did not break, the integrity of the antique tanks. Once it is racked to this room, the beer is left to slowly cool over days and weeks.

The brewery itself is a family affair, sharing a driveway with Neuner's mother's house. There's a resourcefulness required to make beer thousands of feet above sea level in such an old brewery. The onsite museum highlights some of the ways the brewery has modernized, but the methods still employed are quite traditional in comparison to most American craft breweries. The brewery is, in some ways, closer in spirit to some of the original brewery operations of the mid-1800s.

The first American lager breweries were built by German and Czech immigrants, and the August Schell Brewing Company in New Ulm, Minnesota, is one of the oldest still owned and operated by a family. The brewery was founded on a wooded hill a few hours outside Minneapolis in 1860, its grounds boasting an estate and pet peacocks in a throwback to the family's Continental origins.

Schell's founders and owners cut deep cellars and devised complicated methods of harvesting river ice to provide the coldest possible environment for their beer. Like Mittenwald, Schell's has experienced generations of brewing technologies since its founding, from brewing beer seasonally without refrigeration with yeast brought over from the homeland, to using all types of "modern" inventions like vacuum fermentation, steam-injected mashing, ice-filled "schwimmers," and many other pieces of equipment and practices

Fig. 3.1. The very cold lager cellar at the Brauerei Mittenwald, Germany.

now outdated. The decommissioned ammonia refrigeration system that replaced the ice harvesting operation is a mass of cast iron equipment permanently entwined in the brewery's structure. Many of the other technologies have been enshrined and documented in the museum attached to Schell's "bier halle."

"It's not an easy space to work with," said owner and former head brewer Ted Marti. "That one's on me," he said as we pass under the Maypole and past an outer wall with the end of a horizontal tank poking through, birds roosted mockingly in the outer insulation. Years back, Marti had tried to add a few tanks to the nineteenth-century building and had come up a few centimeters short in his measurements.

Yet through it all, the Schell and Marti families have persevered in brewing lager. Prohibition saw them creating "near beers" that were meant to be spiked at one of the speakeasies in town. The brewery has been brewing with gelatinized corn since its founding, and added a line of more traditional, all-malt beers in the 1980s. Another more recent shift has introduced some American craft beer styles into the Schell's lineup. Fermentation and conditioning times have crept down over the generations, but Schell's beers still spend weeks in a mixture of vertical and horizontal tanks.

Most Americans, even those with a love for American lager, haven't had the opportunity to try Schell's Deer Brand beer. That's something that ought to change!

In this two-tank approach it is important that the right amount of yeast is present during lagering. Too much yeast will quickly lead to autolysis, resulting in off-flavors and poor foam retention in the finished beer; not enough yeast will lead to incomplete reduction of acetaldehyde and diacetyl, which will also lead to off-flavors in the final product. A cell count of around three million cells per milliliter is the target that avoids either of these outcomes.

Working with Lager Yeast in Modern Breweries

The decision matrix for modern lager brewers changed with the invention of the unitank, or conical fermentor, in the second half of the twentieth century. While this solved many issues it also created a set of new challenges that needed to be addressed. Traditional lager fermentation was inefficient, slow, and expensive. As brewing entered the modern age, a desire for efficiency changed many of the variables for brewing lager beer. While advances like refrigeration and sanitary tank design have increased the brewer's ability to control fermentations and create consistent beer, many other advantages meant to increase brewery efficiencies have had knock-on effects that present challenges for the continuation of traditional lagers.

Traditional slow fermentations, with their long conditioning times and low osmotic and hydrostatic pressures, have no place in most modern breweries: taller tanks, higher starting gravities, warmer fermentations, single-culture strains, shorter tank times, and higher attenuation requirements make it easier to brew more lager quickly and efficiently. Yet these tools also encourage a consistency that approaches homogeneity. Many classic lager sensory characteristics are process and fermentation driven, and are often linked to outdated technologies. Brewers that wish to produce traditional tasting lager will have to decide how to best use their equipment to meet the needs of their preferred lager yeast. Designing a fermentation program that accounts for these variables is a real challenge.

We find that most brewers use a method that fits roughly into one of three types of primary fermentation program (table 3.1). There is a traditional method where the temperature remains cold the entire time; a modern hybrid method where fermentation starts cold but is allowed to warm at the end; and a more industrial method where temperatures are warm for the entirety of the fermentation.

Every adjustment to temperature, yeast nutrients, pressure, aeration, and pitch count will have positive and negative sensory impacts. Unfortunately for brewers, there is no single correct answer to these questions, and the sensory impacts are a tradeoff. For example, while a colder fermentation will decrease ester and fusel alcohol formation, it will also increase the possibility of diacetyl, acetaldehyde, and sulfur aromas. Lager brewers must find the balance of flavor characteristics they feel is suitable for their beer and adjust their inputs accordingly.

Cold and warm are relative, and dependent on equipment. For our purposes, we'll consider cold fermentation to be 41–54°F (5–12°C) and warm 54–64°F (12–18°C).

Table 3.1

Pros and cons of various lager fermentation programs, with timeframe assumed starting with 12° Plato (1.048 OG) wort

Method	Pros	Cons	Average timeframe for beer
Traditional: always cold 41–54°F (5–12°C) 46–50°F (8–10°C) most common	"More traditional" Higher CO_2 levels at end of primary fermentation Longer shelf life	Longer to pass diacetyl rest, more sulfur & other off-flavors Less vigorous fermentations Greater time commitment	5–8 weeks
Modern hybrid: cold start followed by raise in temperature toward end of primary ferm., typically at ~50% of original gravity 41–54°F (5–12°C) start Allowed to rise as high as 64°F (18°C) by end	Faster, vigorous primary fermentation helps with diacetyl reduction while also limiting ester and fusel formation Warmer temperature for dry hopping give better hop aroma extract Quicker turnaround of beer due to shorter lagering time	Potential repitch issues Less CO_2 in solution presents challenges for natural carbonation Warmer end-stage of fermentation reduces overall yeast health	3–5 weeks
Warm fermentation: higher temperatures throughout 54–64°F (12–18°C)	Fast primary fermentation Requires little to no lagering time Potential for most stereotypical "clean/neutral" character with top pressure	Yeast health issues Increased ester and fusel alcohol production Natural carbonation likely not possible Top pressure must be applied during fermentation for "clean/neutral" character	1–3 weeks

TYPES OF FERMENTATION

Traditional fermentation: always cold; 41–54°F (5–12°C)

The traditional method of fermentation maintains a low temperature throughout, often with a cooling step at the end of primary fermentation. Historically, the cooling step would have occurred naturally as heat generated by fermentation subsided and the cold environment reduced the beer's temperature further. Here lies one of the big challenges with traditional fermentations. Decreasing temperatures during fermentation slows the metabolic process of yeast, slowing the rate at which off-flavors like diacetyl are reduced. Healthy yeast and the correct cell count are vital to ensure proper diacetyl reabsorption.

The advantage for brewers in the past, of course, is that these conditions would have been ideal for prolonging the lagering process, the slow yeast metabolism facilitating a continuous fermentation and allowing the beer to last through the long summer months. Krausening during secondary fermentation would have extended the maturation process by adding more fermentables to continue the slow fermentation. A modern brewer can mimic the natural process of cooling beer in a cellar by cooling wort down to 39°F (4°C) at a rate of 2°F (1°C) per day at the end of primary fermentation (Narziß 1966, 21).

Lagers brewed in this fashion tend to have the lowest ester and fusel alcohol character, as well as favorable fusel alcohol to ester ratios (see p. 84). Colder primary fermentation results in less cell multiplication and therefore less yeast biomass production. At the same time, yeast health will be maximized because fewer yeast cells are competing for the same nutrient pool. Colder temperatures solubilize carbon dioxide (CO_2) in beer at higher rates, which also helps to reduce ester formation. Higher levels of dissolved CO_2 benefits naturally carbonated lager, because higher levels of CO_2 at the start of the process means less CO_2 will be needed for full carbonation at packaging. Furthermore, because more CO_2 is solubilized in colder liquids, less top (head) pressure needs to be applied to the beer to contain the desired amount of carbonation. The reduced top pressure provides a healthier environment for yeast, reducing the chance for autolysis. We will talk more about natural carbonation in chapter 5.

The main disadvantage to the traditional cold fermentation method is the slow metabolic activity of yeast causing a buildup of off-flavors. It may take weeks before diacetyl is completely removed, perhaps even longer for stronger beers. There will be a long and noticeable change in these beers week after week as acetaldehyde and sulfur compounds are slowly metabolized. These issues are amplified with natural carbonation methods. Spunding traps off-flavors from primary fermentation, while krausening creates an entirely new (secondary) fermentation with its own potential for off-flavors. In these cases, more lagering time will be needed for maturation.

Cold fermentations with natural carbonation are best completed using a two-tank process that separates primary fermentation from maturation and lagering. By racking beer to a secondary tank, beer is removed from the bulk of yeast in the primary tank. When using a single tank, yeast dumps and regular monitoring of tank pH should be taken to prevent and monitor for autolysis. Cold temperatures alone will not suffice to prevent autolysis.

Modern hybrid fermentation: 41–54°F (5–12°C) start; allowed to rise as high as 64°F (18°C) by end

In a modern hybrid fermentation, fermentation starts cold but is allowed to warm toward the end of primary fermentation. The modern hybrid approach takes advantage of a cold start to fermentation, which limits ester and fusel alcohol production while more quickly reducing off-flavors at the end of primary fermentation as the beer warms. Typically, the temperature is raised when 50% of the total original extract is consumed. At this point, the cooling of the tanks is stopped to allow the wort to naturally rise in temperature through fermentation, or raised to a higher set point.

Raising the temperature only at the end of primary fermentation avoids the increased ester and fusel alcohol production seen in fermentations that are warmer all the way through. The late warm stage in the hybrid method also accelerates the metabolism of off-flavors like diacetyl, sulfur compounds, and acetaldehyde. This reduces the time required for lagering; typically a hybrid fermentation will require a shorter period of time at close to freezing temperatures than a traditional fermentation. The hybrid method might also be advantageous for specialty beers like hoppy lagers, because the warmer temperatures at the end of fermentation will allow for better dry hopping extraction. (Dry hopped lagers are discussed more in chapter 7.)

There are downsides to raising the temperature though. Generally, raising the temperature will cause unrealized changes that can affect the overall flavor and aroma profile of the finished beer in ways that may be at odds with creating traditional-style lagers. Warmer temperatures at the end of fermentation, while temporarily enhancing yeast health and increasing yeast metabolism, lead to yeast health issues when primary fermentation is complete and available nutrients are consumed. The process will reduce long-term yeast viability and potentially create repitching issues, although not to the same extent as entirely warm fermentations. This also creates problems for natural carbonation. If naturally carbonating these beers, higher top pressure will be needed to get to full carbonation. A combination of reduced long-term viability and increased secondary fermentation top pressure can lead to increased yeast autolysis. Monitoring for an increase in pH will help identify if this is an issue. Krausening might be a better solution, as it introduces healthy yeast once the beer has cooled to a more appropriate temperature where lower top pressures can be used. A slow cooling of the beer at the end of primary fermentation will help alleviate the need for these higher pressures.

Warm fermentation: 54–64°F (12–18°C); higher temperatures throughout
The warm fermentation method keeps the temperature of the fermentation on the higher side throughout the entirety of the process. In general, a relatively warm pitching temperature accelerates yeast metabolism, increasing yeast health and biomass production. The result are beers that have fewest off-flavors (warmer fermentations expedite the reduction of diacetyl, sulfur compounds, and acetaldehyde, among other off-flavors), albeit with the potential to create high levels of esters and fusel alcohols. These fermentation profiles also tend to create beers with less aromatic character, lighter body, and less bitterness (de Clerck 1957, 409).

Styles like California common take advantage of the esters and other fermentation characteristics that lager yeast strains produce at warmer temperatures. However, warmer lager fermentations are most often used by large industrial brewers who employ higher temperatures to speed up the brewing process. In these cases, the esters and fermentation characteristics are often undesirable; adjusting fermentation parameters is key to keeping these flavors in check.

Brewers who wish to ferment warm to speed up fermentation while minimizing the formation of esters and fusel alcohols can take advantage of top pressure. Top pressure can be used for the entirety of the fermentation process, as long as it is applied within twenty-four hours from the start of primary fermentation. Using top pressure in this way should not be confused with bunging, or spunding, a tank for carbonation purposes. The application of top pressure at the beginning of primary fermentation limits the creation of sulfur compounds, esters, and fusel alcohols, whereas bunging for natural carbonation can trap these flavors in the beer. Top pressure increases the level of carbon dioxide in the fermenting beer, which reduces the number of decarboxylation reactions that are a key reaction step in the formation of fusel alcohols and esters (Pires et al. 2013, 1944).

Top pressure is frequently recommended as part of warm lager fermentations to help keep fusel alcohol, ester, and sulfur compound levels within normal limits while reducing other off-flavors (Annemüller, Manger, and Lietz 2011, 364). This provides the "clean and neutral" yeast flavors that are often associated (perhaps stereotypically) with American light lager.

However, top pressure is only one variable present in warm lager yeast fermentations. Industrial lager fermentations are often paired with high starting gravities and massive tanks, factors that tend to skew fermentations to produce esters and fusel alcohols. So, while we often associate industrial-scale lager production with the lightest and most neutral beers, some of the largest brands are strongly associated with their ester profiles, particularly notes of apple and banana. American light lager has more fermentation character than it usually gets credit for, albeit significantly less than it would if top-pressure fermentations were not used.

The biggest problem with the warm fermentation process is the stress it creates on the yeast. High biomass production quickly depletes nutrients, forcing yeast to compete for them; combine this with high pressures and high attenuation and the conditions can quickly cause yeast to autolyze. Thus, for beers that have gone through a warm fermentation, a long lagering process will be unhelpful at best and actively detrimental at worst. A quick and very cold crash process is recommended to drop out the yeast and eliminate the potential for autolysis affecting the finished beer. Repitching such yeast may be impossible.

Given that beers which have undergone a warm fermentation program don't lager well, they require a faster approach. The best process substitute for the slower, colder lagering process of the more traditional methods is likely a warm, fast, "clean and efficient" fermentation. Jean de Clerck notes that a rapid fermentation leads to greater coagulation of suspended solids, which results in drier and brighter beers that are less subject to raw material defects (de Clerck 1957, 409). All these factors combined have led to a modern method that produces the "cleanest and most neutral" light lager beers.

Fermentation Variables

There are many factors that influence lager beer fermentation. We'll address the most important variables and explain how they affect the fermentation process and flavor profile of lager (table 3.2). While each factor will affect the final beer, the relative degree to which each factor influences various fermentation compounds will vary.

AERATION

Both ale and lager yeast have a similar recommendation for oxygen wort content of around 8 mg/L (Ockert 2006a, 13), but lager yeast generally has up to twice the recommended pitch rate. This means that each pitched cell will have half the available oxygen compared to ale yeast of the same wort. This is partly what leads to a lower rate of cell multiplication in lager fermentations: low biomass growth requires less oxygen, and low oxygen encourages low growth rates (Mathias Hutzler, pers. comm.). Low growth leads to lower ester and fusel alcohol formation, leading to a more neutral yeast aroma.

Table 3.2

Factors affecting selected fermentation compounds

	Esters	Fusel alcohols	Sulfur compounds (SO$_2$, H$_2$S)	Acetaldehyde
Aeration				
Higher[a]	↑	↑	↓	↓
Lower[b]	↓[c]	↓	↑	↑
Free amino nitrogen (FAN)				
High	↑	↓[d]	↓	↓
Low	↓	↑	↑	↑
Pitching rates				
Higher[b]	↓	↓	↓	↑[e]
Lower[a]	↑	↑	↑	↓[f]
Top pressure				
Higher	↓	↓	↓	↑
Lower	↑	↑	↑	↓
Temperature				
Higher	↑	↑	↑[e]	↑
Lower	↓	↓	↓[f]	↓
Wort gravity (original extract)				
High, >14°P (>1.057 SG)	↑	↑	↑	↑
Average, 10–14°P (1.040–1.057 OG)	...	...	↓	...
Low, <10°P (<1.040 SG)	↓	↓	↑	↓

[a] Assuming higher biomass production.
[b] Assuming lower biomass production and sufficient lagering.
[c] Esters will increase if aeration is insufficient.
[d] Excessive FAN will increase fusel alcohols.
[e] But reduced faster through metabolism at end of fermentation.
[f] But reduced slower through metabolism at end of fermentation.

When using sterile air to aerate wort, the temperature of the knockout is very important. The ability of oxygen from air to become solubilized in wort is proportional to the temperature of the wort. It's nearly impossible to get enough oxygen in solution to reach the target of 8 mg/L at 59°F (15°C), but it becomes progressively easier as the wort gets cooler. As a consequence, providing enough oxygen using sterile air at ale fermentation temperatures may not be feasible.

Aeration, or lack thereof, and how it is applied can affect a fermentation program and the subsequent aging and lagering decisions in important ways. Brewers who follow "traditional" or *Reinheitsgebot* practices are not able to add oxygen or yeast nutrients, which makes warmer fermentations challenging because higher fermentation temperatures facilitate higher biomass production, potentially requiring more resources than the wort can properly supply. This depletes nutrients and creates long-term vitality issues. To put it another way, fermentations that rely on air aeration without added nutrients will benefit from a cold and slow fermentation that inhibits cell multiplication.

At Urban Chestnut Brewing Company in St. Louis, Missouri, owner and brewer Florian Kuplent is a strong proponent of using air instead of pure oxygen when aerating wort. His main concern is that pure oxygen is toxic to yeast, and overoxygenating wort is a significant risk when brewers aren't testing their wort dissolved oxygen (DO) levels. An additional benefit when using air comes from the large volumes needed to hit proper DO levels, because the increased flow of air helps to mix and homogenize the wort.

There are other long-term flavor changes that come from overaerating lager wort. A balance needs to be struck between having high yeast vitality, which will create fewer esters and fusel alcohols, and avoiding excessive biomass production that will increase these compounds. Bear in mind that, with lager yeast, yeast health is not necessarily directly linked with fermentation speed.

FREE AMINO NITROGEN

Yeast nutrients are a key component of healthy fermentation. Free amino nitrogen (FAN) levels in wort are generally regarded as perhaps the best index for predicting the health and vitality of yeast during fermentation (Stewart, Hill, and Russell 2013, 207).

About 70% of wort FAN is derived from the malting process, while the remainder is formed during mashing. A mash rest in the range 104–122°F (40–50°C) will maximize the formation of FAN. This mash temperature may be beneficial for decoction brewers or step-infusion brewers, depending on the malt being used and the type of beer being brewed.

The amount of FAN consumed by yeast is directly proportional to its biomass growth. The rate and level of biomass growth is a key differentiating factor between lager and ale yeast fermentations. Traditional lager fermentations can have half the biomass growth of a typical ale fermentation. Warmer lager fermentations have similar levels of biomass as ale fermentations, which accounts for some of the vastly different FAN malt recommendations between European and American maltsters.

Proper fermentation requires sufficient nutrients to achieve full attenuation. However, both high and low FAN levels can be problematic for lager fermentations. The amount of FAN suggested for proper fermentation varies depending on yeast and gravity, but 150–200 mg/L is generally considered a reasonable range. Higher-gravity worts will have higher FAN levels than those of weaker gravity.

Since they produce so much less FAN, using 100% European malts is unlikely to result in a wort with too much FAN. These malts are more likely to cause an issue with too little FAN, especially in lower-gravity beers where the limited FAN content of the malt can easily be diluted below healthy levels. Yeast viability and vitality will suffer if not enough FAN is available, leading to many off-flavors and autolysis. For most modern malts, this is an unlikely scenario, but when using high percentages of adjuncts extra nutrients may be needed.

Too much FAN can be just as much of an issue for lager. Excess FAN will lead to a higher ending pH, as well as increased concentrations of diacetyl and 2,3-pentanedione, esters, and fusel alcohols in the later stages of fermentation (Hill and Stewart 2019, 6). Fusel alcohols can be biosynthesized following amino acid utilization via the Ehrlich mechanism; accordingly, high FAN levels encourage yeast to employ this metabolic pathway.

PITCHING RATES

Pitching lager yeast differs significantly from ale yeast. While ale yeast cells may multiply up to eight times, creating significantly more biomass than was originally pitched, lager yeast cells on average exhibit half that multiplication rate (Noonan 2003, 167). From the viewpoint of practical application, propagating lager yeast can be a time-consuming process and repitching it will not go nearly as far as with ale yeast cultures.

There is little consensus in brewing literature when it comes to pitch rates for lager (table 3.3 has some examples). We've found that average pitch rates for lager are generally in the range of 1.0–2.5 million cells per milliliter per degree Plato (10^6 cells/mL/°Plato), which is higher than most ale fermentations. Even so, there will be fewer total cells at the end of fermentation compared to ale fermentations since the growth rate of lager yeast is lower. In general, we found that those writing about more traditional styles of lager production called for higher pitching rates, while the literature associated with more modern styles of lager fermentation called for lower rates.

Table 3.3
Pitching rate recommendations in published literature (million cells per milliliter per degree Plato)

| Source | Pitching rate (10^6 cells/mL/°Plato), ale vs. lager yeast | |
	Ale	Lager
Fermentation, Cellaring, and Packaging Operations (Ockert 2006a, 96)	0.5–1.0	1.0–1.25
A Textbook of Brewing (de Clerck 1957, 408, 411)	0.48 [a]	1.2–2.4 [b]
Technology Brewing and Malting (Kunze 2014, 427)	0.6–1.2 [c]	1.6–2.5 [d]
The Yeast in the Brewery (Annemüller, Manger, and Lietz 2011, 355)	0.48–1.2 [e]	1.2–2.4 [f]
Yeast (White and Zainasheff 2010, 122)	0.75	1.5

[a] Estimated from slurry 0.2 liters slurry per hectoliter.
[b] Estimated from 0.5–1.0 liters slurry per hectoliter.
[c] Estimated from 0.25–0.50 liters slurry per hectoliter.
[d] Estimated from 20–30 million cells per hectoliter.
[e] Estimated from 0.2–0.5 liters slurry per hectoliter
[f] Estimated from 0.5–1.0 liters slurry per hectoliter

The best traditional lager yeast fermentations have two to two-and-one-half doublings of yeast cells (Mathias Hutzler, pers. comm.). This comparatively low growth rate is part of the reason lager tastes like lager. The reduced rates of cell growth and multiplication with lager yeast leads to less fermentation character with fewer esters and fusel alcohols created. Ale fermentations are skewed toward biomass production, which can highlight fermentation flavors.

For many lager yeast strains it will be a stretch to pitch from one tank into twice the volume for the next generation. For example, a 10 bbl. batch will likely have at most enough biomass to pitch into 20 bbl. of wort for the next generation. Planning out batches of lager requires extra planning to ensure proper pitching volume. In general, the lower and colder the fermentation, the less biomass will be produced, requiring more cells to be pitched to ensure the beer is fully fermented. Conversely, the warmer the fermentation, the more cell growth will occur and subsequently less yeast is required.

Lance Shaner of Omega Yeast notes that the biggest challenge first-time brewers have when ordering lager yeast is not ordering enough. There can be sticker shock due to the added cost of needing two to three times more lager yeast compared to an ale pitch. It's a headache for yeast producers too: double the amount of yeast is needed while at the same time the yeast grows slower than ale yeasts.

The quantity of yeast pitched will directly affect the rate of fermentation and the subsequent conditioning time. All things being equal, lower pitch rates will result in more nutrients, oxygen, and extract per cell and the yeast will therefore have a higher growth rate.

As an experiment, Jack's Abby tested two pitch rates over a year-long study. In this experiment, the times it took to complete primary fermentation and pass VDK[1] testing were compared using two different pitch rates. (In order to pass VDK testing, samples were assessed by a trained sensory panel.) Pitch rates of 1.2×10^6 cells/mL/°Plato and 1.5×10^6 cells/mL/°Plato were used on our House Lager, a Helles-style lager with 12° Plato original extract, fermented at 48°F (9°C), spunded at the end of primary fermentation and held at the same temperature. Both pitch rates were within average recommendations and all other variables remained constant. The results are shown in table 3.4.

Averages from the year-long study show that fermentations for either pitch rate fell within de Clerck's "golden rule" of fermentation (de Clerck 1957, 409), taking 8–10 days to reach terminal gravity. As might be expected, the higher pitch rate did reach terminal gravity faster, by a day and a half. However, both sets of fermentations took the same amount of time to pass VDK testing, indicating that the lower pitch rate resulted in quicker metabolism of off-flavors. However, how these beers develop during lagering is still being studied.

Table 3.4

Fermentation parameter averages between two different pitching rates compared. Data from year-long Fermentation Pitch Study at Jack's Abby

Fermentation pitching rate (cells/mL/°Plato)	Fermentation parameters averaged across all trials for each pitching rate (n = 25)			
	Days from brew date to reach terminal gravity	Days from brew date to pass VDK testing	Total yeast growth (%)	Total peak cells (cells/mL)
1.2×10^6	9.5	19	260	40.0×10^6
1.5×10^6	8.0	19	230	41.5×10^6

Note: All fermentations in 12° Plato lager wort, fermented at 48°F (9°C) and bunged upon reaching terminal gravity.

I   VDK(s), vicinal diketone(s)

On average, higher pitching rates are advisable when fermenting at lower temperatures. Lower pitching rates are more common in warmer fermentations. Since higher temperatures facilitate higher growth rates, less yeast is needed and fermentation profiles begin to look more like their ale counterparts. For very fast fermentations, high temperatures are combined with high pitch rates.

Controlling for one variable can often cause a change in another variable that might not be ideal. Finding the right balance for the flavor profile of your beer will be important. For example, an increased pitch rate will lead to lower acetaldehyde and ester formation (assuming also a lower biomass formation) but at the same time it will increase ethyl acetate levels, reduce yeast viability, and increase the number of dead yeast cells, posing challenges for future batches. While lower pitch rates increase viability and yeast sedimentation, this will likely be paired with higher biomass production that yields more esters and acetaldehyde.

Diacetyl is a double-edged sword. Faster fermentations create more diacetyl in primary fermentation but the warmer temperatures means this diacetyl is more quickly reduced; and in slower fermentations the reverse is true. When performing a warmer/faster fermentation, it is important to ensure diacetyl has been removed before proceeding to cooling, because by the end of primary fermentation yeast viability is generally diminished and diacetyl conversion will be challenging at cool temperatures. The time it takes to reduce diacetyl is highly variable and dependent on many factors. At Jack's Abby we have many different fermentation programs and beer styles. On average, our fastest fermentations pass VDK testing in less than two weeks, while a more typical traditional fermentation plan takes on average three to four weeks to reach this stage.

In the end, maybe a better way to look at yeast pitching rates is to consider how your other variables will affect the fermentation. Pitching rates should be informed by the fermentation plan, rather than the other way around.

TOP PRESSURE

Pressure considerations will apply to nearly all lager fermentations to some degree. Most traditional fermentation plans involve a secondary fermentation under top pressure, while more modern higher-temperature fermentations often use top pressure for primary fermentation.

Cylindroconical tanks exert physical effects on lager fermentations. Hydrostatic pressure increases the CO_2 concentration of fermenting beer, which in turn reduces ester formation. Even though these tanks are often associated with improved fermentations due to their ability to create convection currents that promote yeast growth (which promotes esters), the increased carbon dioxide content tips the scales toward lower ester formation (Annemüller, Manger, and Lietz 2011, 364). At Weihenstephan, this factor is one reason why the brewery ferments its wheat beer in short horizontal tanks and its lager in tall vertical tanks. The reduced pressure for the wheat beer promotes ester formation, while the taller tanks for the lager reduces ester production.

When top pressure is applied from the start of primary fermentation, it has the side effect of reducing the production of sulfur compounds, esters, and, to a lesser effect, fusel alcohols (Annemüller, Manger, and Lietz 2011, 364). The main cause of this is the increase in dissolved CO_2 under higher top pressure. Carbon dioxide has a stronger effect on ester formation than temperature does (Yang 2019, 170). This should not be confused with adding top pressure for natural carbonation at the end of fermentation. The top pressure applied at the end of fermentation has the opposite effect by containing the off-flavors that have already been created in the tank and increasing the amount of time needed for lagering.

Yeast cell vitality suffers minimally when using gauge (applied) pressures of 4.4 psi (0.3 bar) or lower (Annemüller, Manger, and Lietz 2011, 164). Over 4.4 psi and lager yeast becomes stressed. The higher the pressure the higher the negative impact will be. Performing a secondary fermentation under pressure often requires gauge pressures higher than 5 psi. In these cases, it is important to ensure that cell counts are appropriate and that the total volume of yeast cells is not too high. Three million cells per milliliter is a recommended value to maintain enough yeast for the secondary fermentation but few enough to avoid autolysis. Yeast in the cone of a vertical fermentor will quickly autolyze under hydrostatic pressure; removal of this yeast is important and may require consistent management.

Open fermentors offer a dramatically different environment from tall cylindroconical tanks. Many smaller traditional breweries in Germany and Czechia prefer to use these types of tanks for primary fermentation. Their short stature offers some advantages to lager yeast, creating an environment with very low pressure that supports yeast health and viability.

At the Únětický pivovar (Únětice Brewery) outside of Prague, all beers are fermented in open tanks. These tanks sit in the middle of the brewery, completely exposed to the atmosphere. The tanks are only a few feet above the path, inviting those who walk by to quickly view the tanks, taking care they don't fall in.

With so many open tanks at Únětický pivovar, the various stages of fermentation can easily be identified, an important fact that the brewers note helps them better understand how their fermentations are proceeding. At first, fermentation features white rings of foam that reach the top of the wort (fig. 3.2). Over time, the krausen ebbs and flows, changing its character. Eventually, the highly oxidized foam at the top turns brown, marking the end of primary fermentation.

Figure 3.2. "White rings" stage of open fermentation at Únětický pivovar near Prague, Czechia.

TEMPERATURE

Very small changes in temperature can dramatically alter fermentation performance and flavor formation. Two key reasons for this are temperature's influence on biomass production and on dissolved CO_2. As temperature rises, biomass production increases and CO_2 in solution decreases; as temperature lowers, biomass production decreases and CO_2 in solution increases. Higher concentrations of CO_2 inhibit yeast growth and limit the synthesis of acetyl-CoA, reducing the main substrate available for ester formation.

Reduced CO_2 and concomitant increased biomass production promotes the formation of esters, fusel alcohols, and acetaldehyde, while reducing sulfur compound formation. Higher temperatures increase the expression of genes that allow for certain amino acids to be transported into the yeast cells from the surrounding wort; the presence of these amino acids in the cell in turn encourages the formation of fusel alcohols that are necessary precursors for ester formation (Pires et al. 2014, 1944). However, not all temperature increases are equal. Engan and Aubert reported in 1977 (quoted in Pires et al. 2014, 1944) that increasing the fermentation temperature from 46°F to 50°F (8°C to 10°C) increased ester production significantly less than when the temperature was increased from 50°F to 54°F (10°C to 12°C), the latter step up increasing ester production as much as 75%.

Biomass production and CO_2 concentration are two variables that will have a major impact on how fermentation will proceed. Temperature offers a key way to adjust these variables and influence the rate of ester and fusel alcohol formation, as well as affecting long-term yeast health. A hallmark of traditional fermentations is their low biomass production. Brewers of these types of traditional lagers may prioritize many other variables to minimize biomass production, which leads to the types of low-ester, low–fusel alcohol flavor profiles desired in these beers.

Some of the coldest fermentation temperatures in the lagering world are to be found in Czech breweries, with a long and slow primary fermentation in the 44–46°F (7–8°C) range. This cold primary fermentation is combined with the famous Czech H-strain yeast, which has a propensity for creating diacetyl. The very low temperatures make it challenging for the yeast to subsequently convert diacetyl; thus, this combination often leads to a noticeable diacetyl flavor contribution, often considered a desired character that is integral to many Czech lagers. With enough time, however, the yeast can remove diacetyl; so, to avoid diacetyl while using the H-strain at low temperatures, very long lagering times need to be employed. To consistently achieve the same amount of diacetyl, testing through lagering should be routinely employed to know when the desired level is reached. Filtering and/or pasteurizing the beer will maintain that level permanently.

Harvesting and Repitching Lager Yeast

Yeast collection and repitching methods have a significant impact on yeast health. When an open, horizontal, or other non-conical tank is used, collecting lager yeast can be quite challenging. Yeast will often need to be manually collected in some fashion, often with scoops, squeegees, or other improvised tools. Lager yeast that is top-cropped will eliminate most process stresses, including temperature, ethanol, osmotic pressure, and hydrostatic pressure. However, top-cropping is a relatively uncommon process for lager brewers and yeast is generally collected at the end of fermentation. Yeast that is skimmed from the top of lager tanks is usually considered to be high in impurities that are not desired in subsequent fermentations and therefore such yeast is discarded.

Yeast collection and pitching is easier when using conical tanks, though lager yeast does offer some specific challenges. When cropping yeast from a cylindroconical tank, particularly when naturally carbonating the beer, significant amounts of dissolved CO_2 will be in the yeast. This high concentration of CO_2 is unhealthy for the yeast on its own; taking into consideration that these cells are under significant hydrostatic pressure as well, it makes for a particularly challenging environment for yeast cells. Thus, it is extremely important to remove the yeast that settles in a spunded (bunged) tank as soon as possible. Yeast that settles in the cone of a fermentor is under significant stress regardless and the added top pressure from natural carbonation captured in a spunded tank only compounds the issue by keeping the dissolved CO_2 levels high. In order to get the most accurate flow rates, back pressure will need to be applied to avoid false readings that will occur due to the CO_2 creating bubbles in the flow meter.

Due to all the stresses associated with the end of fermentation, yeast should be immediately removed for subsequent fermentation. Lager yeast strains, particularly the very popular 34/70, tend to exhibit considerably decreased viability and reduced glycogen and trehalose stores within 48 hours of reaching terminal gravity. Interestingly, 34/70 shows little difference in these levels after primary fermentation is over and it has been stored between 39°F and 50°F (4°C and 10°C) under beer prior to repitching; but, as one might expect, significantly lower levels are seen when it is stored at 77°F (25°C; Somani et al. 2012, 126–128). Yeast stored longer than 96 hours at temperatures above 41°F (5°C) will have lower than acceptable glycogen content and viability (McCaig and Bendiak 1985, 119).

For lager brewers who implement a raised temperature at the end of primary fermentation, there is an unintended consequence for repitching yeast, particularly when pitching directly from one tank to another. The yeast harvested will be warmer than the initial fermentation temperature and any drop in temperature of more than one degree Celsius (approx. 2°F) has the potential to cause temperature shock and facilitate sedimentation of the yeast. Cold shock can increase the number of dead cells, decrease the number of budding cells, decrease attenuation, and increase the final pH (Annemüller, Manger, and Lietz 2011, 359). In one study, lager yeast slurries stored at 39°F (4°C) for more than 20 hours showed increases in pH, FAN, and total ion levels, all tell-tale signs of autolysis. It is recommended that any yeast slurry above pH 4.9 not be used (Layfield and Sheppard 2015, 134–135).

Many brewers who use lager yeast tend to limit the number of generations of their strains. When it comes to lager yeast in modern brewing, the common wisdom is that 5–10 generations should be the maximum. Lager yeast is more prone to undergo mutation. Some of the factors that cause this issue stem from how lager yeast is treated in modern brewery operations, namely, fermenting lager yeast in tall conical tanks and harvesting the yeast from the bottom of these tanks. Brewers who top crop or harvest yeast after racking beer to a secondary tank will likely see fewer health issues with their yeast. While each fermentation exposes yeast to stress and cellular damage, the long-term viability and vitality across multiple generations of yeast is most dependent on how the yeast is handled and a strain's fermentation stress tolerance (Jenkins et al. 2003, 7).

At Live Oak Brewing Company in Austin, Texas, Chip McElroy and Dusan Kwiatkowski feel comfortable repitching their yeast for significantly more than five to ten generations. One key reason for this is Live Oak's use of horizontal lagering tanks for primary fermentation. This tank choice allows for very low-pressure fermentations and maximizes yeast health. After the beer is transferred to a secondary tank, yeast is pulled out of the primary tank. The process of getting yeast out of the horizontal tanks is precarious: long custom-built devices help brewers scrape the yeast from the back of the tanks and into a bucket. This bucket is then used to transfer the yeast to a keg, which will then be pushed into the next batch of wort. The yeast collected in this process is ideally pitched the same day or within 24 hours.

For head brewer and owner Tim Wilson of East Rock Brewing in New Haven, Connecticut, several attempts to keep healthy yeast for more than ten generations have all ended in poor results. Wilson has found that after ten generations, while there is still a strong initial fermentation, the yeast struggles to fully attenuate to the expected target. There would be obvious benefits to being able to repitch lager yeast for longer, including the expense and logistics of bringing brewing new yeast into the brewery.

Presumably, at one point in history, lager yeast was repitched indefinitely. It's unclear if the mixed cultures that predated pure single strains were healthier or if brewers demand more of their yeast with the industrialization of brewing. Even so, there are still breweries that continue to pitch yeast for many more generations than are typically recommended. Mathias Hutzler is aware of breweries that go up to 100 generations with their lager yeast. The one caveat here is that these breweries do perform "yeast rest and recovery" steps where the yeast is aerated to rebuild strong cell walls and increase vitality. This essentially mimics yeast propagation but without using a new culture (M. Hutzler, pers. comm.).

Lagering

Storing and aging is so closely associated with brewing lager that it has given the beer its name. Lagering refers to the time between the end of primary fermentation and when a beer is packaged. We won't dive into the surprisingly controversial debate over how long a beer needs to be cold stored to be considered a lager. We refer to lagering solely by the above definition, even if it only takes a small amount of time.

The historical realities that necessitated the long, cold storage of beer no longer exist, but many of the same goals of lagering remain. Time and temperature are two variables that modern lager brewers will need to control when planning their secondary fermentations. There are four main purposes to lagering beer (Ockert 2006a, 97):

- Flavor maturation; eliminating the undesirable flavors and creating desirable ones
- Clarification through the sedimentation of yeast and other insoluble materials
- Chill stabilization by promoting the creation of protein tannin complexes that can be removed by sedimentation or filtration
- Development of carbonation

Clarification, stabilization, and carbonation can be objectively measured in the lab with relative ease. What counts as appropriate flavor maturation, however, can be subjective. How taste is affected by maturation times and temperatures invites a more artful approach. Even brewers who can find the time and are determined to lager their beers for weeks or months often struggle with the words to describe the changes that are happening to their beers. The science of maturation is complicated and the changes that occur are hard to document scientifically, especially regarding how they relate to the flavor and aroma profile of the finished beer.

One thing is certain when it comes to flavor maturation: yeast is the key component. Such modifications only happen in the presence of yeast. Yeast metabolism effects these changes, thus, the type of yeast that is employed will be the determining factor in how these beers age. The changes that occur in the lagering tank are often not well understood and can take unexpected turns. As an example, it is not uncommon for an increase in hydrogen sulfide and vicinal diketones to be observed during the first week of lagering (Masschelein 1986, 214).

FACTORS THAT DETERMINE LAGERING TIME

When it comes to flavor maturation, the time required for lagering will vary depending on a number of factors, including the strength of the beer and the amount of added materials, particularly hops and adjuncts (table 3.5). But the most significant variable that determines the time and temperature of lagering will be how the primary fermentation was conducted.

Table 3.5
Major factors that determine lagering time

	Effect on lagering time	
Variable	Longer	Shorter
Colder primary	X	
Warmer primary		X
Naturally carbonated	X	
All malt	X	
Adjuncts and dry hopping		X
Higher strength	X	
High pitch rates		X

The colder the primary fermentation, the longer the lagering time needed. Cold fermentations take a long time to finish cleaning up diacetyl, acetaldehyde, sulfur compounds, and other off-flavors. Colder temperatures slow biomass growth, leaving fewer cells and more nutrients behind in wort. The colder the primary fermentation, the "warmer" the lagering needed, that is, a temperature lower than primary fermentation but high enough to ensure yeast metabolism is still active.

Diacetyl is a particular problem with colder fermentations; certain lager strains also have a higher propensity to produce diacetyl. The slow metabolism of yeast at low temperatures can take weeks to resolve the presence of diacetyl. This is a feature in many Czech beers, for which diacetyl is a welcome component of the sensory profile. It's prized in these beers for its texture as well as its flavor, as it is believed to round out and soften these assertively hopped beers. However, finding the right balance can be tricky. Diacetyl should not be a dominant flavor—it is there to balance the beer's bitterness and body. The flavor threshold of diacetyl is around 50–100 parts per billion (0.05–0.1 mg/L) and Czech brewers note that levels over 100 ppb are not to style.

The brewers at Pilsner Urquell use diacetyl as a means to determine when their beer is finished lagering. The beer is filtered and pasteurized around the five-week mark to ensure that a consistent diacetyl character is preserved. (In the early days of the COVID-19 pandemic beer sales were dramatically slowed, causing longer lagering times that made ensuring this constant level of diacetyl particularly difficult.) Czech brewers also pay close attention to the final attenuation to help monitor for potential diacetyl issues. When a beer doesn't reach its normal attenuation due to less healthy yeast that can't finish the fermentation, a likely side effect will be increased diacetyl.

With a warmer primary fermentation, less lagering time will be needed. Yeast in warmer fermentations metabolize off-flavors faster and longer lagering is therefore not necessary. Yeast at the end of a warmer primary fermentation will also be less healthy and more likely to autolyze during lagering. Warmer temperatures increase biomass and thus increase competition, reducing nutrients and leaving wort inhospitable; colder conditions will be needed during lagering to help remove dead and unhealthy yeast. Dead yeast will create their own off-flavors as well as cause poor foam and long-term aging problems. With warm fermentations, long lagering times are, at best, unnecessary and will often do more harm than good.

The next biggest factor in determining lagering time will be the choice of carbonation. Naturally carbonated lagers will need longer lagering times than force-carbonated lagers. Natural carbonation simply takes more time to accomplish and the off-flavors that are created during this process become trapped in the beer. This can only be helped by giving sufficient time for flavor maturation.

However, the above are just guidelines. There is little consensus about the exact time any particular lager needs. For every positive flavor contribution from lagering, a corresponding negative reaction may be a consequence, particularly oxidation reactions and autolysis. Long-term lagering must be designed with such potential downsides in mind. There is a balance to be struck between creating "fresh" and "aged" lager flavors.

FINDING THE RIGHT BALANCE: TIME VERSUS TEMPERATURE

Kevin Davey, brewer of Gold Dot Beer in McMinnville, Oregon, believes that lagering temperature is potentially more important than the length of time, so he tries to lager his beers at as cold a temperature as possible without freezing the beer. Very cold temperatures during lagering dramatically improve yeast sedimentation and chill stabilization. This method of lagering makes a lot of sense for the modern hybrid and warm fermentations (table 3.1), as it helps to speed up lagering time. When lagering more traditional beers with natural carbonation it's important to ensure that all flavor maturation is completed before cooling the beer to near freezing: once the temperature falls below 32°F (0°C) yeast activity will stop. There is little use in prolonging lagering at such cold temperatures.

When determining the appropriate lagering temperature, consider the four main objectives of lagering—flavor maturation, clarification, stabilization, and carbonation—and which are to be achieved. For flavor maturation, choose a warmer temperature in the 35–46°F (2–8°C) range. To address clarification and stabilization, very cold temperatures, even down to the freezing point of the beer, are recommended.

Lisa Allen founded the aforementioned Gold Dot Beer in partnership with Kevin Davey on the site of McMinnville's long-running and popular Heater Allen brewery, where Allen had worked for many years, rising to head brewer in 2017. Allen strongly believes that the most important ingredient she adds to her beers is time. On average, Allen conditions her beers for up to eight weeks. A big part of this decision relates to clarity and allowing yeast to drop, but she also notices a softer flavor in beers aged this long. During the slowest days of the COVID-19 pandemic, Allen was able to taste the Heater Allen beers as they aged up to twelve weeks—they continued to mellow and develop in flavor, mouthfeel, and texture. Heater Allen's more traditional temperature program doesn't have a diacetyl rest or warming at the end of fermentation, so it can take weeks for undesired flavors to dissipate. Heater Allen beers are still brewed in what is now Lisa and Kevin's brewhouse at Gold Dot Beer. Today, the brewery also incorporates horizontal lager tanks for aging, which helps clarify and stabilize the beers.

Adam Goodwin, the founder of Charles Towne Fermentory in Charleston, South Carolina, has started brewing more lager styles, notably an American light lager called Yacht Party. For such a small brewery, lager brewing is a huge investment in time and capital. Goodwin explains that not only can he produce three IPAs in the same amount of time as one lager, the lager is also regularly sold at a lower price. Goodwin's enthusiasm for lager is clear, because the additional time and cost can be a hard pill to swallow. But there are workarounds when time is an important factor (*see* "The Long and Short of It" sidebar).

The Long and Short of It: Suarez Family Brewery and Human Robot

Potentially the largest difference in lagering times we've discovered is between Suarez Family Brewery and Human Robot, two excellent American lager-focused breweries.

Dan Suarez from Suarez Family Brewery in Hudson, New York, allows his beers to condition for up to four months. Important to this process is transferring the beer to a secondary after primary fermentation. The main priority for this long conditioning period is to produce bright and clean beer by the end of lagering that can be served unfiltered. A further benefit is the reduction of sulfur to a delicate flavor. Indeed, the flavor can be a bit shocking or harsh early in the lagering, even after several weeks. The brewery's Pilsners also have a significant hop character that needs time to develop.

Andrew Foss, head brewer at Human Robot in Philadelphia, has found a way to create great lagers that usually only spend three weeks in tank from brew to packaging. Foss's fermentation philosophy is to have the minimum yeast growth possible, limiting multiplication to one-and-a-half to two times. To do this, Human Robot limits the oxygenation of the wort to 15 minutes during knockout. The start of fermentation is paired with top pressure at 15 psi (1.03 bar) throughout the fermentation process, which helps to reduce unwanted fermentation products of esters and fusel alcohols. This is one method that can help speed up the fermentation process at the same time as limiting the production of off-flavors that would otherwise need significant lagering time to resolve.

At the Austin Beer Garden Brewing Co. (ABGB), lagers take about seven weeks to produce. ABGB is notable for its dedication to filtering beer, so this extended maturation process is not driven with clarification in mind. During lagering, the brewers notice a reduction in grassy and grainy malt flavors and a reduction in sulfur compounds. They believe there is a sublime quality to ABGB's aged beers, and that time is one of the reasons the beers taste so close to their European counterparts.

ABGB is perhaps an outlier when it comes to steadfastly filtering. For many smaller breweries, time spent lagering is often used as a clarification step to achieve bright, non-hazy lagers. Because many of the US craft lager brewers we talked to do not filter or centrifuge their beers, long aging times are required for these beers to properly clarify. Having yeast in solution is considered a negative flavor contributor by most lager brewers. Even when we talked to producers of *Kellerbier* and other yeasted lagers, many commented that the shelf life for such products is considerably reduced, a stark difference to ale producers who often use yeast to improve the shelf life of their products. By the time lager yeast makes it to a bottle or keg, its viability and vitality is poor.

Taking these points into consideration, it's clear that there is little reason to bother with extended lagering times with modern warm-fermented lager. The high fermentation temperatures expedite fermentation and reduction of off-flavors, and clarification and chill haze concerns are alleviated by numerous process additives and filtration systems. Typically, these beers are also force carbonated.

KNOWING WHEN LAGERING IS DONE

One simple test to determine if fermentation and lagering are nearing an end is to simply check for yeast in suspension. Particularly for non-powdery or Frohberg yeast strains (e.g., 34/70), once fermentation and the conversion of off-flavors is complete, the yeast tends to drop to the bottom of the tank. It is important to know your strain's behavior and understand how it reacts during the lagering process.

Some brewers that employ very cold primary fermentations mentioned to us a phenomenon where their lagers dramatically change around the four-week mark. Owner and brewer Tom Beckmann of Goldfinger Brewing in Downers Grove, Illinois, notices a significant increase in bitterness and yeast character around this time, which quickly mellows afterward. Goldfinger's beers never get above 50°F (10°C) throughout the entire fermentation process and are released at around seven weeks of age on average. It's possible that this timeframe marks the end of maturation and a settling of yeast in the tank, or that tank temperature changes that occur around this time change the convection patterns of the beer.

For any style of lager fermentation, there certainly comes a point when lagering has gone on for too long and the "aged" flavors begin to work against the beer. Florian Kuplent of Urban Chestnut cautions against lagering beer for too long. In the case of Urban Chestnut's modern hybrid fermentations, Kuplent notes that once diacetyl has been removed more bad than good will happen. Autolysis or other problems in the beer will be indicated by an increase in pH. This will happen faster in lager that is warm-fermented and under top pressure, whereas it will happen slower in lager that is cold-fermented slowly and is under lower pressure.

At Victory Brewing in Downingtown, Pennsylvania, release times are based on a rigid structure controlled by the brewery QA/QC laboratory. Every new release is monitored and tested continuously to determine the best time to package the beer. The two main compounds that the lab focuses on are diacetyl and sulfur dioxide. Standard curves that mark this progress are used to identify if they are seeing problems for future fermentations. On average, most of Victory's lagers that employ a modern hybrid fermentation program require three to four weeks before being ready to package, but beers will be held if they are determined to need more time.

At Schanzenbräu in Nuremberg, Germany, lagers are produced through a modern hybrid fermentation approach utilizing a single conical tank for fermentation. After primary fermentation, the beer is cooled to 30°F (−1°C) and yeast is dumped regularly. Currently, the beers at Schanzenbräu take 21 days on average from brew day to packaging. Owner and brewer Stefan Stretz explained that the brewery is working to reduce this time to as close to 14 days as possible, potentially by using a filter or other mechanical yeast separation process. In Stefan's view, once diacetyl has been removed and direct tank cooling is employed, the goals of conditioning have been met and there are strong ethical and moral considerations to be more efficient and use less energy.

YEAST HEALTH DURING LAGERING

A comprehensive study and review by Masschelein (1986) reveals what happens in a lagering tank during secondary fermentation. Samples were taken from a large brewhouse horizontal tank at the end of primary fermentation and again after 40 days' lagering; the yeast was removed and the beer samples analyzed to compare the major biochemical characteristics between the sample times and location in the tank from where the samples were extracted (table 3.6). The results show some dramatic changes happening during the lagering period.

Table 3.6
Comparative analysis of beer samples taken from the middle and bottom of a 400 hL horizontal tank after fermentation and after 40 days' lagering

	End fermentation		40 days storage	
Analyte	**Middle**	**Bottom**	**Middle**	**Bottom**
pH	4.0	4.1	4.15	5.0
FAN (mg/L)	58.0	60.0	80.0	700
Isohumulones (mg/L)	26.0	27.0	27.0	32.0
Anthocyanogens (mg/L)	49.0	51.0	50.0	60.0
Color EBC	7.5	7.5	7.5	10.0
Invertase (nM glucose h^{-1} mL^{-1})	70.1	75.1	100.0	1,000
Glucosidase (nM nitrophenol h^{-1} mL^{-1})	0	0	0	5

The data illustrate the dramatic changes to markers of yeast health after 40 days, particularly for beer at the bottom of the tank. The large increases in beer pH, FAN, and invertase activity levels clearly show that yeast viability is reduced and autolysis is occurring. There are some who postulate that these events might be part of the flavor profile of traditional lager beer as well as contributing to mouthfeel and body. While autolysis and poor yeast health may very well create a specific flavor profile in lagered beer, brewers must consider the many potential sensory challenges when dealing with autolysis. Many studies have shown the negative consequences of autolysis, which affects microbiological stability, head retention, and flavor stability in finished beer (Bamforth 2023, 3–11).

This is another example of a potential "off-flavor" defining the greatness in certain beers. It's an interesting theory and could help explain why beers that have been aged for a long time develop flavor profiles that defy easy characterization and are unattainable using short maturation periods. But care should be taken to mitigate yeast health issues during lagering. Enough yeast needs to be in solution to perform maturation, while too much will cause excessive autolysis; a value of 0.5–1.0 million cells/mL is recommended (Back et al. 2020, 148). Colder temperatures will further reduce metabolic activity and slow autolysis.

Reduced hydrostatic pressure during lagering will help as well—many brewers argue that horizontal lagering tanks are a must for this reason. However, depending on the size of your tank, horizontal tanks are not always necessary and may even cause more problems. For example, at Jack's Abby, we have 300 bbl. horizontal lagering tanks that are taller than many of our smaller unitanks. There would be no hydrostatic pressure advantage to lagering in a 15-foot-tall horizontal tank versus a 15-foot-tall vertical tank, especially when the vertical tank makes removing yeast that much easier. In addition to being inefficient to crop, the horizontal tank also promotes more surface area contact between yeast cells and beer, which has the potential to lead to the uptake of off-flavors via autolysis.

AUTOLYSIS

Autolysis signals yeast death. When dead, a yeast cell's membranes fall apart, allowing uncontrolled enzymatic degradation of cell structures and contents; eventually, the cell wall is compromised and the cell ruptures, leaking its constituent chemicals into the surrounding medium.

For lager brewers, autolysis is a constant threat. When yeast health becomes so poor that autolysis begins, the final beer is invariably negatively affected. As yeast cells autolyze, proteases and fatty acids are released into the beer, which results in poor foam stability (Back et al. 2020, 172). Other substances produced that end up in the beer may introduce off-flavors such as salty, meaty, sulfurous, and bitter that can degrade a lager beer's flavor quite noticeably.

Identifying when autolysis is occurring is a vital part of the lagering process. A simple test to determine if there are signs of significant autolysis in yeast slurry is to centrifuge a sample and measure the pH of the liquid on top of the cells (i.e., the supernatant). If the pH is 0.5 higher than the beer's pH, significant autolysis has occurred (Ockert 2006a, 26). Autolysis is a common issue for lager brewers using a single tank, particularly if that vessel is spunded or used in conjunction with top pressure. The pH of beer produced this way should be closely monitored at the end of fermentation as a precaution.

Autolysis is a more common risk when brewing lager than when brewing ale due to lager's significantly longer conditioning periods. This is a reason why lagering time should be planned in accordance with the primary fermentation method. Long lagering times can be more detrimental to the finished beer when unhealthy yeast is left in the tank.

Berthold Bader from Alpirsbacher Klosterbräu explained the conditioning process at his traditional brewery in Germany's Black Forest region. Although the Alpirsbacher brewery is relatively large, producing 200,000 bbl. a year, it still employs a traditional lagering process. In this setup, 2,400 hL lagering tanks with no direct cooling sit unjacketed in a cold room held at 32°F (0°C). These tanks are nearly 20 meters tall, or a little under 66 feet. It's important that the beer is cold going into these tanks because the tanks' large size and lack of direct cooling make it more difficult to control the temperature inside. The significant hydrostatic pressure of these tall tanks in addition to their indirectly cooled nature means that autolysis is a significant worry. Yeast must be dumped from the bottom of these tanks every two to three days. Alpirsbacher's beers are lagered for four to six weeks before they are packaged.

Naturally carbonated beers will require longer fermentation times. Spunding will lengthen primary fermentation, although not to the degree that krausening will lengthen the maturation stage because krausening induces an entire secondary fermentation. The pressure created through natural carbonation will stress yeast and slow the rate at which it reduces off-flavors, delaying the time until the beer can be thoroughly cooled. Careful monitoring of yeast viability post-carbonation will be important to ensure no autolysis is occurring.

SULFUR COMPOUNDS

No conversation about lager fermentation is complete without spending a disproportionate amount of time discussing sulfur. Most sulfur compounds are generally considered to be off-flavors resulting from fermentation issues. Certainly, there are sulfur compounds in beer that will always have this negative association, including hydrogen sulfide (H_2S), dimethyl sulfide (DMS), and mercaptans, all of which can be off-putting at low levels. Sometimes, however, more nuance is required to understand sulfur's contribution to finished beer, particularly when it comes to sulfur dioxide (SO_2).

It may surprise many American brewers, but SO_2 is a highly coveted and important part of German lager fermentation and flavor profile. It's striking to note that SO_2 production is often enthusiastically encouraged in German lager brewing due to its preservative qualities. For instance, a leading German brewing text recommends that the SO_2 concentration in finished beer should be 5–10 mg/L. It's been shown that increasing the SO_2 content by 5 mg/L can add two months of shelf stability (Annemüller, Manger, and Lietz 2011, 198).

While there are numerous variables in the brewing process that can affect the production of sulfur compounds, the single biggest factor determining the amount of sulfur compounds in the finished product is the yeast strain. Every yeast strain has a different propensity for creating sulfur compounds. Lager strains can produce as much as 20 mg/L of SO_2 under certain conditions; by comparison, top-fermenting yeast strains generate less than 2 mg/L of SO_2 (Back et al. 2020, 139). Since SO_2 is considered an off-flavor over 10 mg/L, the potential total SO_2 content can be a significant sensory component of a finished lager beer (Annemüller, Manger, and Lietz 2011, 198). The flavor of SO_2 is generally described as "struck match," "flinty," or "young white wine" and is often associated with a "fresh" character in beer.

Yeast naturally makes sulfite as a step along the sulfate assimilation pathway, which ends with the reduction of sulfite to sulfide and the synthesis of homocysteine, an intermediate needed to form sulfur-containing amino acids (methionine and cysteine). At the start of fermentation, the yeast uses the abundant amino acids found in wort, so it doesn't need to assimilate sulfate and create sulfite. As amino acids in the still-fermenting beer are depleted, the yeast increases the activity of the sulfate assimilation pathway. Most of the resulting sulfite is immediately utilized by the yeast as it finishes the fermentation stage. When fermentation nears the end and the yeast growth phase ends, the yeast's amino acid requirements are reduced and this sulfite begins to build up in the cells. Excess sulfite is a precursor to SO_2 formation.

Warm lager fermentations run the highest risk of excess SO_2 and H_2S due to the yeast's exponential growth. For this reason, very fast fermentations that end abruptly can see high levels of sulfur remaining in the beer—when yeast growth stalls, no more sulfur is absorbed by amino acid synthesis. Fermenting at 60°F (16°C) appears to result in maximal sulfur formation (Wurzbacher et al. 2005, 11). Yeast selection and process changes (such as utilizing top pressure) will be very important if fermenting lager at warm temperatures.

The stronger and healthier a fermentation, the less SO_2 will be produced; the weaker and slower a fermentation, the more SO_2 will be produced (Back et al. 2020, 139). Thus, most variables that are optimal for fermentation health tend to decrease SO_2 production. There is a balance that needs to be considered to find the level of SO_2 production that best suits the desired flavor and aroma profile while at the same time ensuring a strong fermentation. The catch here is that the variables that limit sulfur happen to increase ester and fusel alcohol production because biomass production increases under those conditions (Wurzbacher et al. 2005). A key factor to SO_2 production is the yeast generation number, because SO_2 creation tends to increase over the course of successive repitches as yeast health tends to decline. Lower pitching rates and lower aeration levels also tend to increase SO_2 production for the same reason.

Once compounds like SO_2 or H_2S are present post-fermentation and then trapped in a tank via bunging there are limited options to remove them. Warmer temperatures and oxygen ingress will expedite the breakdown of sulfur compounds, but those are two factors that are not ideal for the long-term stability of beer. When lagering beer at cold temperatures with limited oxygen, sulfur compounds break down in a very slow, linear manner. It will take a long time, potentially months, to get below the flavor threshold (Dvořák et al. 2008, 145–146).

Yeast with high viability results in a fermentation that creates very low levels of SO_2. This is most notable in yeast that is freshly propagated under ideal growth conditions so that the cells have all entered the exponential growth stage, also known as *assimilated* yeast. Assimilated yeast is theoretically the healthiest yeast that will be used in a brewery. In order to achieve a satisfactory fermentation velocity and sufficient SO_2 content in the finished lager, a suggested compromise is to pitch the wort with a mixture of assimilated yeast and blend with yeast from a previous fermentation (Annemüller, Manger, and Lietz 2011, 200). When we were visiting Schönramer, brewer Eric Toft described blending assimilated yeast with post-fermentation yeast in batches of their beer for this very reason. However, significant time and attention needs to be dedicated to pitching yeast in this manner.

Blending assimilated yeast with post-fermentation yeast will likely be problematic for many small breweries. The logistics are challenging, as assimilated lager yeast needs to be constantly available. If consistent SO_2 levels are desired, a simpler solution is to always blend batches of beer using assimilated yeast into other batches of beer using non-assimilated yeast. Assimilated yeast can also be used in a brand for which SO_2 considerations are not important. At Jack's Abby we brew a year-round *Radler* for which having no sulfur content is not a concern, so we aim to use assimilated yeast in these batches.

Aeration has a significant effect on SO_2 production. In general, less aeration leads to more SO_2 production; more aeration leads to lower SO_2 production. This variable is fairly straightforward to control when it comes to single-batch fermentations. Aeration becomes more complicated when many batches of wort from the brewhouse are blended together prior to fermentation. Again, a balance between yeast health and SO_2 production needs to be considered. Aerating all batches will lead to reduced SO_2 levels, while just aerating the first batch leads to the highest SO_2 levels. A compromise can be found by aerating the first and second batches 50% and not aerating batches three and four (Back et al. 2020, 141).

Another potential option to control sulfur characteristics in a more consistent manner is to perform primary fermentation with a low-sulfur-producing yeast strain, followed by krausening the beer with a secondary strain that has a high propensity to create sulfur. In conversations with Mathias Hutzler, he noted that one yeast in particular, a Saaz-type "dusty" yeast from Dortmund (TUM 66/70), was an obvious choice for krausening with this method.

When it comes to flavor profile, many American brewers agree with their German counterparts and find a small amount of sulfur refreshing. John Lenzini from Schilling Beer Co. in Littleton, New Hampshire, is one such brewer, noting that the right amount of sulfur has a similar effect on a beer as bittering hops. As with hop bitterness, too much can be overpowering; just the right amount is a natural and integral part of balancing many styles of lager.

The most famous beer with intentionally high sulfur content is the Helles from Augustiner-Bräu in Munich. There is much debate about the origins of this flavor, and there are two leading theories as to how the brewery is able to create it so consistently. The first theory is that the yeast used at the brewery is genetically similar to the 34/70 strain, but with a mutation that causes the yeast to produce more SO_2. The second theory is that the brewery performs its primary fermentation with a more neutral strain of yeast and uses a different high-sulfur-producing strain for secondary fermentation. Regardless, sulfur is a key component to the flavor profile of this delightful beer.

ATTENUATION

Attenuation is the proportion of fermentable sugars converted into alcohol and CO_2 by yeast, as measured by the progressive decline in wort extract. A beer with a higher degree of attenuation will tend to be drier and less sweet, while those with a lower degree of attenuation will tend to be perceived as sweeter. While there are many factors in the mash and raw materials that will affect the attenuation potential of a beer, yeast and healthy fermentation is ultimately responsible.

And this is particularly significant, as attenuation is an important part of the flavor profile of modern lager beer. A trend toward higher attenuation can be observed in modern German lager styles like Munich Helles, which are being driven to higher degrees of attenuation than ever before. High attenuation leads to drier, more drinkable beers, be they Helles or American adjunct lagers (for which high attenuation is often the most assertive flavor characteristic). For many in the business of marketing ever-lighter beers, higher attenuation has the added benefit of reducing carbohydrate content (i.e., calories) compared to similar strength beers of lower attenuation.

There are some all-malt brewers who believe that extreme attenuation can actually provide perceived sweetness by increasing the alcohol content. In higher concentrations, ethanol can provide a slight but perceptible sweetness. While this is a popular trend in Helles lagers, some brewers believe that driving attenuation too far takes away from the malt complexity of their beers. Steve Holle, founder of KC Bier Co. in Kansas City, Missouri, likes to use a lager strain that is slightly lower attenuating compared to 34/70 to leave more residual sweetness. In combination with decoction mashing, KC Bier's lagers exhibit an assertive malt character.

For Czech brewers, attenuation goals differ significantly from their German counterparts because they aim for much higher finishing gravities. The attenuation rate of Czech pale lagers tends to hover around 70%, in contrast to German pale lagers where the norm is quickly approaching 85%. Attenuation is an important factor in how Czech beers are hopped. High hopping rates are used to balance the high residual extract so that the finished beers have ample hop character. This sweet and bitter balance is a key characteristic that differentiates Czech lager. The mouthfeel and foam that comes from this type of fermentation is full and dense.

Tips for Homebrewing

When attempting to ferment lager at home, the best advice we can give is to control those variables that are of greatest consequence to lager yeast health. Also keep in mind de Clerck's "golden rule": fermentation should take 8–10 days at a constant temperature.

When planning out your fermentation program there are three main factors that need to be carefully controlled to ensure healthy yeast:

1. Oxygenation rate
2. Pitching rate
3. Temperature

Jan Brücklmeier, author of *Bier Brauen*, advises that homebrewers should not trust the "pitch cell count" that comes from any commercial yeast source. Unlike some ale strains that can overcome low cell counts when pitched, lager yeast will not properly ferment if underpitched. Brücklmeier considers underpitching to be the single biggest issue for homebrewers brewing lager. He recommends a yeast starter to make sure there is enough active yeast. When weighing the pros and cons of pitch rates, you should always prefer overpitching to underpitching.

Dried lager yeast strains should be seriously considered. Dried yeast packages historically have had a poor reputation for quality. Seminal books from the early days of homebrewing in the US, such as Greg Noonan's *New Brewing Lager Beer*, posited dried yeasts as the least desirable choice due to challenges with bacterial contamination during the drying process (Noonan 2003, 97). Happily, this is no longer the case and today's dried yeast strains offer the same quality as those available in liquid form. For lager, where strain selection is generally not as big of a concern, dried yeast can offer advantages over liquid yeast.

Dried yeast allows a homebrewer to aim for a more precise cell count based on weight. While some very nifty new liquid yeast packages are on the market, you still won't know exactly how many cells you are adding.

Adding the proper amount of oxygen to aerate wort is challenging in a homebrew setting but, again, dried yeast here is advantageous. A dried yeast does not require oxygen as it's packaged ready to ferment under a high state of aeration. It also reduces the risk of problems from overpitching because cells in a dried yeast package already have all the nutrients and oxygen they need and won't need to compete for resources.

As a homebrewer, you may want to repitch your yeast, even if it was originally a dried strain. However, don't repitch lager yeast unless you have a microscope and can check the viability of the yeast.

When it comes to temperature, less is better . . . albeit it's a gamble and a bit nerve-racking when attempting temperature control at home. You will find that when performing primary fermentation, you will make better beer at 45°F (7°C) than at 55°F (13°C), but targeting 50°F (10°C) will generally be the best approach at balancing yeast growth and health with fermentation by-products.

Always ferment with a primary fermentor and rack to a secondary for conditioning. This will help alleviate autolysis issues, particularly if yeast was overpitched. Brücklmeier recommends racking beer from the primary fermentor when it is about two degrees Plato residual extract (roughly 8° degrees specific gravity) above the target finishing gravity. This helps minimize oxidation issues and will provide enough extract left to spund, if you wish to naturally carbonate the beer (*see* chap. 5).

GOT DECOCTION?

OF ALL THE PROCESSES USED BY LAGER BREWERS, DECOCTION MASHING INSPIRES SOME OF THE MOST CONTRADICTORY OPINIONS. Mystique and misunderstandings abound when it comes to this mashing process that is uncommon outside of Central Europe and practiced by only a handful of modern American brewers.

There is precious little consensus when it comes to the necessity of decoction. It's generally viewed as a traditional means for deepening malt complexity in darker lagers, but with the caveat that plenty of great malty lagers are produced without decoction. The closest to a consensus we could find on the subject came from maltsters—most maltsters seem to agree that performing a decoction mash on well-modified modern malts is unnecessary to produce high-quality beer. The common wisdom is that decoction evolved as a method for brewing with poor-quality malt and has been made obsolete by modern malting innovations. Decoction offered a practical way to increase the extract obtained and control attenuation either up or down depending on the brewer's goals.

And yet decoction mashing continues, with an appreciable cost in time and money, at many breweries across Germany and Czechia. Surely these famously pragmatic Continental brewers must have good reason for this expenditure of resources. These breweries have access to modern highly modified malts that would work well with infusion mashing. Brewers who decoct often explain that the process imbues their beer with a complexity of flavor that would be unattainable by any method other than decoction. Meanwhile, brewers of infusion-mashed lager smile and roll their eyes a little at the notion that such an outdated process could still be worthwhile. Plenty of award-winning lager is produced without the trouble of decoction; in fact, two of America's most award-winning lager producers, Chuckanut Brewery and Austin Beer Garden Brewing Company, both eschew the process. For these breweries, malt complexity is derived through the careful selection of malts and corresponding mash programs.

Unfortunately, there are few studies on record that adequately compare the sensory effects of infusion mashing and decoction mashing. Only two research papers could be found on the topic, and these two researchers came to opposite conclusions. In one pilot beer experiment run by a maltster, two otherwise identical *Maibocks* were brewed, one decocted and the other infusion mashed. An analysis of the two beers' characteristics and sensory profiles found nearly no difference between the two beers.[1] However, the recipe that was used for both batches contained 12% specialty malt; such a large amount of specialty malt means that the often subtle changes from decoction might very well go unnoticed. The majority of decoction mash lager brewers we talked to only use base malt—no caramel or crystal malts—to brew Maibock-style beers, a stark difference in recipe formulation from the experiment. This experiment highlights the inherent challenge in using different mash processes for the same raw materials. Different mashing processes should inform recipe and raw material decisions, meaning that recipes that are built for infusion processes may not be suitable for a decoction (and vice versa). This is a blind spot of this single study.

A similar experiment by a team of Czech researchers at Pilsner Urquell compared four different mash programs. This experiment *did* show there was

1   Thomas Kraus-Weyermann and Horst Dornbusch, "Are decoction mashes still necessary?" *Brauwelt International*, March 5, 2021, https://brauwelt.com/en/topics/brewhouse/642726-are-decoction-mashes-still-necessary [subscription required].

a strong variation among the four batches, but it too used exactly the same materials for the grist in every mash program (Enge et al. 2005, 160). While the authors didn't specify the precise makeup of the grist, it can be inferred that it consisted of malt from Czech barley varieties "that are not as modified" (Enge et al. 2005, 159). Therefore, it is not surprising that there were noticeable variations in these beers, since undermodified malts were used with infusion mashes that would be unable to properly convert the grain.

If nothing else, the two experiments highlight both the complexity of the question and the limited research done to compare decoction mashes versus infusion mashes. The impact of decoction is certainly situational and factors from recipe design to raw material to process will affect the extent of that impact. There is no simple answer that will satisfy both proponents and opponents of decoction. The decision on how to mash often seems to be deeply personal and not necessarily based on any scientific research.

Of course, American craft brewers who have an interest in brewing great lagers have been running their own experiments for years, decocting their beers on brewhouses of all types. A handful of American lager breweries are designed with decoction mashing in mind, such as Live Oak Brewing Company in Austin, Texas. Owner Chip McElroy chose a BrauKon brewhouse partly because the German manufacturer was so comfortable building a decoction-ready system. And while some of Live Oak's beers feature single and double decoctions, its other pale lagers are simply step mashed. McElroy and Live Oak's head brewer, Dusan Kwiatkowski, value the ability to choose specific mashing programs as a method for coaxing specific characteristics out of their beers.

For every notable American lager producer that decocts, there's an ample number of others who brew great lagers with simpler mashing plans. Yet even in those simpler programs, multistep infusion programs are usually preferred over single infusions for brewing lager beer. This effectively mimics the rest steps of a decoction mash, helping to create wort more similar in style to decoction mashes.

So why should you consider decoction in your brewery? When is it appropriate and when is it not? What are some methods for trying decoction out on systems not designed for it? We set out to answer these questions in the hopes of uncovering the secrets surrounding decoction mashing. We'll explore the history of this process to better understand the reasons behind its development, as well as how the process has changed over time. We'll also examine decoction mashing with modern techniques and raw materials.

Modern brewers decoct with sensory impact in mind rather than out of any necessity. As a method of conversion, decoction is inefficient and it is not surprising that breweries wanted to improve their efficiencies through infusion mashing and temperature-controlled step mashing as more highly modified malts became widely available. This efficiency is not without sacrifice, however. Gains in efficiency were at the expense of some sensory and quality impacts that had come to be prized in these beers. Typically, brewers use decoction as a means to control their mashing and often do so with varying goals in mind. So, while many pale lager breweries in Germany use decoction to increase attenuation, their counterparts to the east in Czechia use decoction to decrease attenuation.

When it comes to hops, there is seemingly no limit to the methods and lengths American brewers will go to create unique processes that differentiate their beers. Malt does not seem to inspire such lengths; if anything, most US brewers are concerned with streamlining and simplifying their mashes. As brewers continue to demand malts capable of being converted through simple infusion mashing, the variety of interesting heirloom barleys and specialty malts is at risk of disappearing. While maltsters may not want brewers to think they *have* to decoct their malt, they all agree that flavor changes in the finished beers are intrinsic to decoction.

As the industry in the US approaches 10,000 breweries, having the ability to differentiate your beers is an advantage. With so much similarity of process and ingredients, decoction offers an opportunity for lagers to stand out while incorporating unique flavors. Adding decoction steps may not add any more time than adding a dry hopping regimen. For a small brewer, the added time needed for mashing might well prove to be worth the effort.

Malt Before Mashing

Before malt hits a mash tun, it is important to understand that the three types of malt modifications are a shared responsibility between brewers and maltsters. When deciding between decoction and infusion brewing the first step is to understand the three types of modification—cell wall (cytolysis), protein (proteolysis), and starch (amylolysis)—which we covered in chapter 2 (pp. 40–43). How the responsibilities of the types of modification are shared between the maltster and brewer directly affects the choices a brewer has to make when mashing and has an impact on the sensory qualities of a finished beer.

The share of responsibility for modification between brewer and maltster has shifted over time. Classically, decoction brewers assumed an equal share of modification with maltsters. Matt Riggs of Riggs Beer Company in Urbana, Illinois, laid out a classic textbook explanation from his German brewing school experience, depicting these relationships between maltster and brewer with two inverted triangles, the width of the triangle indicating the level of responsibility (fig. 4.1).

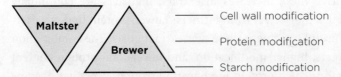

Figure 4.1. Historical shared responsibilities for malt modification between maltster and brewer.

In the historical example shown in figure 4.1, the maltster is fully responsible for cell wall modification, equally responsible with brewers for protein modification, and minimally responsible for starch modification. The brewer assumes the opposite share of responsibilities.

This relationship has changed. Modern malts are, in general, highly modified, arriving at breweries with full cell wall modification and protein modification. Modern well-modified malt means the relationship between maltster and brewer looks more like that depicted in figure 4.2.

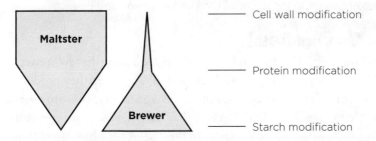

Figure 4.2. Modern shared responsibilities for malt modification between maltster and brewer assuming highly modified malt.

Barley breeding, malting technology, and brewery requirements have contributed to drive these changes in malt modification. Some of these changes are surprisingly recent—there has been a noticeable increase in malt modification even in the last few decades of the craft beer movement in the US. As the number of breweries using single-infusion mashes has increased exponentially, maltsters have responded by producing malt that is better suited for this mashing style. Today, most craft malts are highly modified, with levels of extract quickly approaching 82% (fine grind, dry basis), a once unthinkably high value even with a simple infusion mash (Evans 2021, 5).

Since a single-infusion mash brewer does not have the ability to compensate for lack of malt modification, it is important that the malt that arrives at the brewery be ready to use.

In order to drive these increases in extract, maltsters are continually refining the varieties they select from farmers. Lower-protein barley varieties have become useful to achieve these new extract goals. The combination of increased extracts, higher modification, and lower total protein content creates a situation in which protein modification from brewers has become either irrelevant or detrimental. Not only are protein rests generally not necessary, but protein rests might in fact be harmful to the final quality of beer by overmodifying the proteins, reducing levels of foam-positive proteins and extracting increased levels of fatty acids that contribute to foam-negative characteristics (Bamforth 2012, 29–32). It is particularly important that brewers who perform a protein rest consider if the malt they are using needs more protein modification. More harm than good might come of this process when using well-modified modern malts.

Brewers who want to employ step infusions or decoction mashes need to be well acquainted with malt specification sheets. Knowing the modification levels and potential extract of a malt will dictate what temperatures and mash durations are necessary to get the ideal level of conversion and extract.

What Is a Decoction Mash?

Producers of traditional German and Czech lagers are among the few brewers in the world bothering to carry on with decoction. The beers they produce this way range from deeply malty to stunningly crisp and dry. These brewers may not be able to agree completely on why they decoct, but most agree that there is a degree of added malt complexity in their beers for which decoction is responsible. Efficiency in mash extract is another common answer given, particularly for Czech brewers working with less-modified malts.

A decoction mash is a procedure in which part of the mash is separated from the whole and boiled or heated close to boiling. The boiled portion (known as the decoction) is then reintroduced into the main mash, which raises the main mash temperature. This process can be repeated, resulting in single-, double-, and triple-decoction programs (and potentially more, although more than three decoctions is rare).

Boiling part of the mash during a decoction process has both a mechanical and sensory impact. The boiling of grains breaks down the cell walls of barley and exposes the proteins and starches within the grain. For less-modified malts, this allows more of the extract to be solubilized; this step is usually unnecessary for highly modified malts. There is also an added benefit from boiling to the flavor of the beer, as the portion that is decocted can contribute significant sensory impact.

The decoction is performed in a separate vessel, either a dedicated piece of equipment or something repurposed from other parts of the brewhouse (de Clerck 1957, 272–274). While a decoction mash needs two mashing vessels so that the decocted portion of the mash can be boiled separately, this doesn't necessarily mean that the brewery must acquire an extra vessel. In some smaller brewhouses the wort kettle doubles as a mash kettle, allowing decoction programs to be carried out in a two-vessel brewhouse. However, because of the extra time required, this arrangement may not be practical if many batches of beer need to be brewed.

Privatbrauerei Stöttner, in the Mallersdorf-Pfaffenberg municipality, is a classic nineteenth-century German brewery that performs a decoction mash on all its lagers, even though it is only a two-vessel brewhouse (plus a whirlpool). The Stöttner brewers feel the commitment to beer quality justifies the significant additional time needed to perform it on their system. As beer styles in Germany are changing and consumer preferences are shifting toward Helles, they appreciate how important mashing is to their final product and what the brewer's responsibility is to the modification of malt.

There are many different types of decoction programs. The number of decoctions, temperatures targeted, mash amounts taken for decoction, and length of boil are all variables under the control of the brewer. While it wasn't unusual to see three or more decoctions in older brewing styles, there has been a marked shift toward fewer or no decoctions as brewing and malting technology has improved. The mash rest temperatures that decoctions are taken at has also shifted, particularly as an increased understanding of enzymatic activity and temperature control has allowed brewers to be more particular about the goals of their mashing programs. Not every single, double, or triple decoction is the same. For example, there are various ways a double-decoction mash might be performed. We'll discuss how and why this may change.

One major trend for how decoction and infusion mashes have been conducted over the last century led to the term *Hochkurz* mash. Essentially meaning "high and short" mash, this involves mashing in on the higher temperature side, generally above a protein rest, to start the mash at saccharification temperatures. This type of mashing reduces the total mashing time by mainly focusing on amylolytic reactions. There are many types of Hochkurz mashes, from double-decoction methods to infusion methods, but they all roughly conform to this protocol. The definition of "short" could be considered subjective, since a Hochkurz double-decoction, for example, still takes a considerable amount of time compared to an infusion mash. Its significance stems from the fact that it is relativity shorter than the mashing programs that preceded it.

TRIPLE DECOCTION

Classically, three decoctions was a standard practice that worked best when malts were poorly modified and brewhouses had limited temperature control. The classic triple-decoction mash program had three rests that hit the optimal temperature ranges for the three main groups of mash enzymes, starting with an acid rest (or phytase rest; p. 155), moving up to a protein rest, and ending at a saccharification rest (fig. 4.3). In the triple decoction shown in figure 4.3, there is a mash rest for the first and second decoctions. This allows for some saccharification of the malt before it is boiled. This is likely a more modern addition, as resting at set temperatures would have proven difficult without temperature probes. The rest allows for more attenuation than would be achievable without this rest.

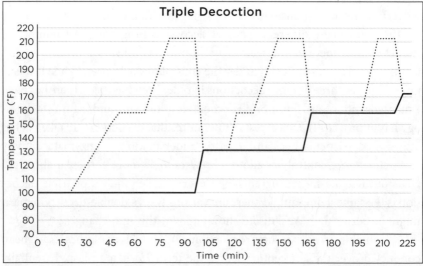

Figure 4.3. A traditional triple decoction that employs an acid rest, protein rest, and single saccharification rest.

While there are still some breweries where the triple-decoction mash process makes sense, generally this only applies to those who continue to brew with undermodified malts. A triple-decoction mash is used to maximize extract; the natural consequence of this is the wort will have low attenuation and the beer will have higher residual extract after fermentation. Brewers who use this type of mashing program utilize high hopping rates to help balance the sweetness from this residual extract.

DOUBLE DECOCTION

A double-decoction mash is more common in modern decoction processes. For the most part, it has replaced the triple-decoction mash method, even with undermodified malts. Generally, the acid rest is eliminated in a double-decoction mash. The two decoction steps are set at the protein rest and a single saccharification temperature for less-modified malts, which will also lead to low-attenuated worts (this is typical in Czech double-decoction programs). Alternatively, in the case of well-modified malts, two saccharification rests, one for β-amylase and one for α-amylase, are employed, which leads to highly attenuated worts.

One modern double-decoction method is the Hochkurz double-decoction mash, which eliminates both decoctions for the lower-temperature acid and protein rests and instead employs two decoctions during the β- and α-amylase saccharification rests (fig. 4.4). By avoiding the acid and protein rests, the Hochkurz double decoction reduces the potential negatives of foam and flavor stability issues associated with decocting modern malts. This type of mashing is used to brew pale beers of high attenuation. This represents the longest type of Hochkurz mashing since it still incorporates two decoctions.

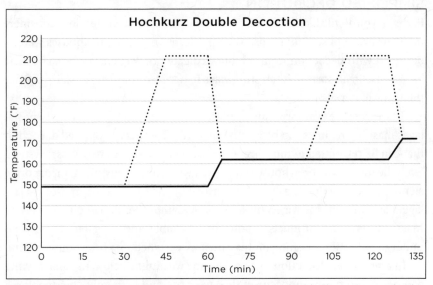

Figure 4.4. The simplest and fastest option for running a double-decoction mash. This assumes a highly modified malt is used.

One brewery regularly using undermodified malts is Live Oak in Austin, who imports slightly undermodified malts straight from Czechia. Live Oak's flagship Pilz employs a double-decoction mash involving a protein rest and saccharification rest.

At Privatbrauerei Stöttner, the goal for the Helles is high drinkability. The beer must exhibit high attenuation, low sweetness, a low finishing gravity, and no off-flavors. To achieve this, Stöttner performs a double decoction with the first rest at 131°F (55°C). The mash temperature is increased to 144°F (62°C) after returning the first decoction to the mash. A second decoction is then performed. This mashing program allows for higher attenuation, which the brewers at Stöttner believe is essential for the drinkability, or *Süffigkeit*, of their beer.

SINGLE DECOCTION

In a single-decoction mash program, one decoction portion is removed and boiled and then reintroduced into the main mash. The decoction step can happen during any given mash rest: typically, the decoction is taken during the protein rest for lower modified malts and a less attenuative beer, and at the saccharification rest for higher modified malts and a more attenuative beer (fig. 4.5). The single-decoction mash can be simplified to make it easier for most brewhouses to accomplish.

SIMPLIFIED DECOCTION

Perhaps you'd still like to decoct, but it just doesn't seem feasible considering your brewhouse limitations. Most modern American brewhouses weren't designed with decoction in mind, but dedicated brewers have "broken" their brewhouse in all sorts of interesting ways in order to coax specific flavors from their raw materials.

These creative workarounds are testament to a shared belief that special lager mashing regimes can be worth the hassle. There is a simplified decoction that can be retrofitted to most brewhouses, even a standard two-vessel system. Even the most basic brewhouse setups can, with some adjustment, incorporate elements of decoction mashing for sensory impact. In fact, many world-class lagers are brewed this way. Will Meyers of Cambridge Brewing Company in Massachusetts has produced endlessly drinkable and delicious lagers that undergo decoction mashing on his infusion-designed pub brewhouse system.

In a simplified decoction, such as the one we outline below, the final mixing of a decoction mash can occur in the lauter tun and with only one step. For a two-vessel system, the wort kettle will double as the mash/decoction cooker.

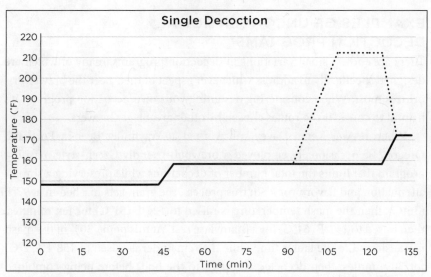

Figure 4.5. A single decoction that employs two saccharification rests. In this example, the decoction is taken during the α-amylase rest, which is suitable for highly modified malts and a more attenuative beer.

For systems that have the capability for multistep-infusion mashes, generally no modifications or adjustments need to be made to the brewhouse. For the tank that is being used for the decoction, steam jackets should be carefully observed to ensure that the remaining mash sits above the steam jacket. If there is only one steam jacket, a small decoction portion might not cover the entire steam jacket.

To perform a simplified decoction, raise the entire mash to 158°F (70°C) following your usual mashing procedure. Transfer 75%–80% of the mash to the lauter tun. Bring the 20%–25% that remains in the kettle to a boil. After it is boiled (typically for 15–30 minutes), the decoction portion is transferred to the lauter tun and thoroughly mixed into the mash. Theoretically, the entire mash should be at 172°F (78°C) after mixing. In this simplified decoction process, the added time is around an hour compared with an infusion mash.

One alternative to this process is to keep the mash at 149°F (65°C) and transfer 40%–50% of the mash to the lauter tun. The remaining 50%–60% is brought to a boil and then reintroduced into the lauter tun, causing the entire mash temperature to rise to 172°F (78°C). This is more consistent with how a Czech pub brewer might decoct their mash. In both cases, mash is only transferred in one direction, simplifying the amount of movement and time required to perform the decoction step.

EXAMPLES OF UNCONVENTIONAL DECOCTION PROGRAMS

There are endless small variations in decoction programs, many of which are designed specifically to address whichever aspect of their beer the brewer prioritizes most. When considering designing your own decoction program, it's helpful to consider the routes chosen by other great lager brewers.

When brewer Kevin Davey still worked at Wayfinder Beer in Portland, Oregon, he occasionally employed a brewpub-friendly Czech-style mashing program that limits the total number of decoctions while preserving a similar attenuation and flavor profile. In this process, the grain gets mashed in at 97°F (36°C), then the mash temperature is raised to 124°F (51°C) for ten minutes, then raised to 147°F (64°C) for a β-amylase rest. At this point, 30% of the mash is transferred to the lauter tun, while the remainder is raised to 158°F (72°C) for 30 minutes, then decocted (brought to the boil) before being combined with the mash in the lauter tun.

The brewers at Human Robot in Philadelphia use a hybrid double/enhanced decoction mash. This method simplifies the process by only having to pull out one decoction while still raising the temperature of the mash twice. For this method, after mashing in and resting, a double portion of the normal decoction quantity is moved to the kettle to boil. After boiling, half of this decoction is then returned to the non-decocted portion, raising its temperature. The remainder of the decoction portion continues to boil for another rest time until all the mash is combined (fig. 4.6). Depending on the rest temperatures desired, it's important to ensure that saccharification is at a satisfactory level since so much mash will be decocted (fig. 4.7).

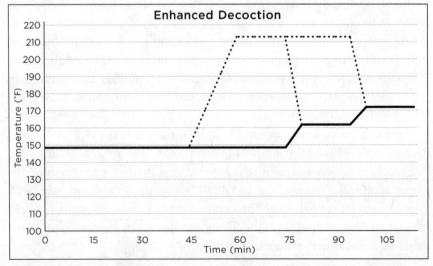

Figure 4.6. A hybrid double/enhanced mash. After the initial saccharification rest, 40%–60% of the mash is separated out for decoction and then reintroduced into the main mash in two intervals.

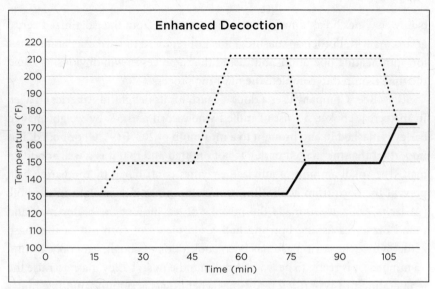

Figure 4.7. A hybrid double/enhanced decoction that employs a protein rest. The 40%–60% portion of the mash is separated out for decoction and then reintroduced into the main mash in two intervals. Note that the decocted and non-decocted portions are given time at saccharification temperature.

DOUBLE/ADJUNCT MASH, OR CEREAL COOK

The practice of decoction followed those German brewers who emigrated to the US in the nineteenth century, becoming intertwined with the classic process for American adjunct lager. Decoction mashing helped solve some of the challenges those early American brewers faced when using North American raw ingredients. Brewing with rice and corn (maize) presented significant problems for infusion-mash brewers. An understanding of decoction mashing allowed brewers to surmount these difficulties and create a new style of American lager in the process.

One special type of mashing process that's similar to all-malt decoctions comes from historical American lager brewers: the double mash. The double mash, or cereal cook, is a way to gelatinize unmalted grains (typically corn and rice, although any unmalted grains can be used) so that they can be incorporated into the mashing process. The term double mash was coined because brewers typically employed a separate cereal cooker alongside the mash kettle used for their barley mash.

In the double mash system, the chosen adjunct grain is heated past gelatinization temperature, often being brought all the way to the boil. After the cereal cook is finished, it is returned to the mash kettle, which helps bring the entire mash up to the saccharification rest temperature (fig. 4.8). Now combined, the barley enzymes break down the starches liberated from the gelatinized cereal grains. As with decoction mashing, it is not required to have a separate vessel for both heating operations, but using the same vessel will obviously extend the time required to complete the mashing process.

Riggs Beer Company uses a double mash for its delightful American Lager. In the cereal cooker, a grist of milled whole corn and 5% by weight malted barley is mashed in and brought to a minimum of 203°F (95°C) or boiled. It is important that the malted barley is not omitted and that it is a well-modified malt. The small amount of amylase enzymes contributed by the barley help prevent the corn from congealing and clumping as it is brought to the boil. (At Jack's Abby, we've made the mistake of leaving out the barley malt and found ourselves fishing bowling ball–sized pieces of corn out of the mash kettle.) Once the corn mash has been cooked long enough, generally around 15 minutes, it is ready to be transferred into the main barley mash to raise the temperature to 149°F (65°C). At times when Riggs is running multiple brews and using two vessels is prohibitive, the cooked corn mash is cooled down to the initial mash-in temperature of 149°F and then the main barley grist is mashed into the same vessel and it is all thoroughly mixed. In addition, Riggs takes advantage of the cereal mash to add undermodified barley malt. This process helps to ensure they utilize grains that would otherwise be useless, so maximizing the Riggs farm's barley production.

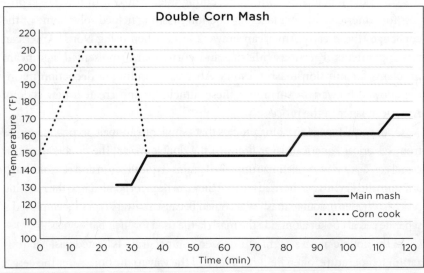

Figure 4.8. A double mash, or cereal cook. An unmalted grist (e.g., corn, or maize) is separately mashed and boiled before being introduced into the main barley mash.

F.X. Matt Brewing Co. in Utica, New York, is one of the oldest family-owned breweries in the US. The brewery still uses its 500 bbl. brewhouse to produce Utica Club, the first beer sold in America after Prohibition. The beer is still brewed with a significant portion of corn grits, which are cooked in a large horizontal cereal cooker that can process thousands of pounds of corn or rice at a time. The recipe has not changed dramatically over the years but has been adapted to replace six-row barley malt with two-row. The corn grits the brewery uses have ~1% oil content, in contrast to flaked corn, which contains none. Scott Grenier, the assistant brewmaster, explains that the oil helps to build flavor and enhance Maillard reactions. The grits are boiled with a portion of barley malt for thirty minutes before being added to the main mash, which raises the mash temperature to that of the regular step-infusion program.

Alternatives to Decoction: Single- and Step-Infusion Mashes

As malting technology and malt quality continually improved, the additional resources of time, energy, and equipment required to perform a decoction mash made it a much less attractive option for many breweries. This caused a significant shift in the industry away from decocting in favor of infusion mashing. In single- and step-infusion mashes, no part of the mash is moved to additional tanks or brought to a boil.

For a single-infusion mash, all of the malt is blended with a single hot water infusion with the sole purpose of hitting the saccharification rest temperature, generally in the 145–160°F (63–71°C) range. A step-infusion mash uses multiple hot water infusions to hit successive protein and saccharification rest temperatures (and other rest temperatures deemed necessary). In this, the step-infusion method mimics decoction, but no part of the mash is separated or boiled. With modern malts, a step-infusion mash is a simpler and more effective way of hitting various enzymatic mash rest temperatures to achieve the desired wort profile.

At Art History Brewing in Geneva, Illinois, Greg Browne created a modified step-infusion mash program using his standard two-vessel infusion brewhouse. For his lagers, Browne mashes in at 144°F (62°C) for 30 minutes with a very thick mash. He then adds near-boiling water until the mash temperature reaches 160°F (71°C) and rests the mash for a further 30 minutes. Browne ends the mash by adding boiling water until the mash tun has no room left, with the mash temperature reaching as close to 170°F (77°C) as possible. Thorough mixing is required in order to ensure that the temperature of the mash is homogenous.

History of Decoction Mashing

There are some common misconceptions about the history of decoction mashing that have contributed to some of the misunderstandings surrounding the role of decoction in the production of modern lagers. Many theories attempt to explain the origins of decoction mashing and what, if any, problems it was intended to address. One challenge comes from overlaying our modern understanding of lager beer, malt quality, and mashing principles in attempting to explain these origins.

Here are a few points commonly (mis)understood as explaining the historical use of decoction:

- Decoction mashing was useful for gaining consistent extracts from poorly modified malts.
- Decoction mashing allowed brewers to optimize the enzymatic activity of malt by hitting different rest temperatures.
- The decoction method was developed at a time when brewers didn't use thermometers; the boiling portion was a way to consistently hit mash rest temperatures ideal for enzymatic activity.

That these conditions no longer exist for modern brewers is often cited as a reason for why decoction mashing is an obsolete and unnecessary process. Those historical realities were not completely unique to lager brewers, however, so these assumptions should be questioned. Brewers from other brewing traditions developed methods of mashing that were arguably more effective, at least from an efficiency viewpoint, even though they faced similar challenges as their German and Czech counterparts.

What accounts for the importance and longevity of the decoction process among lager brewers in particular? For a complete understanding, we need to take a closer look at the raw material composition and overall sensory quality of the beers these brewers were making.

HISTORICAL LAGER, MALT, AND MASHING PRINCIPLES

Bavarians weren't always prolific beer brewers, having preferred wine up until the 1400s. In fact, Bavarians switched to brewing largely because the local climate had changed and grape production was no longer viable. Keen to manage this new industry quickly, the Bavarian government enacted laws to monitor the emerging brewing trade, not least the Reinheitsgebot and Brauordnung (p. 13). Two key factors that likely contributed to decoction's origins lay in unintended consequences from these various brewing laws: a ban on summer brewing and a tax system that taxed the production rather than the sale of beer (Jan Brücklmeier, pers. comm.).

An understanding of decoction's history requires letting go our modern understanding of lagers as clean, highly attenuated, magically effervescent beers. That this has become the definition of lager is thanks to the achievements of generations of lager brewers. Stoneware mugs of the late medieval era would have been filled with lager that was sweet, dextrinous, and underattenuated. It would not have needed to be particularly interesting to look at either, given its presentation in those opaque mugs under caps of foam. These hardly recognizable ancestors to modern lager were themselves far from the modern lager brewer's definition of Süffigkeit, but they laid the foundations for many lagering traditions like decoction.

To avoid brewing during the summer, these early brewers had to create beers that would survive for months until brewing could recommence in the fall. This is no small feat for any brewer, then or now. Decoction mashes may have offered Bavarian brewers an advantage by producing highly dextrinous worts that would allow for a slow fermentation process. Mathias Hutzler of the Technical University of Munich (TUM) notes that prolonged fermentations lasting months would have been ideal for ensuring beer didn't turn sour in storage (M. Hutzler, pers. comm.). Highly dextrinous worts with a high protein content would have provided food and nutrients for yeast to survive on for extended periods (Thausing 1882, 423).

Early brewing laws were also often enacted to place limitations on trade for reasons of economic protectionism. In southern Germany, this created a brewing community insulated not only from competitive imports but also from outside influences from other brewing cultures. While brewers elsewhere were using wheat, honey, and other simple sugar sources, common brewers in Bavaria had to learn to make do with barley. Only royal households were allowed to brew with wheat.

Barley is now touted as the best, highest-quality ingredient for brewing beer. But our appreciation for barley as an ideal grain for brewing is a modern one. The evidence suggests that the proscriptions against brewing with grain other than barley was due to barley's inferiority as a food source. While the husk of barley is important for proper lautering, it also has the negative effect of making it more challenging to access starch within the kernel. Since brewers who followed the Reinheitsgebot could only use barley, they needed a way to better access the starch within the grain. The single biggest modification challenge early brewers needed to deal with was cell wall modification (p. 42), for which decoction mashes were a ready solution.

ADDRESSING EXPLANATIONS FOR THE ORIGINS OF DECOCTION

How do we apply historical context to our current understanding of the origins of decoction mashing? Let's take a look at each of the three common explanations for the origins of decoction mashing that we outlined earlier on page 138.

- *Decoction mashing was useful for gaining consistent extracts from poorly modified malts.*

While this statement is true, the meaning of *extract* is often misunderstood. Our modern focus on efficiencies means this tends to be interpreted as meaning decoction led to increased enzymatic modification at the various decoction steps, allowing for stronger beer to be brewed. But we need to differentiate the effects of extract and modification. Extract refers to the amount of solubilized material that is transferred from grain to wort regardless of fermentability. Crucially, modification determines what compounds comprise this solubilized material. While decoction likely did increase the amount of extract obtained from undermodified malts, it also likely produced a wort with reduced fermentability and a lower attenuation limit compared to infusion mashing. While more starch and protein may have become solubilized, the conversion into fermentable extract would have been reduced since there would have been limited enzyme activity. In some ways, decoction mashing seems better suited for modern highly enzymatic malt, since the decoction itself involves temperatures that destroy enzymes. Poorly modified malts with limited enzymatic activity would be at an even greater disadvantage after repeated decoction.

- *Decoction mashing allowed brewers to optimize the enzymatic activity of malt by hitting different rest temperatures.*

This statement is at best misleading and probably just incorrect. Decoction does improve the mechanical modification of barley. Boiling grains of a malt with poor cell wall modification will physically rupture their cell walls. Brewers would have been much more likely to understand physical versus enzymatic modification, relying on what they could see happening. For example, milky colored wort at colder temperatures would begin to clarify at warmer temperatures as proteins and starches start to be modified. For any brewer inspecting the spent grain after mashing is complete, a rudimentary assessment of how efficient the mashing process could have been made. Was there still white starch within the kernels and did the grain still taste sweet?

Of course, the opposite effect would have been achieved regarding enzymatic modification, something the brewers would not have comprehended. Boiling grains decreased the overall enzymatic activity of the grain: although the mashes may have hit various enzymatically important temperatures, they would have had fewer enzymes available to modify the mash. A step-infusion mash would have had the same benefit of hitting multiple temperature rests but also would have preserved the enzymatic potential of the mash. So, while decoction mashes did result in more mechanical modification of the malt, they arguably resulted in less enzymatic modification.

We know from the historical record and we can infer from other sources (Federated Institutes of Brewing 1897, 148; Mikyška et al. 2022) that Bavarian malt was so undermodified that it could have over 20% "dead" kernels (i.e., completely unmodified). Medieval Bavarian malt and beer had a reputation for inferior quality, which was a likely consequence of early laws limiting trade and competition. The incredible challenge of solubilizing extract from these variable quality malts would have made any reliable method useful, no matter the effort. If the main goal of decoction was cell wall modification to expose extract, regardless of (or being ignorant of) protein or starch enzymatic conversion, beers with high extract and low fermentability would have been the result (Thausing 1882, 422–423).

- *The decoction method was developed at a time when brewers didn't use thermometers; the boiling portion was a way to consistently hit mash rest temperatures ideal for enzymatic activity.*

When considering the origins of decoction, while it's true that various temperature steps may have been convenient guidelines, it is a mistake to assume they were instructional. Considering that repeated decoctions at set intervals have the ability to raise the mash to various rest temperatures ideal for enzymatic modifications, it is easy to take the leap and assume that decoction was intended for this purpose. Given what little was known about the science of beer brewing at the time decoctions became accepted practice, this was not likely to have been intentional.

Preindustrial brewers who performed decoction mashes had little comprehension of the chemical reactions they were creating. An understanding of mash enzymes and the corresponding rest temperatures that take advantage of their activity didn't become standard brewing knowledge until the end of the nineteenth century. Well into the twentieth century, many brewers still didn't fully grasp the enzymatic processes in their mash tuns. And while there was a time when using decoction methods may have led to brewers to perform mash temperature steps in line with modern practice, it's unlikely that they evolved for this purpose.

While the temperature of the boiling portion of a decoction can be assumed to be a constant temperature, the same can't be said for the non-decocted portion. Even with temperature probes available today, it can be challenging to hit target mash temperatures consistently and reliably during a decoction mash. Basic heat loss in a modern insulated vessel can throw off even the best temperature-programmed mash. This is a significant error in almost all standard decoction mash temperature graphs, which omit fluctuations in temperature of the non-decocted portion at the point when the decoction is removed. (The decoction charts shown in figures 4.3–4.7 are arguably only possible when the non-decoction and decoction portions are both temperature controlled.) For historical brewers with poorly insulated mash tuns and who needed extended periods of time to heat the decocted portion, hitting consistent and accurate temperatures seems unlikely.

Furthermore, even if temperatures could be controlled and exact rest temperatures reached that correspond to the enzymes' optima, enzymatic activity was constantly degraded every time a portion of the mash was removed and boiled. If it was important to use the boiling point of a liquid to standardize the rise in mash temperature, a much simpler solution would be the addition of boiling water. It would have served the same purpose and had the same advantages of only having to heat a small amount of liquid while also preserving enzymes in the mash.

SO WHY DECOCTION?

The answer to why early brewers decocted is likely less impressive than we'd like to believe. Considering the limitations of barley malt, which, at that time, was the only malt most Bavarian brewers were permitted to use, along with the traditional cessation of brewing during the summer, the decision to decoct seems understandable. What might be considered by a modern brewer to be excessive processing of malt probably gave more reliable extract for early lager brewers. (There are written records from the Middle Ages of mashing taking upward of 14 hours [Pattinson 2011, 108]). For the types of beer that needed to be brewed and the malts available, the goals of Bavarian brewers historically would have been significantly different to those of their ale brewing contemporaries and modern lager brewers. Lagers that had to be brewed to survive months of conditioning in very cold cellars during the summer would have needed a high protein content to keep yeast healthy and a dextrinous wort for slow and steady fermentations. The decoction methods described would have led to both these results.

Bavarian breweries eventually earned a reputation for quality, and decoction was one of the processes that contributed to the quality of that beer. Lager brewers who chose to decoct unknowingly ended up making better beers for reasons they didn't properly understand. Repetition, luck, and an ever more discerning customer base eventually honed the process to one that created consistent results. But these beers were not yet the refreshing lagers we prize today. Ironically, the use of decoction mashing by modern German brewers is for completely different reasons, more often employed to create high levels of attenuation and a crisp, dry beer. It takes a modern understanding of chemistry and biology to use decoction to coax a more attenuative wort from the mash tun.

Changes to Lager over Time

The attenuation found in some well-known beers still around today has changed dramatically since the nineteenth century. One example is Munich's famous Paulaner Salvator, a *Doppelbock* brewed since the seventeenth century. The apparent attenuation of Salvator grew from 45% in the late nineteenth century to 74% in the late twentieth century. During this time the original gravity of the beer dropped as the alcohol percentage increased. This beer is typical of the changes that have occurred to lager over the last 150 years.

Attenuation statistics for Paulaner Salvator (Pattinson 2011, 113–114):

1853	1.099 OG	6.0% ABV	45% attenuation
1890	1.073 OG	5.8% ABV	62% attenuation
2004	1.075 OG	7.5% ABV	75% apparent attenuation

DECOCTION STARTS TO BE QUESTIONED

By the end of the nineteenth century, improvements in malting and refrigeration technologies meant that Bavarian brewers could begin to consider options
for mashing other than decoction. No longer did beers need to be brewed with
the intent to store them for months over the summer. Malted barley began to
be processed in a way that dramatically improved its overall modification. For
the first time, German brewing scientists were debating the merits of decoction,
citing the limited gains in extract over infusion mashing despite the extra time
and resources it required. There was a growing sense that decoction brewing was
an optional and unnecessary process for brewing lager. Dr. Wilhelm Windisch, a
leading German brewing scientist, advocated for a change in mashing procedures
away from the arduous mashing regimes typically used by Bavarian brewers. His
arguments, published in various issues of the *Wochenschrift für Brauerei* from
the early 1880s onward, were debated in numerous *American Brewers' Review*
articles near the end of the nineteenth century.

Economic and environmental conditions in Bavaria had contributed to the
perseverance and proliferation of decoction mashing over the centuries. Until
the twentieth century, Bavarian malt was primarily noted for its dark color
and intense malt flavor that was particularly suited to dark lagers (de Clerck
1957, 12). This was despite the fact that brewing scientists of the late 1800s
had been recommending German maltsters mimic the growing and malting
conditions of English brewers, in conjunction with brewers adopting infusion
mashing (Thevenot 1897, 242). How the malt was dried and processed was
considered key to improving its modification. In England's milder climate, the
drying of grains would have been possible under slower, less intense heat. Jean
de Clerck notes that England produces fine barley of all nearly pure varieties and their malts didn't need a protein rest because they contained more
soluble nitrogen through prolonged floor aging and kilning (de Clerck 1957,
12). In addition, cooler germination temperatures allowed for more even and
complete modification.

But by the time this advice came out, Bavarian brewers were set in their
ways. They had earned their reputation with consumers, who held expectations
of the beers they were buying. Fresh, foamy beers that were highly carbonated
were the norm in Bavaria, in contrast to the milder, less carbonated ales of the
UK. In an American article comparing ale and lager mashing programs, a distinction was made to explain why they differed, stating "the desire in England
is to have as little albumen [protein] as possible in the beer, whereas for our
beer we require the largest possible amount of useful albuminoids in order to

get the desired foam" (Thevenot 1897, 242). The mashing programs were at least partly responsible for the differences.

It is unclear if extract gains from decoction mashing have ever been that significant. British brewing experts in the late nineteenth century, while clearly very impressed with the ambitious mashing programs of German breweries, still couldn't rationalize the expense and time required to perform the process. E. R. Southby, in *A Systematic Handbook of Practical Brewing*, asked the question about whether the bother was worthwhile, writing, "The decoction system of mashing is an excellent one, but I doubt whether the extra five percent of extract obtainable by it, will prove a sufficient inducement to any of the brewers of this country to alter their plant" (Southby 1885, 301).

That such a notable figure in German brewing as Wilhelm Windisch was an early skeptic of decoction mashing did not go unnoticed in the US. The great Dr. Robert Wahl, writing in the *American Brewers' Review*, remarked, "Yet Windisch holds himself 'justified and obliged' to advise this conservative class [the German brewer] 'to make material changes in the process of decoction brewing or to abolish it altogether.' . . . A daring thought, truly!" (Wahl 1897, 281–282). For those that wished to continue decoction mashing, Windisch (quoted in Federated Institutes of Brewing 1897, 146–148) began proposing decoction methods that reduced the time of boiling as well as limiting the amount of time mashes were held below saccharification temperatures—a potential forerunner to a modern Hochkurz mash program. Windisch only acknowledged that more traditional methods must be used when defective malts with over 20% ungerminated barley were used (Federated Institutes of Brewing 1897, 148).

Bavarian brewers never fully gave up decoction brewing. However, how and why they decocted changed over time and it would realistically take another fifty years until the arguments made by Windisch started to become standard practice for lager brewers. By 1957, an analysis of Pilsner brewers showed they were beginning to drop the number of decoctions to brew such beers. Any advantage of extract through decoction mashing was beginning to be eliminated: it was found that there was only 2% better extract when comparing triple-decoction to a double-decoction Hochkurz mash with lightly modified malts and only 1% better extract than an infusion mash using highly modified malts (de Clerck 1957, 278).

Perhaps the biggest transition away from decoction mashing occurred in the 1970s when a combination of macroeconomic issues challenged the industry. Germany, having essentially rebuilt its brewing industry from scratch following WWII, saw an unusually large percentage of breweries needing to be rebuilt in the 1970s. The timing coincided with a period of significantly increased energy costs that forced brewers to rethink their energy usage when designing new breweries (Jan Brücklmeier, pers. comm.).

Regardless of how decoction became considered "traditional," and whether it was ever strictly necessary, its role in producing classic lagers remains important. The reasons for decoction and its mode of implementation may have changed, but it has undeniably had an impact on lager evolution. It has remained crucial for producing many of the world's classic lager brands, and its subtle sensory impact is still being used by savvy brewers to differentiate their products.

MODERN MISCONCEPTIONS OF DECOCTION

From a modern perspective, there is confusion about how and why decoctions continue to be used in breweries. Brewers often assume that decoction is a method for "solving" issues with poor malt or to increase extract. Even with the lowest-modified modern malts, cell wall modification is no longer a significant factor for why brewers choose to decoct. Modern decoction methods are designed to optimize enzymatic activity. While mechanical modifications still take place during decoctions, this aspect is less important with modern raw materials.

Decoction mashing is often seen through the lens of German decoction mashing programs used to brew pale lagers. These programs often only use saccharification rests, regardless of decoction process, and result in highly attenuative beers. It's then assumed that decoction mashing leads to beers with a high degree of attenuation and low residual sugar content (Ockert 2006b, 168), which, for the majority of modern decocted beers may very well be the case.

Yet, decoction mashing does not result in a singular outcome. Variations in the degree of malt modification and the temperature rests employed will lead to variations in the worts produced. There are decisions that can be made on how to decoct that quickly change the complexion of a beer from poorly to highly attenuative. In contrast to the archetype of pale German lager, it is common for dark lager styles and Czech lager styles to exhibit a relatively low degree of attenuation and high residual extract. Nowadays, brewers can combine consistent and high-quality malts with a newfound control over their decoction mashes and resulting worts. We'll discuss how to manage all these variables.

Czech Decoction Methods

Present-day Czech brewers who still use comparably undermodified malts with a double- or triple-decoction mash are the closest example to historical decoction mashing traditions found in modern brewing. Low apparent attenuations are expected when using these methods, because the continual degradation of enzymes in the mash through decoction results in reduced enzymatic activity that can only convert a portion of the starches into fermentable sugars.

Even with the well-modified malts that are currently available in Czechia, decoction mashing will create worts with lower attenuation limits than those created by simple infusion mashing. Decoction mashing remains a key factor in the characteristic flavor and mouthfeel of Czech lagers. Unlike their German counterparts, who prioritize the saccharification rest, Czech brewers focus less on maximizing starch conversion and employ decoctions with protein rests to help with the relatively low protein modification of their malts, resulting in beers with higher residual extract.

Considerations for Decoction

There are many considerations to take into account when decocting. The inputs for the brewhouse will be important; for example, the water-to-grist ratios and the use of roasted or very dark malts. Practically, there needs to be some thought put into how the mash will be agitated and what piping and pumps are needed to move grain.

Before many of those questions can be answered, there's the matter of whether decoction will aid in the execution of the brewer's vision. There are, of course, tradeoffs that need to be considered when making this decision.

DECIDING TO DECOCT

Deciding whether to decoct a beer is a choice that should incorporate many independent considerations. Certainly, in the case of undermodified malts, practical considerations need to be made for getting full extract and enzymatic conversion that results in full protein and starch modification. For the modern lager brewer equipped with well-modified malt, the decision is based on the nuanced sensory impact decoction can have on the finished product. When using well-modified malt, decoction is best understood as a flavor-changing process rather than a modification process (Ashton Lewis, pers. comm).

Decoction can impart a uniquely deep malty character to lager, highlighting a fullness of flavor that contrasts with a highly attenuated, dry beer. Various mashing protocols can help alter the relative proportions of different sugars formed in the wort, leading to changes in fermentation profiles and finished beer specifications. These changes also allow brewers to use heritage, craft, or raw grains in their brewhouse.

The biggest advantage of decoction may very well be the ability of brewers to use unique heritage malts and raw grains that are bred for flavor rather than efficiency. With an increasing number of craft maltsters providing these raw materials, even the largest maltsters are starting to react to changing demands. Ashton Lewis of Rahr Malting points out that craft brewers continue to have different goals than the largest breweries, for whom maximized modification is the first concern. Craft brewers are becoming quite technical when it comes to malt specifications and these new requirements are changing how even the largest malting houses approach their craft.

However, there are a few potential problems that can arise from the use of decoction. Overmodification is an unintended potential consequence that should be avoided. Decocting a mash made with highly modified, low-protein malt can produce thin beers with low foam stability. Kevin Davey, now at Gold Dot Beer in McMinnville, believes that decoction can be either a blessing or a curse for a finished beer. Done wrong, the beer will be thin, without foam protein, and lacking in malt complexity; done right, the beer is nuanced, drier but still well rounded and balanced. This insight reflects the challenges of making the right choices for rest steps and ensuring the proper assessment of modification when decocting. The main pros and cons of decoction mashing are summarized in table 4.1.

Table 4.1

Summary of the pros and cons of decoction brewing

	Pros	Cons
Decoction mashes	More efficient; potential higher extract and/or attenuation Increased flavor contributions and Maillard reactions Better foam potential as a result of Maillard reactions Stronger fermentations due to increased FAN, resulting in lower levels of esters, acetaldehyde, and sulfur compounds Can help control "overconversion" of malt by degrading enzymes	Potential for overmodification, particularly of proteins—can result in poor foam retention Requires more time and increases energy costs Potential for excessive hot side aeration; a more significant issue with double and triple decoctions Potential astringency from boiling grain in the decocted portion(s) Thermal stress can cause flavor stability issues (not hot side aeration)
Non-decoction mashes	Simpler, easier to manage, fewer variables Requires less time and energy than decocting Not necessary; the use of modern high-quality malts generally sufficient in terms of modification and flavor potential	Loss of some flavor contributions from boiling process Less control over mashing, marginally less extract and attenuation potential (particularly compared to single infusions) Limits raw materials that can be used in the brewhouse

DESIGNING A GRIST FOR DECOCTION

When designing any beer, the recipe should inform the process, and the process the recipe. Modern decoction methods give brewers unprecedented control over their mashes. Our goal is to inform your decision about what plan might be best for your beer using your brewhouse and chosen raw materials. There are many great brewing texts that provide examples of various decoction mash programs, listing the temperatures and lengths of rests complete with graphs as visual aids.[2] If you want to create a high-fructose wort that will highlight ester formation, there is a decoction mash process for it; similarly, there is a decoction mash for creating a non-alcoholic beer. Need to gelatinize adjuncts? Increase β-glucan degradation? Dial in attenuation? Yes, there are decoction regimens suited for all these needs.

Questions to answer for any beer recipe:

- What is the degree of modification of the malt and or adjuncts that are being used? Do you need to further modify the cell walls and protein, or gelatinize the grain?

---

2   A few good sources that can be found in the bibliography are Kunze (2014), de Clerck (1957), Ockert (2006b), Back et al. (2020), and Basařová et al. (2017).

- What flavor profile is desired?
- What is the target attenuation for the finished beer?
- Are specialty barley malts required (e.g., crystal/caramel, roasted, or dextrin malts) to get the desired flavor and color?

Perhaps the most noticeable recipe difference between those who decoct and those who don't is the use of specialty malts. A common trend among brewers who perform decoction is a tendency to limit or avoid altogether the use of specialty malts like crystal/caramel. Rather, mash programs are designed to feature the malt character and attenuation that the finished product requires. Even deeply malt-forward beers like Oktoberfest and Maibock brewed this way tend to use little to no specialty malts.

For most decoction brewers, simplicity reigns when it comes to designing a grist recipe. At KC Bier Company in Kansas City, Missouri, Steve Holle describes his philosophy as creating flavor by using a lot of a little. Other than his Dunkel Lager, which uses a touch of caramalt and Carafa® for color, most of his lagers develop their flavor from just three base malts: Pilsner, Vienna, and Munich.

It is true that specialty malts like melanoidin malts can lend similar flavor characteristics. However, they also generally decrease attenuation and "drinkability" by imparting a heavier body and more sweetness. With highly modified malt, decoction effectively produces a beer that tastes "full" but is inherently more drinkable than a beer brewed using caramel or melanoidin malts. Triple decoctions with direct fire and undermodified malt can result in beers with a similar body and sweetness as can be found in beers brewed with specialty malts.

Even for beers that do require specialty malts, less will be needed when performing a decoction. Brewers who decoct utilize both the sensory impacts as well as the attenuation impacts to mold a beer to their preference. As an example, Schilling Beer Co. of Littleton, New Hampshire, uses on average half the specialty malts in its lagers compared with its ales, estimating a maximum of 7%–8% specialty malts in the grists for any of its lagers.

Even when it comes to intensely malty beers like Dunkel, brewers often use limited amounts of specialty malts to develop the flavors. Matt Riggs prizes the flavor, aroma, and body he gets from using darker base malts with a multi-decoction process. He finds that using specialty malts with his Dunkel results in a cloying sweetness rather than the drier, more attenuative character he prefers.

MALT MODIFICATION

The most important consideration for determining a decoction process will be understanding the modification level of the malt that will be used. The type of malt and its modification will dictate how it should be mashed. Modern, highly modified malts generally need limited mashing programs and often have complete protein modification, reducing or eliminating the need for a protein rest. On the other hand, decoction mashes do offer the ability to utilize certain older-style malts, like those produced via floor maltings in Czechia, or other heritage or local malts that have more variability. Malts with high β-glucan levels or with poor modification can be used with the right decoction steps.

There are important downstream effects when employing a decoction mash program due to working with undermodified malts. Many traditional decoction programs incorporate a protein rest, and the subsequent increase in FAN that promotes yeast health will result in beers with reduced levels of esters, acetaldehyde, and diacetyl. The continual boiling of the decocted portions of the mash will also reduce the amount of DMS in the finished beer (Enge et al. 2005, 162).

Eric Larkin at Cohesion Brewing Company in Denver, Colorado, wanted to combine his appreciation of Czech malt with his desire to use local ingredients. He partnered with a maltster to make a special Pilsner malt with locally grown barley that is undermodified and resembles Czech malt more than most modern malts. This undermodified malt allows Cohesion Brewing to perform double and triple decoctions in most of its beers. For the Cohesion 8° light lager, while the mash only undergoes a single decoction, Larkin has found it's still necessary to have a protein rest and a step infusion before the main decoction. The brewery's current flagship beer, Cohesion 12°, is a triple-decocted Czech-style pale lager: from mash in to runoff takes five and a half hours.

When employing a decoction process that has a first rest temperature lower than saccharification temperature, common practice is to allow the pulled portion of the mash to rest at saccharification temperatures before being brought to a boil (de Clerck 1957, 273). This helps ensure better conversion of starches to fermentable extract and will limit the negative consequences of destroying a large portion of mash enzymes through boiling. This short saccharification rest can be seen when looking at a triple-decoction mash program, such as the one shown in figure 4.3, where the decocted portion is first held for 15 minutes at 160°F (71°C) before being brought up to 212°F (100°C).

Perhaps the most notable effect of decoction happens when multiple steps are performed. For Czech brewers who want to classify their beers as *České pivo* a minimum of two decoction steps is required, though many brewers still use a very traditional triple decoction.[3] This process is directly linked to the caramelization that creates the deep color and robust body typical of these beers. Unlike modern craft brewers who often use caramel/crystal specialty malts, the use of these malts by traditional Czech brewers is generally less common.

The more recently established craft brewers we met in Czechia tended to prefer double over triple decoctions and, as such, adapted their grist recipes to compensate for this change, with the use of more specialty malt becoming acceptable. Still, whether traditional or craft, a multidecoction mash utilizing a less modified malt results in a beer with lower attenuation due to the thermal inactivation of enzymes during decoction. As a consequence, Czech lagers generally have a fuller body and robust sweetness that is frequently balanced by increased bittering of up to 40 IBUs.

Cell Wall Modifications

Cell wall modification considerations for brewers generally arise when using unmalted grains or malts with low modification. Poor harvest years can result in high β-glucan levels that might cause trouble for infusion mash brewers. Cell wall modification would have been a much more significant consideration for historical brewers.

At Riggs Beer Company, brothers Matt and Darin Riggs grow their own six-row barley and malt it with the help of another local farmer. This type of vertical integration is unusual today but reminiscent of how many breweries historically would have been responsible for malting their grain. In the barley grown and malted at Riggs Beer Company, it's not unusual to see a fine/coarse extract difference (F/C difference) of up to 5%; this is three times the maximum F/C difference recommended for properly modified malts. Centuries ago, farmers and maltsters would have had to deal with even worse cell wall modification levels. In a preindustrial brewhouse, brewing with malt like this would have required significant boiling of the grains to break down the cell wall to extract starch from the grain. As farmer-brewers, the Riggs brothers anticipate these variables and are able to incorporate poorly modified grains into a corn-based double mash process for their flagship beer, American Lager (p. 136).

Protein Modification

Protein modification, while traditionally a shared responsibility between the maltster and brewer, is much more likely today to be performed by the

---

3   Czechia's highest volume beer, Pilsner Urquell, still uses the triple decoction method. The terminal gravity of this beer is 5° Plato, which we calculate as 62% apparent attenuation.

modern maltster (figs. 4.1 and 4.2). Brewers wishing to perform traditional rest steps need to pay close attention and understand why and how they are performing them.

Malt with undermodified protein is not necessarily an issue as long as a brewer plans to perform a protein rest to compensate for this factor. In fact, the best foam retention is often a result of employing a protein rest with undermodified malt rather than the newer low-protein barley malts typically used today. It is important to understand the outcome of using traditional techniques with unsuitable modern malts. Modern barley cultivars have been bred to reduce protein levels, allowing for more starch in the cells, which in turn allows for more extract. Low levels of total protein combined with a high degree of modification means that modern malts often have lower than ideal foam capacity. Bamforth (2012, 29–32) notes that "more highly modified malt yields beer with lower foam stability and that low temperature mash stands should be avoided." Sufficient protein breakdown and FAN production can still occur at relatively high mash temperatures. There is significant and maximal free amino nitrogen (FAN) production at 131°F (55°C) and the FAN production is decreased by 30% when mashed in at 149°F (65°C).

Another potential downside to a protein rest is an increase in the buffering capacity by the phosphatase enzymes. Without a protein rest, the pH level will drop faster during fermentation and allow for a beer of lighter color and higher colloidal stability (Back et al. 2020, 69). Skipping a protein rest allows for a lighter, brighter beer, which is generally seen as a positive by lager brewers. (Though hazy beer is all the rage, clarity is still prized in lager beer.)

Czech brewers are significantly more likely than their German counterparts to perform a protein rest during a decoction mash. The reason for this is twofold. First, the malt in Czechia is of a lower modification and performing a protein rest results in beers with high foam potential. Second, with the desire by many Czech brewers for higher residual extract it makes sense to minimize saccharification time.

The type of malt will also be a factor when determining whether a protein rest will be useful. Often, barley with the lowest protein content is reserved for pale and Pilsner-style malts, leaving the high-protein barley for the production of darker malts. While much of this high-protein barley might go to specialty malts, maltsters are also more likely to use them for darker base malts like Munich (Matt Riggs, pers. comm.). Mashes with a higher protein content will naturally perform better with a protein rest.

Also active at protein rest temperatures are enzymes involved in fatty acid metabolism. There is the risk of extracting foam-negative hydroxy fatty acids from well-modified malts during a protein rest that become solubilized in the finished beer. High mashing temperatures as well as short mash durations can reduce the hydroxy fatty acid content (Kunze 2014, 235). During mashing, lipid enzymes, including lipoxygenase (LOX), are not degraded at 149°F (65°C) for up to 30 minutes (Schwarz and Pyler 1984, 52). With highly modified malts there is the potential for excess hydroxy fatty acids; the implication of this is that brewers should avoid using a β-glucanase rest during mashing because such conditions favor residual lipoxygenase (LOX) activity, resulting in undesirable reductions in beer quality (Evans 2021, 34).

Starch Modification

There are two main enzymes responsible for breaking down starches, α-amylase and β-amylase. Limit dextrinase is involved to a lesser extent. Each amylase has its own optimal temperature range, and therefore a different range of fermentable sugars is produced when a mash is held at different temperatures. Optimal activity for α-amylase is between 149°F and 160°F (65–71°C), while optimal β-amylase activity occurs between 140°F and 150°F (60–65.5°C). Single-infusion mash brewers will only be able to prioritize one of these temperature ranges. The highest attenuation beers come from mash rests at 149°F (65°C), which favors β-amylase activity.

For highly attenuated modern lagers, starch modification is the priority. Traditional mashing programs likely only had a single saccharification rest. Modern lager brewers generally perform two saccharification rests to hit the optima for both α- and β-amylase activity, regardless of whether a step-infusion or decoction mash is being performed. By performing a β-amylase rest before an α-amylase rest, higher attenuation can be achieved.

But attenuation is only part of the equation when deciding on rest temperatures. Worts created with mash programs favoring either α- or β-amylase can theoretically have the same fermentability, but, because each amylase creates different types of sugars, the fermentation character of these worts can be quite different (Evans 2021, 111). For example, worts with lower maltose and higher glucose levels will encourage yeast metabolic pathways that favor ester formation.

Unlike when performing a single-infusion mash, the saccharification rest in a decoction mash is limited to the exact amount of time allowed for a rest temperature. Unlike a decoction mash, which typically finishes at around 172°F

(78°C)—hot enough to deactivate all mash enzymes—less control is available during an infusion mash, which continues to be enzymatically active and not directly under the control of the brewer, potentially staying within an active temperature range during the vorlauf, initial sparging, and runoff. Thus, using a single-infusion mash on 100% highly modified base malts at a β-amylase temperature rest will result in a beer with high attenuation. In decoction mash programs, sufficient time needs to be allowed for full conversion, potentially hours. Adjustments will need to be made when changing mashing programs from infusion to decoction for this reason.

At East Rock Brewing Company in New Haven, Connecticut, brewer and owner Tim Wilson confirmed that, with his infusion mashing system, even a 10-minute rest at 146°F (63°C) leads to around 85% apparent attenuation. This high attenuation is responsible for the distinctly dry finish of East Rock's Lager and Pilsner. While ten minutes doesn't seem like a long mash time, with infusion mashing the brewer has to consider the time taken to mash in and conduct the vorlauf and runoff, during which the mash is within a temperature range where some mash enzymes are still active.

Phytase/Acid Rest

The phytase enzyme is not generally associated with malt modification, but it is important when talking about triple-decoction mashes. The original mash-in rest for a triple decoction was "blood" temperature, that is, close to 100°F (38°C), a temperature where phytase is active. This enzymatic process creates a weak organic acid that slowly drops the pH of the wort to a more beneficial level.

Depending on the water source, particularly for very soft water, mash pH was often a problem. Pilsner Urquell is famous for still using this mash rest. The very soft water of Pilsen made hitting the ideal mash pH challenging. However, the process is quite time consuming, and often many hours are needed to get the required pH drop. Today, even if the mash-in temperature corresponds to the acid rest, it is likely not utilized as an actual acid rest since it would require hours to complete. Modern water treatments and pH adjustment, including biological acidification, generally replace the need for an acid rest.

EXTRACT AND ATTENUATION

One advantage of decoction is the increase in extract obtained, which can be substantial when working with undermodified malt. (For fully modified malts the increase will be modest at best.) Decoction will almost always lead to more extract because boiling the kernels will expose starches that would otherwise be locked in the grain. Whether or not the additional extract leads to more attenuation and alcohol production depends on the raw materials used and the mashing program. While both undermodified and highly modified malts will have increased extract, the gains with undermodified malts will be more dramatic.

Andreas Husel, brewmaster at Klosterbrauerei Ettal in Germany, notes the contradiction between extract and attenuation in his beers. For Ettaler beers, the double decoction process yields different results when making a golden lager compared to a *dunkel* (dark) lager. In Husel's experience, double-decocted golden lagers are extra dry and attenuated while his double-decocted dunkel lagers are sweeter and less attenuated. Likely the modification of the base malt for these two types of beers will be a determining factor in the resulting attenuation. Highly modified malts will have enough enzyme activity to dry out beer even when a significant portion of the mash enzymes are boiled, while malts with less diastatic power, like Munich-type malts, result in fuller, less attenuated beers.

Eric Toft from Schönramer claims that he sees a 1–2 percentage point increase in extract and attenuation with his single-decocted beers compared to single-infusion or double-decocted beers. Unlike many who argue for decoction for reasons of tradition, to add fullness of body, or to create melanoidin flavors, Schönramer golden beers are decocted for this added degree of attenuation. For Toft, attenuation is the key driver for his decisions regarding mashing. He's experimented with different mashing protocols but has found his single decoction process yields the highest extract and eventual attenuation. The increased attenuation and extract combined with an increase in melanoidin compounds create a remarkably dry beer with a full-bodied mouthfeel.

In Toft's experience he finds no attenuation advantage with a double- or triple-decoction mash. There are a few reasons this might be the case. First, there is little potential extra extract in modern commercial malts, some of which can arrive at breweries with a potential extract level of 82% (coarse grind, dry basis). The highest theoretical value of 84% (coarse grind, dry basis) doesn't leave much extract to be found through decoction. Second, the additional decoctions likely reduce overall conversion efficiency as more of the mash enzymes are destroyed through boiling. In a study in Italy comparing double and single decoctions, it was found that single decoctions provided a higher fermentable sugar content (an increase of 5.3 g/L, or about 0.5° Plato) corresponding to a 0.25% v/v alcohol increase (Montanari et al. 2005, 178).

The type of malt is also a key factor in the attenuation of lager beer. Matt Riggs notes that when he first started brewing Helles with a special variety of German malt, the first few batches he brewed had an apparent attenuation beyond his preferred 85%. Herein lines one of the challenges of working with highly modified malts for lager brewers who are used to long mashing regimes. To reduce the apparent attenuation down to a target closer to 80%, Riggs compensated by reducing the time for the β-glucan rest.

Attenuation in Czech versus German Lager

Using highly modified malt with a decoction process will lead to highly attenuative and extracted wort, while using undermodified malts will create highly dextrinous wort with low attenuation. Double- or triple-decoction mash programs with undermodified malt tends to result in comparably sweeter beer. This phenomenon can still be observed today in the Beer Judge Certification Program (BJCP) guidelines. The average apparent attenuation of three Czech styles compared to the roughly corresponding German styles highlights the difference.

Comparison of average apparent attenuation of Czech- and German-style lagers

	Pale (Pilsner) lager	Amber lager	Dark/dunkel lager
Czech	70%	70%	70%
German	79%	80%	74%

For the Czech lagers, likely all the styles would be made with similarly undermodified malts, while the German beers would use highly modified malts for Helles and Pilsner and a slightly less-modified Munich-style malt for Dunkel.

The BJCP style guidelines also highlight another unlikely observation about Helles and Pilsner. While many drinkers generally perceive German Pilsner as drier and more attenuated than Helles, the beers themselves may possess the opposite attributes. This is the case with the Helles and Slow Pour Pils at Bierstadt Lagerhaus in Denver. The strong bitterness and hop aroma of a Pilsner can fool the palate and suggest a perceived dryness. Bierstadt's Helles tastes full-bodied, malty, and sweet, whereas Slow Pour Pils tastes dry, bitter, and fine. In reality, the Helles has a higher attenuation compared to Slow Pour Pils, but the double decoction process Bierstadt uses for the Helles creates deeply complex malt flavors that suggest sweetness.

Eric Larkin at Cohesion Brewing finds his beers have a 68%–70%

apparent attenuation when triple decocting his custom undermodified malt. That's a far cry from the trend around Munich in Germany, where Helles brands regularly approach 90% attenuation. Decocting undermodified malts will inevitably create challenges for full starch conversion because the limited enzymes available will be constantly degraded before the saccharification rest is reached, particularly in a traditional triple-decoction mash program.

MAILLARD AND CARAMELIZATION REACTIONS

Maillard and caramelization reactions both occur during decoction. While these two reactions are similar, there are slight differences between them. Maillard reactions occur between amino acids and sugars, while caramelization is the oxidation of sugars without amino acids. Both require heat, though at different temperatures. Maillard products such as melanoidins also serve to enhance foam stability. Much like alpha-acids or iso-alpha acids, Maillard products can form polar complexes with proteins and/or counter the negative effects of lipids (Back et al. 2020, 170).

The products of Maillard and caramelization reactions will have flavor impacts on the finished product. Aromas range from toasty, malty, nutty, chocolatey, and sweet, among others. Wort composition and the type of heat will affect how such flavors develop. The flavor development of pale wort will differ from that of darker worts.

Maillard reactions generally don't occur until 284°F (140°C), while caramelization reactions begin from 230°F (110°C) for fructose, 320°F (160°C) for glucose, and 356°F (180°C) for maltose. The heating source a brewery employs will have a significant impact on the intensity of these reactions. Many modern brewhouses are designed to use low-pressure steam, which may affect the rate and intensity of resulting Maillard reactions. Low-pressure steam at 1 bar (14.5 psi) has a temperature of 230°F (110°C), whereas steam at 3 bar (43.5 psi) is 289°F (143°C), and steam at 10 bar (145 psi) is 363°F (184°C).

Some brewers claim that steam is too gentle and the Maillard and melanoidin reactions require direct fire for the best impact. Propane, natural gas, and wood all have burn temperatures just below 1,100°F (593°C). For this reason, Bill Wesselink and Hagen Dost at Chicago's Dovetail Brewery swear by direct fire decoction. The intense heat created by direct fire helps to promote the Maillard and caramelization reactions in the decoction boil. Steam will result in a much more limited number of reactions by comparison.

Decocting with direct fire does pose an extra set of complications. Grain kernels are prone to sticking to the kettle surfaces and burning. A standard mash mixer blade likely isn't sufficient to mix and prevent sticking and burning. At Dovetail, a chain is dragged along the surface of the heated area to help physically move the grain that sticks to the metal surface. This device, a "schlepcetcher," is like those used in many a Franconian brewery kettle. Special maintenance needs to be performed on this setup. The constant mechanical action of the chain on the superheated metal wears the metal surfaces down and requires constant repair.

For dark beers, a protein rest should be considered even when brewing with modified malts. Significant Maillard reactions in the decoction will utilize FAN, and more FAN will be needed for yeast health (Back et al. 2020, 78).

DARK MALTS AND ASTRINGENCY

When decocting, astringency is an important consideration. Boiling the barley husks extracts tannins and polyphenols, which can contribute astringency to a finished beer. Malt is generally credited with providing 70%–80% of the polyphenols found in wort (with hops providing the remainder), a factor that is influenced mostly by barley variety and, to a lesser extent, by the growing region and soil conditions (Mikyška, Dušek, and Čejka 2019, 149). Malts from North American barley tend to have a stronger impact than those from European varieties. While we haven't heard too many decoction brewers talk about astringency concerns, this potential needs to be considered.

It should be noted that not all tannin extraction is necessarily negative. The right quantity can give a nice balance, adding depth of flavor to the beer. Tannins are commonly added to wine and beers that have aged in wood. Sensory analysis will be key to determine if a decoction process causes unwanted bitterness or astringency.

In a Czech experiment, using all traditional Czech barley varieties, the concentrations of polyphenols were tested across four mashes that each used a different method: infusion mash, and single-, double-, and triple-decoction mash. The decocted beers had on average 10%–20% more polyphenols in the finished beer compared to the infusion-mash beer. The amount of anthocyanogens, an important "pro-tannin" for beer stability, nearly doubled for all decoction mashes compared with the infusion batch (Enge et al. 2005, 160–162). Conversely, it has been reported that when dehusked grains were used in decoction mashes, the absence of husk material led to a 10%–15%

reduction in tannins and an 8%–10% reduction in husk bitter substances (Narziß 1966, 19). Tannin extraction may also be mitigated by the heating process, as proteins degraded and coagulated in the boil precipitate in combination with tannins from the husk.

Multistep-decoction mashes are the norm for many brewers of dark lagers, but most brewers do not recommend using large quantities of highly roasted malts during the decoction process. Decoction brings with it the potential to extract harsh, bitter, and astringent flavors and aromas. Part of this is caused by Maillard reactions that intensify dark malt flavor. Brewers have recommended that when larger proportions of roasted malts are required for beers made using decoction mashes, the malt should be added at the end of the decoction before transfer to the lauter tun. There is little downside to adding the roasted malts at this stage as they do not require any modification nor do they add fermentables to the mash.

For lighter beers, extended boiling of the grain can lead to more noticeable astringency. Brauhaus Riegele in Augsburg, Germany, takes special measures to prevent this. The brewery has installed a mill that separates out the husk from the barley. Once the beer goes through its mashing protocol, the husks are reintroduced to the mash to allow for lautering.

One other consideration related to astringency comes when using a mash filter. For brewers that use hammer mills or otherwise heavily milled grain where husk material is broken down, decoction may only offer limited benefits. The large husk surface area makes astringency issues more prominent and there will likely be no benefits in terms of efficiency or extract. The boiling process will do very little to further mechanically break down the kernel of a hammer-milled grain. Berthold Bader at Alpirsbacher Klosterbräu in Alpirsbach, Germany, uses a mash filter, and thus chooses only to decoct wheat beers and not lagers. When using a mash filter there are no efficiencies to be gained with decoction for all-barley beers, but malts with no husk and higher protein levels can still benefit from a decoction.

COLOR IMPACT

Decoction will contribute to the color of the finished beer, sometimes significantly. The main factors that will effect this change are the water-to-grist ratio, the number of decoctions, the length of time the decocted portion is boiled, the proportion of the mash that is decocted, and the type and intensity of heat used. Oxidation of the mash as it is transferred between tanks may also darken the color.

Table 4.2

Factors that impact color during a decoction mash

More Color	Less Color
Thicker mash	Thinner mash
Longer boiling	Shorter boiling
More decoctions	Fewer decoctions
Direct fire heating	Low pressure steam heating
Oxygen pickup	Less oxygen

In the 2005 Enge et al. trial that looked at four different mash programs used on grists consisting entirely of traditional Czech barley malts, the color of the infusion-mashed, and the single-, double-, and triple-decocted worts was 10.7, 10.6, 12.8, and 14.1 EBC, respectively. The progressive darkening of the worts shows the effect of each additional decoction step (Enge et al. 2005, 161).

For comparison, at Jack's Abby we have four different beers around 12° Plato (1.048 OG) that all use a 100% Pilsner malt grist but each has a different number of decoctions. We generally see an increase in color equivalent to 1–2 SRM for each subsequent decoction. These mash regimens involve relatively high water-to-grist ratios, use steam for heating, and the boiling is limited to 15 minutes per decoction:

Citra Brau	No decoction	3.5 SRM
Post Shift	Single decoction	4.0 SRM
Brite as Hell	Double decoction	5.8 SRM
Uberholt	Triple decoction	7.0 SRM

More color pickup is possible depending on how the decoction process is being performed. On the now decommissioned first brewhouse at Austin's Live Oak Brewing Company, Chip McElroy and Dusan Kwiatkowski used to notice significant color pickup from their direct fire kettle. They described the color of the decocted portion transferred back into the main mash as chocolate or coffee like.

Bill Wesselink and Hagen Dost at Dovetail Brewery use a thin mash for their Helles to limit the color increase during the decoction process. This is a common practice by many German brewers who still decoct their palest beers. Conversely, a thick mash can lead to more color pickup from decoction.

For Helles and Pilsner beer, one of the main concerns with decoction is the potential color increase associated with the process. As consumer expectations for these styles are for very low color and "fine" flavor profiles, plenty of brewers feel that these beers should not be decocted. Kevin Düsel, from

Brauerei Rittmayer in Hallerndorf, Germany, explains that while most of his beers are decocted, some of his palest and hoppiest beers are not. He finds that his beers provide a better hop aroma without decoction.

One noticeably consistent German brewing practice is the use of a single-decoction mash for pale beers and a double-decoction mash for dark and strong beers. This is at least partially due to the sensory impact these brewers are trying to achieve through decoction. By implementing a thin mash with single decoction, color pickup is minimized while also creating a highly attenuated beer. For darker malts with less enzymatic potential, the double decoction helps highlight the malt character. This makes sense for styles like *Bock* and Dunkel that typically employ these darker, lower-modification malts, but for which there are also significant consumer expectations for malt character and intensity.

WATER-TO-GRIST RATIO

Water-to-grist ratios for lightly colored beers might be as high as 4.5–6.0 liters per kilogram (L/kg); darker beers are generally significantly lower, in the 2.75–3.75 L/kg range. The water-to-grist ratio will have a significant impact on yields and extract. The highest extracts tend to be around 4.0 L/kg (Back et al. 2020, 73). For ale brewers, these ratios might seem like a significant departure from the norm. Schilling Beer Co. brews European-style ales and lagers, but the brewers notice that their lager mashes are on average considerably thinner than their ale mashes.

Very thin mashes are typical of decoction mash programs used on lightly colored lagers, as they offer a few advantages. A high water-to-grist ratio helps minimize color pickup and increase attenuation. For brewers who brew according to the Reinheitsgebot, there is generally a higher concentration of zinc extracted from a thin mash; this is an important yeast nutrient that is otherwise difficult to produce (Ockert 2006b, 11).

Higher water-to-grist ratios help with the physical act of moving the mash between vessels, which is particularly useful when brewing in a brewhouse not originally designed for decoction mashing. At Denver's Bierstadt Lagerhaus, there is an external calandria that the brewery engineered to use with its 90-year-old copper German brewhouse, which was at one time directly fired. To heat for decoction, the mash needs to be pumped through a tube and shell heat exchanger with tubes no wider than 1 inch (2.5 cm). The thin mash used to brew Bierstadt's Helles and Pilsner has no problem flowing through these tubes.

MASH QUANTITY

A general rule of thumb for decoction is to remove 20%–33% of the mash to be decocted (i.e., boiled) before returning it to the rest of the mash. Why the variation? The difference between the starting temperature of the mash to the next target rest temperature is a key factor. The higher the difference between the starting and finishing temperature when stepping up the mash, the larger the portion of the mash that will need to be decocted. For example, raising the temperature of the combined mash from 149°F (65°C) to 162°F (72°C) will need marginally less mash to be decocted and returned than going from 149°F (65°C) to 172°F (78°C). In addition, unless the main mash vessel is also heated and well insulated, testing may be required to see how much loss of heat there is while decocting. The longer the decoction takes, the more significant this factor will be.

Elevation above sea level may also play a factor, as this changes the boiling point of water and, thus, of the mash. The higher the elevation, the lower the boiling point. If you are boiling at high elevation, you'll need to boil a larger portion of the mash to raise the rest of the mash to the desired set point.

The formula for figuring out how much mash is needed can be found in *A Handbook of Basic Brewing Calculations* (Holle 2003, 41–43):

$$\text{decoction volume} = \frac{\text{total volume} \times (\text{target temp.} - \text{start temp.})}{\text{decoction temp.} - \text{start temp.}}$$

At Denver's higher elevation, decoction mashes boil close to 200°F (93°C). That's a significant difference from sea level, where the temperature of a boiling mash may be as high as 214°F (101°C). Significantly more mash, particularly at higher temperature steps, will be needed to raise the rest of the mash to the desired set point.

DECOCTION PORTION

For the portion of mash that is removed for boiling, it's generally recommended to use a thick mash. The liquid or thin mash portion contains the majority of the mash enzymes, so boiling this portion will make conversion more difficult post-decoction. There are some decoction processes that may incorporate the thin mash in the boil, for example, when limiting enzymatic activity from an overmodified malt. In such cases, ensure saccharification is complete so that there is no need for any further enzymatic activity.

To separate the thick from thin mash, all agitation is stopped and the solids in the mash are allowed to drop. The undissolved solids may need 5–10 minutes to drop to the bottom depending on the size of the vessel. The length of the boil for the decocted portion may affect the outcome of downstream brewhouse operations because boiling the grains for too long can cause the breakup of the kernels. John Trogner of Tröegs Independent Brewing in Hershey, Pennsylvania, has seen lautering issues when decoctions have lasted longer than 20 minutes.

MIXING THE GRAINS

Mixing the grains during decoction is very important. Even in steam-heated systems, grains that are not mixed well are more likely to stick to the heated surface. Poor mixing will also create poor heat transfer and hot spots within the mash.

Overmixing is just as problematic, however. Kunze (2014, 242) recommends mash paddles not exceed peripheral speeds over 2 meters per second, otherwise shear forces are likely to damage the grain. At higher speeds there is also a strong possibility of a whirling effect much like in the whirlpool, which can damage the grain and potentially damage the shaft seal. The whirling effect can also be a cause of significant oxidation.

For small systems where a mixer is not a viable option, an alternative is to recirculate the mash with a pump. While this isn't the ideal method, it will allow for the boiling of grains, proper heat transfer, and constant mixing. Often, a physical shovel or paddle is needed to regularly check that grain isn't sticking to the heated surface. The brewers at Live Oak practiced this challenging manual process on their old two-vessel brewhouse when they chose to decoct. Constant motion of the grains helps to properly mix the grain and limits charring.

A standard centrifugal pump and brewery hose can transfer grains. Higher water-to-grist ratios, combined with strong mixing of grains in the mash kettle, help to minimize the likelihood of clogged pipes and pumps.

HOT SIDE AERATION

The impact of hot side aeration in the modern brewhouse is still being studied. Decoctions, particularly multistep programs, offer many more opportunities for hot side aeration due to the additional movement of grain between tanks. Color pickup and poor lautering are potential downsides of too much hot side aeration. Hot side aeration has been linked to staling and long-term packaging flavor changes.

On the flip side, the heating of the mash degrades many oxidase enzymes, including lipoxygenases, peroxidases, and polyphenol oxidases, which in turn limits the ability of the mash to undergo harmful oxidization reactions even with aeration (Back et al. 2020, 74). Boiling liquids are also less oxygenated.

Some traditional brewers swear by hot side aeration as an integral part of their flavor profile. At Budvar in Budejovice, Czechia, the dual 600-hectoliter brewhouses still use open grants during the lautering process, a step that introduces a controlled amount of oxygen into the wort as it transfers from the lauter tun to the kettle. (A grant is a recessed trough that collects wort between the lauter tun and kettle through an array of valve-operated swan-neck faucets.) Budvar had experimented with removing that process but was unable to recreate the desired flavor profile. It's believed that the oxidation helps to promote reactions between polyphenols and proteins, while at the same time deepening the color of the beer.

One other brewery that in certain circumstances still relies on hot side aeration to develop flavor is Brauerei Hofstetten in Austria. The brewery has recently installed a modern stainless steel brewhouse that takes advantage of most modern brewing practices. However, there are certain beers, like Hofstetten's Granitbock, for which its on-site iron brewhouse that dates back to 1929 is still employed. Using this brewhouse also means using its ancient mill, a belt-driven wonder that rattles the rafters while in use. In order to get the proper mash intensity and color development the brewery was looking for in Granitbock, there is no comparison between the new and old brewhouses. The old brewhouse imparts the right character for these old-school beers.

Figure 4.9. The still-working brewhouse that dates back to 1929 at Austria's Brauerei Hofstetten. Photo courtesy of Brauerei Hofstetten.

Homebrewing Tips

Decoction brewing is not only possible at the homebrew level, in some ways it may be easier to perform than on a large commercial brewing system. The process is part of the homebrewing culture of Germany, but it has also influenced American homebrewers who have gone on to open their own breweries. John Lanzini of Schilling Beer Co. began his fascination with the decoction process as a homebrewer, an experience that compelled him to bring decoction brewing into his own brewery.

DECOCTION HOMEBREWING

Jan Brücklmeier is a Weihenstephan graduate with a diploma in brewing, and the author of the German-language *Bier Brauen*. Brücklmeier explains that most German homebrewing texts are modifications of professional texts, which is why decoction brewing is commonly practiced by German homebrewers. Modifications to the process have been made to simplify the decoction process at home. It's recommended that part of the mash be decocted first and then combined with the main mash. There are two options to make this happen, outlined below. If a golden lager is being brewed, aim for a water-to-grist ratio of 4.0 L/kg. If a darker beer is being brewed, a water-to-grist ratio as low as 2.5 L/kg can be used. The likelihood of the malt sticking to the pot and/or burning will depend on the water-to-grist ratio: the more water (i.e., the thinner the decocted mash), the less likely this will happen. With a high water-to-grist ratio, make sure the vessel is large enough to hold all the volume.

Single-vessel decoction option. Mash into the kettle with 25% of the grist at your preferred water-to-grist ratio at 149°F (65°C) for 15 minutes. Bring this to a boil, and boil for 15 minutes. At the end of the boil, add your remaining mash liquor at 128°F (53°C) together with the remaining grist to make a final combined mash at 149°F (65°C). (The 128°F strike temperature assumes the decoction is at 212°F [100°C] when this step is done.)

Two-vessel decoction option. Mash in 75% of the grist at your preferred water-to-grist ratio into a mash tun vessel at 149°F (65°C). Mash into your kettle with the other 25% of the grist at 149°F (65°C) and rest for 15 minutes. After the 15-minute rest, begin heating the kettle and continue to mix slowly without splashing but firmly enough to ensure no grain is sticking to the bottle of the kettle. Once it is boiling, boil the decoction for up to 15 minutes. As soon as the boil is finished, turn off the heat and transfer the decoction into the main mash. Depending on your burner strength, the timing should be about right to have had a 60- to 75-minute rest in the mash tun at the time the decocted portion is added. Pour the entire kettle portion into the mash tun and mix the mash well to ensure a uniform temperature.

If attempting a double decoction, Brücklmeier recommends performing two saccharification rests versus a protein rest. He explains that heating equipment on the homebrew side may take too long to boil a decoction portion, which would keep the non-decocted portion in a protein rest that is way too long for most malts.

STEP-INFUSION HOMEBREW PROCESS

As an alternative to decoction mashing, a single mash can be performed with the addition of near-boiling water to raise the temperature of the mash.

Step-infusion option. Mash in at 149°F (65°C) with a very thick mash in the 2.0–2.5 L/kg range. Rest the mash for 30 minutes, then add an additional 1.0 L of water per kilogram of grist to raise the mash temperature to 158°F (70°C). Either end the process here or add another 0.5–1.0 L of water per kilogram of grist to raise the mash temperature to 172°F (78°C). Always add the boiling water to the mash, not the mash to the water, and thoroughly mix without splashing and foaming.

The decoction process has been preserved as a feature of many traditional lagers. Its association with these styles has inspired modern brewers to incorporate this, sometimes arduous, process into their brewhouse operations.

Rather than rehash old arguments over its necessity, savvy modern brewers have instead homed in on the sensory impact of decoction. By doing so, decoction has evolved into a specialty process that brings out another layer of complexity from raw materials. In a world where every brewer has access to the same materials, processes like decoction give brewers the ability to put their own stamp on their lagers.

To Decoct or Not Decoct, That Is the Question

Having asked these questions of lager brewers around the world, we've found that their answers lend insight into their philosophies and personalities outside the brewhouse.

Hofbräuhaus Traunstein and Klosterbrauerei Andechs have almost a millennium of brewing experience between them and are both globally recognized for the quality of their traditional beers. Both have significant export businesses and are experimenting actively in the non-alcoholic beer market.

Situated atop an idyllic hill in Bavaria overlooking the quiet, fog-laden countryside, time is an abstract concept at the Andechs *Bierhalle*, especially over a stein of Doppelbock. This space has been hosting thirsty travelers for centuries, and their passage has worn smooth ruts into the stairs leading up to the open-air patio. The monks who still call this place home take care to preserve relics from early Christianity in their beautiful pilgrimage church, which is itself being lovingly restored. The brewery that was once tucked into the cellars of the monastery was moved down the hill and completely modernized and automated in the 1960s. A state-of-the-art system replaced much of the traditional equipment of the older brewhouse, such as the massive cylindroconical tanks that replaced the open fermentation tubs.

Through all that modernization, however, decoction remains.

"We do this as it was done in the past," head brewer Andreas Stürzer tells us. Every batch of Andecher beer is decocted; once for the pale beers and twice for the dark beers.

This is not using tradition as a marketing tool—there are no false copper tops to the brewery's stainless steel brewing vessels. Instead, it is perhaps an embodiment of one of their values: "Our tradition is being progressive and we owe our progress to a long tradition." Decoction is simply understood as an irreplaceable part of Andechs' brewing heritage.

The historically royal Hofbräuhaus Traunstein is a few hours and many worlds away from the hilltop at Andechs. The Traunstein brewery is tucked into a tiny urban center, its courtyard's tight angles presenting quite the challenge for truckers. The small space allotted to the brewery is well-used, containing a beautiful and old five-vessel brewhouse.

Figure 4.10. The modern fermentation equipment at the Klosterbrauerei Andechs.

A thoroughly modern tour through the facility, complete with pyrotechnics and animatronics, highlights many traditional methods still employed by Hofbräuhaus Traunstein. Open fermentation, cold sedimentation tanks, and two-vessel fermentations are elements the brewery believes to be crucial to executing their vision.

Missing from that is decoction, which brewmaster Maximilian Sailer notes as unnecessary with the infusion-ready malt they have readily available. Sailer prizes the beautiful, light clarity of his Helles, which decoction would no doubt change. Glasses of Hofbräuhaus Traunstein's excellent Helles support rambunctious amounts of brilliant white foam that sharply contrasts with the brilliantly clear beer. One in hand, it is difficult to argue anything could improve upon it.

Andechs and Traunstein share something else in common: a clear vision for the beer they aim to produce. The methods they use in service of those visions are different. It is tempting to read these differences as completely incompatible brewing philosophies. But if they both produce world-class beer, it is perhaps unimportant which method is "right." They can both be.

Figure 4.11. A brewing vessel at Hofbräuhaus Traunstein

Thousands of miles away at Austin's Live Oak Brewing, sat in a brewery practically ancient by modern US craft beer standards, I'm still daydreaming about the one stein of Andechs Doppelbock I was able to enjoy before having to rush back to America. Live Oak's brewery offers its own sanctuary, abutting a field of live oak, scrub pine, and the odd disc golf basket. The large, German-built brewery was built in 2015 with decoction in mind. The original two-vessel brewhouse with which the brewery opened in 1996 is now a curiosity of the disc golf course.

Chip McElroy founded Live Oak back in 1996 with Brian "Swifty" Peters in a hilariously compact warehouse. Horizontal fermentation was not so much a choice of tradition as it was a physical requirement of the space. McElroy has a love for Czech beer that saw him become the first American craft brewer to import specialty Czech malt specifically for brewing Bohemian lager. In those early days, Live Oak's flagship Pilz was single-decocted, albeit with a "high-short" Hochkurz mash program.

Swifty works across town now at Austin Beer Garden Brewing (ABGB). He talks fondly of his cross-town neighbor and former partner, freely acknowledging their different philosophies. Whereas Live Oak's new brewery is purpose-built for multiple decoctions, yeast strains, and raw materials, the DNA of that early Live Oak brewery lives on at ABGB. Swifty and his partners founded ABGB with the goal of brewing beer on as practical a system as possible that could transport you to Europe with a sip.

Over half pours of beer (a.k.a. "swifties"), Swifty talks about setting up ABGB as cheaply as possible in 2013 and learning to make world-class beer on the brewery's two-vessel system. The brewery doesn't decoct its beers. The goal at ABGB is to make the best beer as efficiently as possible, achieving what they can with what they have. It fits Swifty's personality, too—direct, to the point, and suffering no fools.

For ABGB, the goal is to keep it lean, which means the systems, the processes, and the beer itself. One of the philosophies Swifty still shares with McElroy is a passion for filtering lager. Both breweries employ lenticular filters, which they believe is key to producing great lager. As two of the most awarded American lager breweries, it would be hard to argue with either of them about their processes.

"It's about what keeps you passionate," Swifty says. There is certainly no single, correct way to make lager. But those that produce the best lager in the world share a vision for their finished product and achieve that vision as they see fit.

5

CARBON DIOXIDE: THE FIFTH INGREDIENT

*A*MERICAN CRAFT BEER HAS LONG TRADED ON THE QUALITY AND PROVENANCE OF ITS RAW MATERIALS. The pioneering "full-flavored," all-malt beers, liberally dosed with Pacific Northwest hops, were (and remain) delicious alternatives to the industrialized, adjunct-laden lagers that had previously dominated the US beer market to the exclusion of all else. Farmers, maltsters, and suppliers have kept the raw materials market stocked with premium, high-quality grain, malt, yeast, and hops for brewers of any scale.

The consumer has taken note. When it comes to being knowledgeable about hop varietal characteristics and terroir, many fans of modern IPA styles rival their wine drinking counterparts. Hushed, geeky speculation about yeast strains and grain bills has escaped the confines of internet homebrewing forums and entered the mainstream food and beverage media. Heady descriptions of beer flavors and their corresponding raw materials have found their way into everything from taproom menus to the slickly executed advertising campaigns of the world's largest breweries.

And yet carbonation, the literal vehicle for these sensations, is not so much overlooked as completely left out of the discussion. The simplest flavor trial can illuminate the outsized sensory impact carbon dioxide has on your beer. Your best beer, without its carbonation, is a shell of its fully realized self.

Attention paid to the quality and sourcing of your ingredients should extend to carbon dioxide (CO_2), the fifth and perhaps least understood ingredient in your beer. The quality, quantity, and sourcing of gas used during force carbonation directly affects the way your beer is perceived by each consumer. Taking it one step further, capturing the natural CO_2 produced during lager fermentation is a pure expression of the quality of your raw material.

Notoriously, the German Reinheitsgebot mandated that only water, hops, malt, and, latterly, yeast could be used in the production of beer. Historically, most brewers in Germany interpreted this law to mean that the addition of CO_2 from sources other than beer production was not allowed. Thus, a lesser-known side effect of this so-called purity law was that brewers in the modern age had to develop methods for natural carbonation that could be scaled up to match the needs of industrial production. Two of these methods, krausening and spunding, are discussed in detail in this chapter.

Of all the techniques discussed in the book, natural carbonation is perhaps the most achievable, and will have the most obvious sensory impact on your finished product. Natural carbonation can be executed with minimal investment in equipment, albeit with significant commitment to quality assurance, quality control, and safety. These investments are also likely to improve the overall quality of your beers.

Understanding Carbon Dioxide Sources

Knowing the provenance of your ingredients should be a must for any brewer who takes pride in their beer. Brewers should afford their CO_2 the same scrutiny they apply to their malt and hops, along with an appropriate appreciation of its origins. While beer labels in the US don't require CO_2 to be listed as an ingredient under Alcohol and Tobacco Tax and Trade Bureau (TTB) regulations, all food and beverage products outside the TTB's remit do require it; this is why your favorite soda lists "carbonated water" as an ingredient. Carbon dioxide is considered an ingredient for most food applications when added from an external source.

Commercial CO_2 supplied to breweries can be from a variety of sources. Whether the CO_2 is a by-product of ethanol production, natural gas recovery, or some other industrial process, continuous care needs to be taken to ensure the quality of gas used. Impurities in CO_2 will end up as impurities in finished beer. This is also true of any carbonation captured during natural beer fermentation, though these impurities will be derived from the raw materials of beer production itself.

While regulations in the US require that food-grade CO_2 be 99.9% pure, the Brewers Association (BA) notes that the final 0.1% represents enough parts per million to pass the flavor threshold of many sensory compounds. As new sources of CO_2 are employed by suppliers, new types of impurities can be introduced. The BA recommends breweries actively communicate with their gas suppliers, have systems in place for managing deliveries, and carry out preventive maintenance on storage and supply lines for CO_2. In addition to these preventive steps, the BA also recommends as a best practice a robust quarterly sensory program for assessing the quality of a brewery's CO_2. This emphasis placed on the quality, sourcing, and continued maintenance of CO_2 systems is reflective of the overall sensory impact of carbonation on finished beer.

With these considerations in mind, many lager brewers simply prefer to err on the side of caution when it comes to introducing carbonation to their beers, sticking to the traditional method of natural carbonation. At Utepils Brewing in Minneapolis, Minnesota, head brewer Eric Harper has used natural carbonation methods since he started in 2017; he learned the process in his previous brewery experience. While Harper doesn't have any data to support the sensory impact of these methods, he has serious concerns about adding commercial CO_2 and its potential contaminants to his finished product.

Because the Reinheitsgebot prohibits German brewers from using CO_2 that is not a natural by-product of beer fermentation, many modern German breweries still use natural methods of capturing CO_2 during fermentation. Krausening and spunding are the two methods most used by traditional German brewers, and these processes have a noticeable impact on the sensory aspects of their lagers.

Impact of Carbonation

How brewers introduce carbonation into their beer has a significant impact on how the beer is perceived by the consumer. Bubble size and volumes of CO_2 in solution all shape the sensory impact of every beer. Many of these variables owe much to whether the beer was naturally carbonated or whether force carbonation was employed. Force carbonation is the act of introducing CO_2 from an external source into a beer, while natural carbonation relies on capturing CO_2 created as a by-product of fermentation.

The impact of natural carbonation on beer might be best expressed by the number of American lager producers who go to the trouble of designing natural carbonation methods in their breweries. When we talked with some of the top lager producers in the US, while not all of them followed every traditional lager brewing technique, nearly every one of them was familiar with bunging devices and used them for at least part of the carbonation process.

BEER FOAM

Foam texture and quality is less easily measured, but there is reason to believe that natural carbonation has a positive impact on both. Many brewers believe that they produce a higher quality, denser, longer-lasting foam with natural carbonation processes. The physical act of force carbonation may be one reason why, because any foam produced during the process of force carbonation before the beer is packaged will not be present once the finished beer is dispensed or poured.

Will Kemper, owner and brewmaster of Chuckanut Brewery in Burlington, Washington, suggests a simple experiment to prove the point: whip your beer in your glass a few times, and notice how less foam is produced with each swirl. "When you start injecting carbon dioxide, you have slight foaming," says Kemper. "Once you create foam out of foam-positive agents, you denature those agents." Kemper reports that his natural carbonation program results in beers with sturdier, longer-lasting foam. His belief that "beer is the sum of subtle considerations" can also be tested by sampling Chuckanut Brewery's excellent lagers. In addition, the carbon dioxide created through natural carbonation improves the separation of precipitated proteins and tannins (Kieninger 1977, 76).

Yeast scientist Mathias Hutzler of the Technical University of Munich noted a pertinent theory that is currently under research. At a microscopic level, biological carbon dioxide will bond to the beer matrix,[1] leading to finer bubbles and a "rounder" character. This is another tempting piece of information to advocate for natural carbonation as a superior method for the quality of finished lagers.

Understanding Carbonation in Beer

Before we discuss how to implement a natural carbonation program, it is helpful to understand some pressure dynamics. These factors are important to understand when deciding which natural carbonation process is right for you

---

[1] The term "beer matrix" is a shorthand way to describe the complex aqueous mixture that constitutes a finished beer. This mixture contains carbohydrates of varying size and complexity, proteins and peptides, hop-derived compounds, and a slew of other organic molecules, including phenolic compounds and lipids.

and your brewery, as well as helping to identify when force carbonation might make more sense for a given beer.

No matter how beer is carbonated, the amount of CO_2 that will remain in solution depends on two variables: temperature and pressure. Understanding how these variables interact is important for designing a natural carbonation program but is ultimately useful for any brewer. A quick look at the solubility of CO_2 under constant pressure but at varying temperatures reveals that colder liquids can hold significantly more CO_2 in solution (*see* table 5.1; a much more detailed chart is shown as table 5.5 on p. 198). While table 5.1 shows the saturation of CO_2 in beer at atmospheric pressure, bear in mind that saturation levels will vary based on the elevation of your brewery, since atmospheric pressure decreases as elevation increases, but the principles of this table still apply.

Table 5.1

Carbon dioxide saturation in water at sea-level atmospheric pressure, 14.7 psi (1.01 bar)

Temperature (degrees)		Concentration CO_2	
Celsius	Fahrenheit	CO_2 g/L	vol. CO_2/ vol. water
0	32	3.38	1.71
1	34	3.24	1.64
2	36	3.10	1.57
3	38	2.98	1.51
4	40	2.87	1.45
6	42	2.77	1.40
7	44	2.67	1.35
8	46	2.55	1.29
10	50	2.35	1.19
16	60	1.98	1.00
21	70	1.68	0.85

Source: "Volumes of CO^2 Gas Dissolved in Water," CO^2 Charts, Zahm and Nagel Co., updated April 2016, http://www.zahmnagel.com/wp-content/uploads/2016/04/Volumes-of-CO%C2%B2-Gas-Dissolved-in-Water.jpg.

In a closed system with a constant volume of gaseous CO_2, such as the headspace of a packaged beer, raising the temperature also raises the pressure; conversely, if the temperature drops so will the pressure. A bottle of beer at 40°F (4.4°C) that is equilibrated to 2.5 volumes of CO_2 will have approximately 12.5 psi (0.9 bar) of applied pressure in the headspace. That same bottle when warmed up to 70°F (21°C) on a shelf will have about 30.5 psi (2.1 bar) in the headspace.

This leads to an insight into why natural carbonation methods for colder fermenting lagers may have developed differently than those of warmer fermenting ales. One advantage to fermenting at cooler temperatures is a lager's ability to hold more CO_2 in solution; at any given pressure, a liquid at 50°F (10°C) can hold considerably more CO_2 than a liquid at 70°F (21°C). Assuming for a moment that historical ale and lager brewers used barrels that held similar amounts of pressure, lager beers would have enjoyed significantly higher volumes of CO_2 in the finished product. This is also a tempting explanation for how English cask ale and German lager developed to have vastly different carbonation levels, something still appreciated in classic examples of both styles today.

To put this all into practice, the colder the product you are trying to carbonate, the less pressure needs to be applied for a given concentration of CO_2 in the finished beer. This is why modern lagers are more suitable for tank carbonation, while warmer-fermenting ales tend to be bottled if they are to be naturally carbonated (outside of cask ale). The difference between typical fermentation temperatures of these two beer types is enough to make this practical; many brewing vessels are not rated to the pressure that would be needed to naturally carbonate an ale.

Determining whether your vessels can withstand the pressure required for natural carbonation is important. The American Society of Mechanical Engineers (ASME) is a professional organization that sets pressure standards and monitors compliance by tank manufacturers. Any vessel designed for over 15 psi gauge (psig) is considered a high-pressure vessel by the ASME and should be manufactured to strict guidelines pertaining to pressure and boiler vessels. To have a high-pressure vessel rated by the ASME, a tank manufacturer needs to be permitted by ASME and have each individual high-pressure vessel inspected.

Most standard tank designs used by breweries have a 15 psig (1.03 bar gauge) tank pressure rating. A beer at 48°F (9°C) degrees and under 15 psig top pressure can hold approximately 2.38 volumes of CO_2; a 70°F (21°C) beer would need approximately 30 psig (almost 2.1 bar gauge) top pressure in order to hold the same 2.38 volumes of CO_2. That's double the pressure rating of the tank! For higher-carbonated products like *Hefeweizen*, tanks designed for up to 43.5 psig may be needed to fully carbonate them in tank.

Even if you plan to use a high-pressure tank to carbonate your lager, it is not recommended to use these high pressures with lager yeast. Usually, naturally carbonated lagers have their temperatures reduced at bunging in order to ensure lower pressure values during the process. High pressures will increase autolysis, can potentially lead to other off-flavors, and will make repitching of yeast challenging.

Ungespundetes Bier

Finely tuned carbonation profiles are a modern convenience. Historically, making a consistently carbonated product would have been difficult. The *ungespundet* style of lager is a surviving style that hints at this history. Meaning literally "unspunded" or "not bunged," an ungespundet lager would have only had the amount of carbonation that it could naturally hold at any given temperature.

This process is still traditional for various brewers in Franconia in south-central Germany. This cultural region boasts the most breweries per capita in the world and it's still possible to find many brewers who still follow very old brewing practices. Often these are *Kellerbier*-type beers, golden in color and served *vom Fass*; directly from a wooden barrel.

A particularly well-known example, Mahrs Bräu U (the *U* standing for ungespundet), is served this way in the brewery's beer garden in Bamberg. Had it not been for the rigorous demands of our research dragging us away on a rainy day in August, we could have tucked into these full, bready lagers long into the night. The soft, fine carbonation of the *vom Fass* version is approximated in the bottle and keg, but really shines in Mahrs Bräu's delightful old Franconian saloon.

Natural versus Force Carbonation Process

There are many factors to consider when choosing between force carbonation and natural carbonation. A brewery may prefer to use either one depending on the situation rather than committing to always using one or the other. Brewing philosophy and final product expectations can often outweigh any potential sensory impact in deciding between these options.

Force carbonation is a fast, easy, and on-demand way of carbonating a beer. Most modern brewers are familiar with the process of adding CO_2 via a carbonation stone, pinpoint carbonator, or top pressure. Significantly less attention is needed during fermentation, cellaring, and routine production processes when force carbonating. It is also relatively fast and easy to control force carbonation; theoretically, it's as simple as hooking up a CO_2 gas tank to a tank of beer.

The terms used for natural carbonation are imported from the German language and are often used interchangeably. For clarity, we distinguish between these terms as follows:

Bunging: The process of closing up a tank, using appropriate and safe equipment, to capture CO_2 in solution.

Bunging apparatus/spunding valve: The physical valve used to safely contain pressure in a tank.

Forced fermentation: A fast fermentation performed under ideal conditions in a laboratory to determine the maximum fermentability of wort.

Spunding: The bunging of a primary fermentation.

Krausening: The bunging of a secondary fermentation, traditionally with the addition of freshly fermenting wort (krausen) but krausening can be performed using other fermentables.

Naturally carbonating a beer is in some ways the simplest way to introduce carbonation to a beer. It's a method that predates quality control programs and fancy measuring instruments. Modern homebrewers likely share some of their methodology with ancient alewives in this respect: by capturing the natural by-products of fermentation, the modern homebrewer can preserve a pleasant carbonation in their finished beer. Of course, this simplicity comes somewhat at the expense of consistency and scalability. When naturally carbonating beer, multiple gravity samples may need to be taken each day to know when to bung and hit your carbonation target. Daily monitoring of the spunding or krausening fermentation needs to occur to ensure proper fermentation, and the impact on carbonation of every transfer or movement of beer needs to be considered.

Certain conditioning processes should be borne in mind when designing a carbonation program, as carbonated beer can be challenging to work with. For example, when using lenticular filters, some brewers have to partially spund using a lower pressure setting that traps less CO_2 in the beer so that the filter can properly operate. These brewers typically top off the carbonation level with force carbonation after filtration.

Dry hopping in a natural carbonation program has its challenges as well. Unfortunately, adding hops directly to the tank and/or using a hop cannon, are not an option—dangerous degassing and foaming can occur when working with a pressurized vessel. Adding hops to an empty fermentor or secondary tank before it is pressurized is an adaptation that some lager brewers adopt. New methods that involve keeping full pressure on the tank and gently adding hops can also be used when using a single tank for primary and secondary fermentation. (See "Dry Hopping Lager" in chapter 2.)

With force carbonation, careful planning is needed to ensure equipment (whether a carbonation stone or pinpoint carbonation unit) is available and the process is completed in time for packaging. Here a natural carbonation program offers a potential advantage, wherein brewers will have multiple tanks of lagered, carbonated beer ready for packaging at any given time.

Table 5.2
Pros and cons of force carbonation versus natural carbonation via tank bunging

Carbonation method	Pros	Cons
Force carbonation	Fast On demand Easy to control Can happen whenever or wherever (with proper equipment) Less oversight required during fermentation and cellaring	Purity of external CO_2 must be strictly monitored Cost of external CO_2 Potential for aeration Larger bubble size Foam stability reduced Potential to strip aromas from beer Special equipment needed Needs tight coordination with packaging schedule
Tank bunging	Running stocks of carbonated beer ready to package immediately Less potential for aeration Higher carbonation levels more easily attainable[a] Purity of CO_2 not a concern No cost of bulk CO_2 Better foam stability	Time and expertise needed What do you do if tank loses pressure? Added variables, potentially less consistent Temperature dependent Potential for yeast autolysis

[a] Since the solubility of CO_2 decreases at higher concentrations, it can be difficult to achieve high levels of carbonation using force carbonation. With natural carbonation, CO_2 has no choice but to stay in solution.

Crowns Fit for Royalty

For centuries, the appearance of beer has been important to consumers. While today's hazy IPA fans have their opacity to cherish, many lager-heads yearn for the sturdiest, most pillowy foam crown possible on their finished beer.

Beer is often described as the only beverage that naturally produces foam. Advertisements have long depicted huge, fluffy clouds of enticing foam on full glasses of beer, and to good effect. Foam can

Figure 5.1. Brewer and owner Tom Beckmann of Goldfinger Brewing Company in Downers Grove, Illinois, taking pride in a proper pour.

be an indication of freshness, vitality, and health, a reminder that the product in your glass is a living one. It also influences a drinker's perception of a beer's quality in subtle ways, which Dr. Charlie Bamforth explores in his American Society of Brewing Chemists (ASBC) Practical Guides series entry *Foam*. An experiment detailed in *Foam* explores the unconscious associations that drinkers from around the world bring with them about the quality and quantity of foam in their glass (Bamforth 2012, 2–3).

We'd argue that more foam means more fun and more deliciousness. In a practical sense, good foam stability and retention is an indication of good brewhouse process during fermentation and carbonation. A sturdy foam cap protects a beer from the environment and allows the steady release of volatile aroma compounds that can heighten a drinker's enjoyment.

Yet, for some reason, there is a certain subset of consumers who have come to equate foam with being "cheated" out of beer. Ironically, you need go only as far as a brewery taking care to present the beer with appropriate foam to hear stories about customers sending back pints. Jack once had to explain to someone that the perfectly poured stein he was delivering during a busy festival did indeed include the appropriate volume and was worthy of (literally) putting his name on.

There is no doubt that unscrupulous operators have tried to sell "cheater" pints and half-liters of beer, using smaller glasses or excess foam as shortcuts. But beyond what foam tells the careful observer about the brewer, foam also provides sensory benefits to the imbiber. Poured with a correct cap of foam, beer's carbonation will slowly and effectively disperse aromas and the cap acts as a protective layer that prevents this carbonation being released from solution too quickly.

In his 1989 documentary series *The Beer Hunter*, Michael Jackson demonstrates a point of pride at the Budvar brewery—the crown of their lager can support a coin! This is something most brewers can only aspire to achieve, but in the meantime we can content ourselves with continuing to educate our consumers about the practical and aesthetic benefits hidden in all those tiny bubbles.

Executing Natural Carbonation

Natural carbonation is a great way to harness traditional techniques that will elevate the quality of your lagers. The techniques required are not overly complicated or expensive, and the results will be noticeable in the finished beer. Key to a natural carbonation program is an understanding of the auxiliary processes and tools required, forced fermentations and spunding valves being chief among them. Designing and implementing a program that works for your brewery brings with it the benefit of consistent data collection and an added layer of care and attention to the cellaring process.

Table 5.3

Pros and cons of bunging methods (spunding and krausening) and bottling to trap natural carbonation

Natural carbonation method	Pros	Cons
Spunding (primary fermentation)	Least amount of cellar process work Limits contact with potential contamination or oxygen ingress Easy to accomplish if proper testing is taking place	Requires forced fermentations and additional lab work Daily/hourly monitoring of primary fermentation to spund at the correct time If spunding timing missed, beer will need to be krausened or force carbonated
Krausening (secondary fermentation)	No need to perform forced fermentations Less lab/daily cellar data requirements Timing of bunging not an issue Allows for full venting of primary fermentation, which helps to remove volatiles/off-flavors faster	Added step to reintroduce yeast and fermentables Potentially significant extra time needed to finish second fermentation Risk of aeration and contamination Potential sluggish refermentation
Bottle conditioning	Works well with higher ale fermentation temperatures Less daily lab and cellar maintenance required to control in-tank CO_2 levels before packaging	Mixing and consistency issues between bottles Temperature-controlled space needed Each and every bottle is a control point versus one control point for tank carbonation—needs a plan in place to ensure all packages pass VDK testing and are properly carbonated

Performing forced fermentations on every batch of beer provides data that will determine when to bung a tank, as well as providing a greater understanding of the fermentation profile of your brewery's beers. Forced fermentations are a great tool for any brewer to understand their wort's theoretical attenuation limit and also to verify that the primary fermentation has been successful.

Knowledge of how a spunding valve works, and how to troubleshoot it, will also make implementing a natural carbonation program considerably easier. A general understanding of how spunding valves work will help you maintain consistency, accuracy, and safety when naturally carbonating your lagers.

BUNGING: HOW AND WHEN

The basic concept of both spunding and krausening is that the CO_2 created during fermentation will be captured as carbonation in the finished product. This is not fundamentally different from bottle conditioning; but in spunding or krausening, the conditioning processes occur pre-packaging, either in the fermentor or conditioning tank rather than in the bottle.

Spunding and krausening are similar processes, with one main difference: when spunding a tank, the CO_2 produced in the primary fermentation is captured; when krausening, the CO_2 is captured during a secondary fermentation, traditionally with the addition of a portion of krausen (freshly fermenting wort, or young beer). For either method, a bunging apparatus is attached to a tank near the end of fermentation, which safely retains CO_2 in the tank to carbonate the beer. When to bung is the key question to answer, but this will depend on several variables. Since the objective is to capture the least amount of CO_2 from the fermentation process needed to meet your carbonation goals, a necessary first step is to define those goals.

1. What is the target CO_2 level? The fermentation temperature and the target CO_2 level will determine a pressure setting on the bunging apparatus or spunding valve.
2. What is the CO_2 content of the beer before bunging? Depending on the temperature at which you are fermenting, there will be varying volumes of CO_2 already in solution. Reference a CO_2 solubility chart, such as the one shown in table 5.5 (p. 198).
   - For example, at 46°F (8°C) and under atmospheric pressure at sea level there will be 1.29 volumes of CO_2 already dissolved in the beer, but if fermenting at 50°F (10°C) only 1.19 volumes of CO_2 in the beer. The warmer the fermentation temperature, the more fermentables will be needed to reach the target carbonation level due to the lower CO_2 concentration in the beer pre-bunging.

3. What is the fermentability or theoretical attenuation limit of the wort? This will be important to know so that a tank can be bunged at the correct gravity. A forced fermentation will quickly identify the attenuation limit of the wort.

4. Consider your tank design and headspace. Taller tanks have more hydrostatic pressure than shorter tanks, which allows the contained liquid to hold more CO_2 in solution. If, for some reason, you only half-fill a fermentor with beer you'll need to compensate for the added CO_2 needed to pressurize the increased headspace volume.

There are various shortcuts to make either spunding or krausening easier to execute for those with limited resources and time. We will outline a handful of sound techniques that will go a long way toward achieving consistent and reliable results.

From a quality standpoint, one cause for concern when dealing with pressurized fermentations is that an increase in pressure during aerobic fermentation can put extra stress on young yeast cells, which can inhibit yeast health and vitality, leading to lagging or stuck fermentations (Annemüller, Manger, and Lietz 2011, 164). Many of the complementary considerations needed to avoid autolysis are discussed in chapter 3.

SPUNDING: PRIMARY FERMENTATION

Spunding is the simplest and most straightforward way of carbonating beer; all that is required is that a spunding valve is put on a fermenting tank at the correct time. Spunding requires less cellar processing than both krausening and force carbonating, and it is the process we use most consistently at Jack's Abby.

Some believe that spunding is a necessary finishing touch on a lager. Brian "Swifty" Peters at Austin Beer Garden Brewing believes that the brewery's beer only begins smelling like European lager after undergoing spunding. Peters believes that the spunding process reduces grassy and grainy flavors while slowly dissipating sulfur compounds, the beer achieving sublimity in the process.

For consistency and quality, knowing when to bung a tank for spunding is essential. Spunding too early will result in pressurizing your tanks for more time than necessary during active fermentation and may capture off-flavors that are normally blown off. As mentioned, increased top pressure puts extra stress on your yeast, which can delay how long it takes for the beer to pass the vicinal diketone (VDK) test. It also may slow conditioning time or potentially inhibit the fermentation completely.

Even more important is ensuring a tank is bunged before it passes the determined target gravity; failure to do so may mean the carbonation target is missed. If a tank is bunged late, there is no option to retroactively fully carbonate the tank via spunding; an alternative method, such as force carbonating, krausening, or bottling conditioning will be required.

What follows is a calculation to determine when to bung a spunded beer. It is based on the formula by Holle (2003, 67) in *A Handbook of Basic Brewing Calculations*. First, determine the required increase in CO_2 per liter in grams to hit your target final carbonation level; do this by subtracting the target final CO_2 level per liter from the existing CO_2 level per liter (both also in grams):

$$\frac{\text{required increase}}{\text{grams } CO_2 \text{ per liter}} = \text{target grams } CO_2 \text{ per liter} - \text{existing grams } CO_2 \text{ per liter}$$

Now convert the required increase in grams of CO_2 per liter into extract in degrees Plato. This can be done by assuming about 46% of total extract is converted to CO_2 and also knowing that degrees Plato is the percentage weight extract in the wort (i.e., 1°P is equivalent to 10 g extract in 1,000 g wort):

$$\text{required extract in °P} = \frac{(\text{required increase grams } CO_2 \text{ per liter}/0.46)}{1,000 \text{ g}} \times 100$$

Now add that amount in degrees Plato to your expected terminal gravity (also in °P) and this will tell you the spunding target gravity (i.e., when to bung during primary fermentation):

$$\text{spunding target gravity} = \text{°P to reach target carbonation} + \text{°P terminal gravity}$$

There are only three variables to identify in the above calculations. The target volume of CO_2 will be dependent on the brewer's goals for the beer. The terminal gravity will be as determined by the forced fermentation test. The only variable that needs to be calculated then is the existing CO_2 in solution. This can be identified by looking at the chart of CO_2 in solution by temperature.

As practice, let's say a beer is fermenting at 50°F (10°C). It will have 1.19 volumes of CO_2 (2.35 g/L). If the target carbonation level is 2.6 volumes of CO_2 (5.14 g/L), that means 2.79 (5.14–2.35) grams of CO_2 per liter need to be added. The terminal gravity has been determined to be 3.2° Plato. Based on these values, the calculation to determine degrees Plato to reach target carbonation will be as follows:

$$\text{required extract in °P} = \frac{(5.14\text{ g} - 2.35\text{ g}/0.46)}{1{,}000\text{ g}} \times 100$$

$$= 0.61\text{°P}$$

$$\text{spunding target gravity} = 0.61\text{°P} + 3.2\text{°P}$$

$$= 3.81\text{°P}$$

In some literature, a theoretical 1.1° Plato (4.3° specific gravity) above terminal gravity is suggested for spunding. This estimate assumes that the beer that needs to be carbonated has no CO_2 already in solution. As seen in the above example, the beer already contains roughly half the carbonation needed in the finished product and so the required additional extract was calculated at 0.61° Plato (2.4° SG). If we assumed this beer had no CO_2 in solution, then this extract quantity would need to be roughly doubled, that is, approximately 1.1° Plato would be needed for full carbonation.

When the beer hits its target spunding gravity, attach a bunging device to the clean-in-place or gas arm of the tank. Calibrate and set the spunding valve to the desired pressure and allow pressure to build in the tank. When the pressure within the tank reaches the setpoint of the spunding valve, the valve will begin to release pressure in the tank. When the fermentation is 100% complete the tank will maintain the set pressure.

Even with constant monitoring, it is nearly impossible to bung every fermentation at the exact right time. Each brewer will need to find a range above the required amount that is acceptable to them. At Jack's Abby we have a range of 1–2° Plato (approx. 4–8° SG) above our target spunding gravity that we feel keeps flavor consistency and allows for a realistic expectation of timing.

At Cohesion Brewing in Denver, Colorado, owner and brewer Eric Larkin racks his open-fermented lagers into horizontal tanks when the extract is about two-thirds finished. This leaves enough residual fermentables to properly carbonate the beer in the secondary tank. Cohesion's beers generally hit about 68%–70% attenuation. For a 10° Plato beer, this should theoretically leave about two degrees Plato in the wort to ferment and carbonate the beer. For brewers that spund, finding the maximum amount of residual fermentation that still gives consistent fermentations will be important.

A well-executed spund is simpler and safer than force carbonating or krausening. Spunded beers are less likely to be aerated during the normal course of cellaring, unlike operations such as krausening that add fermentables or force carbonation that may add oxygen from external CO_2 sources. Once your original brewhouse wort enters a spunding tank, there will be no transferring or special processes, all of which represent opportunities for aeration or infection. You also won't need to worry about yeast health during a secondary fermentation, which needs to be considered when krausening.

At Germany's Klosterbrauerei Ettal in the far south of Bavaria, Andreas Husel explains that his beers are generally bunged around 3.5–3.8° Plato at the end of primary fermentation. In the *Lagerkeller*, he anticipates a finishing gravity of around 1.9–2.2° Plato. Weekly gravity reading will determine when the beer has reached this final gravity. This process is slow and time consuming, particularly at the temperatures used. The tanks during this process are cooled close to freezing. While it takes a long time to finish, the added benefit is the process can happen under very low pressures.

Spunding does increase the risk of yeast autolysis, on account of the extra gauge pressure applied in the tank. Some precautions are likely necessary to prevent this outcome, especially in American breweries where single-tank conical fermentations are the norm. When beginning a spunding program, the pH of the bunged tank should be closely and continually monitored at the end of fermentation. A rise in pH will likely be caused by autolysis of the yeast. Racking the beer to a secondary tank to minimize yeast load is one way to mitigate this issue. Some brewers will cool the beer so that a lower top pressure can be used for spunding. Yeast cell vitality suffers minimally when using gauge pressures of 5 psi (0.34 bar) or lower. Over 5 psi and lager yeast becomes stressed (Annemüller, Manger, and Lietz 2011, 164).

Most traditional Bavarian brewers already take steps to rack and cool beer, negating a need for extra caution. In most US brewhouses where open fermentations are not standard, racking, cold fermentation rooms, constant dumping of yeast, lower pressures, and highly vital yeast are the keys to successful spunding.

Tips for Simpler Spunding

In the event that you can't perform a forced fermentation, you can ballpark the values required for the spunding process based on historical data for attenuation limits. You'll still need a spunding valve and overall familiarity with the spunding process. For most temperatures and average CO_2 volumes, spunding a fermenting tank 24–48 hours before the end of primary fermentation at 12–15 psi (0.82–1.03 bar) gauge pressure should get you close to your goals. You can adjust carbonation to your specifications by either adding external CO_2 or degassing the tank.

KRAUSENING: SECONDARY FERMENTATION

Krausening is a similar enough process to spunding, in that natural carbonation is captured during fermentation in a bunged pressure-rated vessel. Instead of using fermentables provided by the original wort fermentation, krausening involves the addition of extra fermentables after primary fermentation is complete. Fresh yeast is also added in order to finish the secondary fermentation, or refermentation. The attenuation limit of the wort added, the temperature of the wort, and desired target carbonation level will help determine how much wort is required.

In *New Brewing Lager Beer*, Greg Noonan defines krausening as "the German word used to describe the infusion of a strongly fermenting young beer into a larger volume of wort or beer that is past the stage of strong fermentation" (Noonan 2003, 168). This seemingly simple definition hints at uses for krausening beyond just carbonation.

Krausening has a long historical precedent. It was a technique developed as much for carbonating as for helping to finish or extend fermentations. Before single-culture yeasts, microscopy cell counts, and many of the other basic laboratory tests we take for granted today, krausening was a method that could help rejuvenate stalled fermentations and "clean up" fermentation issues.

Krausening is perhaps best understood as a historical precursor to spunding. A better understanding of yeast health and wort fermentability allowed brewers to design spunding programs that require less cellar work than krausening. However, despite the method being uncommon today, there are still plenty of opportunities where krausening instead of spunding makes sense, and there are many world-class lager breweries that still employ it.

We recommend taking an approach that relies on krausening solely for natural carbonation rather than relying on the process to fix improper primary fermentation. Modern laboratory testing, brewing techniques, and QA/QC programs should make relying on krausening for anything other than carbonation unnecessary. Rather, krausening should be used when the procedures make the most sense for a brewery or batch of beer. As krausening requires less active monitoring during primary and secondary fermentation, it is a good choice for brewers who cannot monitor their tanks on a daily schedule and therefore cannot rely on spunding to consistently carbonate their beers. Alternatively, if open primary fermentation is being employed, krausening might be a good solution to carbonate when transferring into the conditioning tank.

Tröegs Independent Brewing in Hershey, Pennsylvania, began krausening its year-round Sunshine Pilsner after taking inspiration from cofounder Chris Trogner's brewery trip to Germany in 2017. After primary fermentation, a krausen addition of 10% is added after the finished beer is cooled to 44°F (7°C). This change added about a week of tank time to the process. Compared to previous versions, the krausened beer had a softer mouthfeel and more delicate yeast flavors that the brewers believe warrants the extra time.

The first question to answer when krausening is the type and amount of wort to add by volume. The higher the carbonation level desired, the more fermentable charge will be required; thus, higher-gravity or highly attenuative worts will provide more fermentables than lower-gravity or lowly attenuative worts. The temperature of the fermentation must also be considered. The colder the primary tank, the more residual carbonation the liquid will hold, therefore requiring less secondary fermentation.

Many recognized brewing texts, including the Master Brewers Association of the Americas' Practical Handbook series, suggest using a 10%–15% krausen volume (Ockert 2006a, 106). Nearly identical advice can be found in brewing textbooks written at the end of the eighteenth century and early nineteenth century. While this estimate generally allows for enough fermentables, this vague value can potentially double the amount of fermentables needed to hit your target CO_2 level and increase the chances of refermentation issues in this secondary fermentation.

When using krausen for krausening, we suggest you rely on the following calculations to help determine how much krausen will be required when krausening a batch of beer. These calculations can be found in *A Handbook of Basic Brewing Calculations* (Holle 2003, 69–72). Note that you must determine the real terminal gravity (real final extract) in the beer, which involves compensating for the lower density of the alcohol present:

$$\text{real terminal gravity} = \text{original gravity °P} \times \left\{ 1 - \left[0.82 \times \left(\frac{\text{orig. gravity °P} - \text{term. gravity °P}}{\text{orig. gravity °P}} \right) \right] \right\}$$

Similar to the calculation for spunding, first determine the increase in CO_2 required and allow for the fact that only 46% of the fermentable extract will be converted to CO_2. This is calculated as grams CO_2 required per 100 g wort, because you then need to calculate that as a percentage of the wort volume to be krausened. Remember that 1 g extract in 100 g wort is 1%, or 1° Plato:

$$\text{required increase grams } CO_2 \text{ per 100 g} = \frac{\text{target g } CO_2 \text{ per liter} - \text{existing g } CO_2 \text{ per liter}}{10}$$

$$\text{volume krausen as \% of wort} = \frac{\text{required increase grams } CO_2 \text{ per 100 g}/0.46}{\text{orig. gravity in °P} - \text{real term. gravity in °P}}$$

Table 5.4 shows the various amounts of krausen needed—indicated as a percentage of total volume of the portion of beer to be krausened—that would be needed to fully carbonate a beer based on the temperature and desired carbonation level of the finished beer. All values in table 5.4 are based on starting from the exact same wort for the krausen with an original extract of 12° Plato (1.048 SG), but shows how the volume of krausen might change depending on when it is pulled from fermentation. Assuming the wort for the krausen has an 83% apparent attenuation limit, and a hydrometer reading of 2° Plato (1.008 SG) at terminal gravity, all the amounts given in table 5.4 are based on using a

1. 12° Plato (1.048 SG) wort 24 hours into fermentation, with a hydrometer reading of 11° Plato (1.044 SG);
2. 12° Plato wort, with its gravity still at 12° Plato;
3. 12° Plato wort on day two, with a hydrometer reading of 9° Plato (1.036 SG).

Table 5.4

Amounts of krausen, indicated by percentage of beer volume to be krausened, that would be needed to fully carbonate the beer

End primary ferm. temp. of beer, °F (°C)	Target carbonation level (vol. CO_2)			
	2.5	2.6	2.7	2.8
	Using 12°P OG wort 24 h after fermentation start, with hydrometer reading of 11°P			
46 (8)	7.0%	7.6%	8.1%	8.7%
48 (9)	7.3%	7.8%	8.3%	8.8%
50 (10)	7.6%	8.1%	8.6%	9.1%
52 (11)	7.9%	8.4%	8.9%	9.4%
54 (12)	8.2%	8.7%	9.3%	9.8%
	Using the same wort at KO at 12°P OG			
46 (8)	6.2%	6.7%	7.3%	7.8%
48 (9)	6.5%	7.0%	7.5%	8.0%
50 (10)	6.7%	7.3%	7.8%	8.3%
52 (11)	7%	7.5%	8%	8.6%
54 (12)	7.3%	7.8%	8.3%	8.8%
	An example when the same wort is at a 9°P hydrometer reading			
48 (9)	9.2%	9.9%	10.7%	11.4%
54 (12)	10.3%	11%	11.8%	12.5%

As the examples in table 5.4 show, there is significant variation in the amount of krausen required when krausening based on your carbonation goals, residual fermentables of the krausen used, and the temperature at which it is introduced.

The values in table 5.4 only take into account krausening from one type of wort with a specific original extract and attenuation limit. Not taken into account are situations where freshly fermenting worts of drastically different extracts or attenuations are used. For example, if the wort used for krausening has a terminal gravity of 4° Plato instead of 2° Plato, significantly more volume of krausen will be needed for the former. This may be why the krausen values recommended in the past were higher than those given in table 5.4. Historically, lagers had only 50%–70% apparent attenuation, so significantly more krausen would have been needed to get the equivalent carbonation, perhaps explaining the oft-repeated values of 10%–15% of the volume of beer to be krausened.

Determining and dosing the krausen quantity is just the first step to proper carbonation. A bunging device to capture the appropriate volume of CO_2 is still required (see next section). Even if the correct amount of fermentables is added, the tank will not carbonate to an exact specification if the bunging device is set incorrectly. Make sure that the pressure and temperature settings match the target CO_2 level.

Healthy yeast is a must to ensure the beer undergoes a vigorous secondary fermentation after krausening. Though the beer may naturally have a high density of yeast cells still in solution following primary fermentation, where most of this cell population is in terms of life cycle means these cells are generally not suited for a secondary fermentation.

The yeast responsible for secondary fermentation should come from the krausen portion. This yeast population should have recently undergone an aerobic primary fermentation with high vitality; assimilated yeast from a propagation should not be used. Krausening is a challenging anaerobic refermentation that relies on a much smaller total cell count compared to a normal primary fermentation. Since there should be no oxygen contact during this refermentation, the yeast used for the process must be healthy enough to finish the fermentation without it. Simply pitching yeast from the end of another fermentation won't get the result needed and will likely result in a stuck fermentation.

The amount of yeast needed is as much about the quality and life cycle stage of the yeast as it is about the total quantity of yeast. A true krausen from an actively fermenting fresh wort might contain 2.0–6.0 × 10⁷ cells/mL, but since it will only end up being around 10% of the total volume of beer following krausening this cell count will be reduced tenfold (Annemüller, Manger, and Lietz 2011, 365).

Although other fermentable sources can be substituted by brewers unconcerned with the Reinheitsgebot, krausen will likely be the best option for a few reasons. Refermentation from a freshly fermenting wort similar to the wort used in the primary fermentation will give more consistent outcomes. Consider that as much as 15% of the total fermentables could come from the krausening process—using similar wort maintains consistency in attenuation and other sensory variables such as color, overall bitterness, and malt character.

Krausening is trickier if you are not regularly producing lager wort, but it is not impossible. One possible option is to create "krausen" by diverting wort in the appropriate volume, pitching with lager yeast, and then sending the entire side stream into the main beer. This process essentially mimics the effects of diverting a partial quantity from a full-size batch. It's important that this side stream still has time for yeast to absorb oxygen from the knockout and finish aerobic fermentation before it's introduced for carbonation.

The main advantage of krausening beer is that little daily attention needs to be paid to either the primary or secondary fermentation. If you don't have the ability to constantly monitor your fermentation seven days a week, this solution makes executing natural carbonation easier. Most of the work is tied to the calculation and execution of dosing new fermentables to ensure secondary fermentation.

Examples of Krausening Past and Present

An interesting past krausening process was preserved in the records at Schell's brewing in New Ulm, Minnesota. While krausening is generally not performed at the brewery today, krausening was historically how the brewery carbonated their beer. Water, dextrose, and hops would be boiled in the kettle before being cooled and added to the beer. This rudimentary wort was sufficient to create enough carbonation to finish the beer.

In the present day, at Schönramer in Germany's far southeast corner, brewmaster Eric Toft chooses to add more krausen than needed to carbonate but allows the refermentation to proceed unbunged for 24 hours. Toft believes that his process helps to scrub the beer and remove off-flavors. After 24 hours, the tank is bunged and the secondary fermentation is allowed to continue. The tanks are slowly cooled down close to 32°F (0°C); only 5 psig (0.34 bar gauge) is needed to fully carbonate at these temperatures. Toft notes that it may take weeks for the fermentation to end. Many breweries might balk at waiting up to a month for a secondary fermentation to finish. However, the low pressures that are needed allow for healthier yeast and lower risk of autolysis.

In the same corner of Germany at Hofbräuhaus Traunstein, brewmaster Maximilian Sailer comments that every beer they brew is krausened with Helles. The spunding valves are set to approximately 5 psig for this secondary fermentation. In order to achieve full carbonation with pressure this low, very cold temperatures are needed to properly carbonate.

WORKING WITH A BUNGING APPARATUS/SPUNDING VALVE

Safety concerns are ever present when working with pressure. The pressure values associated with natural carbonation are no different than those created during force carbonation. However, when naturally carbonating, the increase in pressure happens outside of the operator's direct control. When naturally carbonating beer, the brewer is relying on equipment to properly control the pressure on a tank. It is important to know the ins and outs of how this equipment works.

Manufacturers and distributors have applied various names to spunding valves, such as bunging pressure regulator, bunging apparatus, or bunging device. No matter what it is called, a spunding valve is a pressure-regulating valve that exists to control and *regulate* the pressure created by fermentation in a closed tank. It is usually adjustable by way of tightening or loosening a spring-loaded knob that, respectively, increases or decreases the pressure at which the valve opens.

All fermentation vessels should be installed with a safety device known as a pressure relief valve (PRV). These are designed to ensure your tank won't explode in the event of excess pressure building up. Pressure relief valves should never be used in place of spunding valves when naturally carbonating because they do not regulate pressure other than to open or close based on the set pressure threshold. When a PRV goes off, it often sounds like a "pop, pop, pop," versus a steady flow of air.

Since spunding valves are pressure-regulating valves, they are much like the regulators used to control gas equipment or draft systems. A spunding valve works to regulate the pressure from within the tank based on the amount of pressure exerted by the CO_2 created during fermentation. The spunding valve's ability to reduce pressure varies depending on the amount of pressure the tank is exerting; it will open more when more CO_2 is produced, and open less when less CO_2 is produced.

There are various models of spunding valve depending on the connection type and expected CO_2 flow rate; design features also account for clean-in-place or clean-out-of-place applications. All units essentially function in the same manner and the operation of the valve won't be affected by these variables.

Each spunding valve model will have a maximum flow rate, or blow power, that determines the flow rate of gas the valve can release from a tank. Generally, the different models will refer to a fermentation tank barrelage for which they are appropriate. A manufacturer would recommend, for example, smaller units with the lowest flow rates for tanks around 50 bbl. (~60 hL), medium flow units for 170–430 bbl. (200–500 hL) depending on the type of fermentation, and the largest units for tanks above that. It's best to work with your bunging apparatus supplier to determine the required valve size based on your own fermentation setup.

While quality spunding valves can be expensive, creating a gas manifold to connect multiple tanks is a great way to be efficient with your purchase. It is important to confirm with your spunding valve supplier that the valve is rated to handle the total pressure your manifold would apply. As an example, a valve rated for 200 bbl. should be able to handle five 40 bbl. tank fermentations at once. When creating the manifold, ensure that there are one-way valves on every supply line to the manifold so that gas cannot flow between tanks. A single spunding valve can then be connected to the manifold to regulate all tanks. While each tank

Figure 5.2. A modern spunding valve being used at Müllerbräu.

will be regulated to the same top pressure, each individual tank can be set to different temperatures to hit the individual beer's target CO_2 concentration.

When deciding how many devices to purchase, keep in mind that spunding valves are only needed for a relatively short period per tank. While a lager may sit in a tank for a month, it likely only needs a spunding valve for around a week. While the exact amount of time will vary, the valve only needs to be applied at the end of fermentation until the tank is finished fermenting and cooling has begun.

Bunging a tank for natural carbonation at exactly the correct time is nearly impossible. This means that to ensure tanks end up 100% carbonated, they are bunged when there are more fermentables than are needed. Hence the spunding valves are installed to allow the surplus CO_2 to escape. Once it's confirmed that the secondary fermentation is 100% finished the valve can then be removed.

When it comes to calibrating your spunding valve, Will Kemper of Chuckanut Brewery reminded us that it is important to take into consideration its age. The continuous pressure applied to the spring in the device will change the valve's operation over time, so regularly checking these parts for signs of wear is a good idea. A testing apparatus can be easily assembled with mass market parts and a high-accuracy pressure gauge. A spunding valve can be calibrated by adjusting the spring pressure until it matches the gauge pressure. Do not assume that the regulator or the pre-etched markings on the valve are accurate.

It is important to factor in both the adjustable range of your spunding valves as well as the maximum pressure rating of the vessels you plan to use with them. Often, a spunding valve will be rated for a higher pressure than the tank, which could create a hazardous high-pressure situation if you set the spunding valve for a pressure higher than the tank will support.

Besides safety, you should also consider your tank pressure rating as it pertains to your carbonation target and desired fermentation temperature. Above a certain temperature, the applied CO_2 pressure you would need to achieve the correct carbonation may not be possible (table 5.5). The higher the carbonation level required in your beer, the colder the fermentation will need to be (*see* chap. 3). You must also bear in mind the maximum temperature a beer may reach in the course of normal cellar operations. At 15 psig and 48°F a beer will hold approximately 2.5 volumes of CO_2. However, if performing a "warm" VDK rest at 60°F, 2.15 volumes would be your maximum CO_2 level at 15 psi. An end fermentation temperature of 60°F would need a top pressure of 22 psi to get to 2.5 volumes of CO_2. That pressure would exceed the threshold of most brewery fermentation vessels.

Herein lies one of the largest downsides to a modern hybrid fermentation, or a warm VDK rest, when it comes to spunding. Very high pressures are needed, or a better option might be krausening once the beer has been cooled. There is no reason to do a warm VDK rest if you are krausening because you'll need to wait to pass VDK again after the krausen fermentation.

Table 5.5
Relationship of carbon dioxide concentration (volumes) in beer with temperature and applied pressure

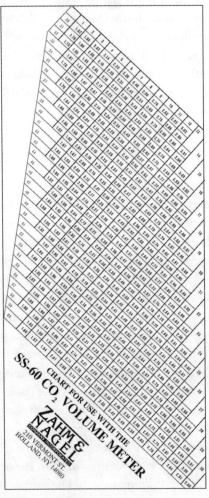

Courtesy of Zahm-Nagel.

Source: Data from Methods of Analysis, 5th ed., (Milwaukee, WI: American Society of Brewing Chemists, 1949).

Notes: Values assume sea-level altitude, beer specific gravity of 1.015

FORCED FERMENTATION TEST

A forced fermentation test is a laboratory-controlled fermentation that quickly yields the attenuation limit of a wort.[2] This information is crucial in a natural carbonation program, as it will help determine when a tank should be bunged to achieve a specific volume of carbonation, or how much fermenting wort should be added during krausening. Understanding a beer's baseline attenuation will provide significantly more control and consistency during bunging. A forced fermentation test is a helpful tool even if not using it to naturally carbonate because it can also alert you to any potential attenuation problems in the beer and give you a chance to address them.

To perform a forced fermentation, wort should be taken directly from your fermentation tank after knockout. Breweries that blend multiple batches need to ensure that the sample taken is completely homogeneous. This might mean taking a sample as much as 24 hours after the brew day: this waiting period allows for enough mixing of batches and dilution water to ensure your sample is representative.

After the sample is pulled, additional yeast needs to be added to the wort. This should be the same yeast strain that you are using to ferment the beer. The simplest way to add yeast is with dried packaged yeast, but this is an added expense. This expense can be avoided by harvesting fresh yeast from a fermentor, though the yeast will first need to be thoroughly separated from any beer or wort in the sample before being added. Even a small amount of liquid can throw off a forced fermentation reading. One method for separating yeast is to apply a vacuum to a sample of yeast in a filter to pull out any liquid.

After yeast is added, the sample should be frequently agitated and kept warm to ensure a fast and complete fermentation. A stir plate is a common and effective method for agitation. Take a gravity reading after 24–48 hours, once all fermentation activity has subsided, to find out what the lowest theoretical terminal gravity will be.

The results of a forced fermentation test will directly dictate when to spund or how much krausen to add. When spunding, the terminal gravity determined by the forced fermentation test will be needed when you calculate at what point to bung the tank (p. 187). When krausening, the terminal gravity will affect the amount of krausen needed to provide the right amount of fermentables.(p. 191).

---

2   Samantha White, "QC 101: Forced Fermentation," QC2 (website), Quality Control Collaboratory, February 26, 2021, https://qc2.beer/blogs/qc2-blog/qc-101-forced-fermentation.

SPUNDING AND KRAUSENING FOR HOMEBREWERS

There are significant safety concerns when using pressurized vessels in a homebrew setting. Using quality equipment appropriate to the task is particularly important. Never attempt to spund or krausen beer in a glass or plastic fermentor. Even most stainless-steel homebrewing fermentors are not designed to hold pressure. Using pressure-rated stainless steel kegs or Cornelius kegs is the recommended option. Spunding/bunging valves with Cornelius keg connections are now available for homebrewers from most homebrew supply shops.

For homebrewers, krausening will likely be a better option than spunding because it will feel much like bottle conditioning. If using malt extract with 75% fermentability for the krausen wort at 12° Plato, you will require about 8%–10% by volume of beer at around 50°F (9°C). For a 5 gal. (18.9 L) batch of beer, this translates to 50–60 fl. oz. of krausen made from this wort.

To create your krausen, malt extract and dried yeast is the simplest option. Dissolve the extract in 170°F (77°C) water, cool the resulting wort down to the temperature that the secondary fermentation will take place at, and add the dried yeast. Wait a minimum of two hours and no more than 24 hours before blending into the main fermentation. This will ensure that all oxygen is scavenged. To blend with the main fermentation, either carefully add the krausen to the beer in your secondary, or place the krausen in the secondary fermentor and rack the contents of the primary fermentor onto it.

If the desire is to keep the alcohol content the same, the original gravity of the krausen wort should match that of the original brew. This will mean that more or less krausen may be needed and you will need to use the quantity of krausen calculation described on p. 191. Additionally, parameters like IBU level, hop flavor and aroma, and malt characteristics need to be considered to ensure that the finished flavor of the blend is on target.

The timing of krausening will also affect the quality of the finished beer. Rack your beer from the primary fermentor to the secondary fermentor a few days after you are sure primary fermentation has reached its terminal gravity. Ensure the beer is as clear as reasonably possible when transferring to the secondary fermentor, because yeast from the primary fermentation will be prone to autolysis as you wait for the krausen yeast to do its job.

If your secondary fermentor is a keg, you can mimic the effects of a horizontal secondary tank by leaving the keg on its side. However, if using a spunding valve, make sure the valve is not covered by liquid or it will not work properly and create a safety hazard.

OTHER TRADITIONAL LAGER TECHNIQUES

*A*S LAGER'S POPULARITY HAS STEADILY SPREAD ACROSS THE GLOBE, IT HAS HAD TO TRAVEL FARTHER, LAST LONGER, AND WITHSTAND MORE EXTREME TEMPERATURES. Modern lager brewers have had to hone their techniques accordingly. Streamlining processes, gaining efficiencies, and preventing beer spoilage have all been integral to lager's world domination. While this may be seen in its most extreme form in the largest of modern industrial breweries, even simple stainless steel cylindroconical fermentors are a replacement technology for older materials and methods.

By striving to make consistent beer as efficiently as possible, some of the largest breweries have certainly accepted "good enough" flavor for their commodity liquids. Some traditional methods, like open cooling and fermentation, are understandably too expensive, risky, and unreliable for most large-scale breweries. Brewers willing to sacrifice their time, effort, and resources to employ such methods are not the norm. Yet they are not as rare as you might think, especially in Bavaria, Franconia, and Bohemia, where centuries of continuous brewing history have preserved many of these techniques. The age and complexity of some of these old breweries conspire to discourage and dis-incentivize some modernization. After all, these methods have created great beer for generations, so why overhaul what works? The perseverance of these methods is also perhaps due to their potential to create lager that surpasses "good enough" on the way to becoming great.

Each traditional lagering method we explore in this chapter has modern advocates and practitioners. It is also fair to point out that at least as many brewers will tell you not to waste time and money trying these methods. Even current practitioners of traditional lagering methods are quick to point out that their processes are best suited for their own breweries and will not yield the same results outside those walls.

While replicating the exact conditions of a historical lager producer's premises may not be preferable or possible, the persistence of many of these methods in some of the world's best lager breweries is noteworthy. In extreme cases, traditional methods have grown to define flavor profiles of certain styles, as is the case for the in-house wood-smoked maltings at Brauerei Heller-Trum that gives Schlenkerla Rauchbier its distinctive flavor. But other subtle environmental pressures, like the curved cellar ceilings built around open fer-mentors and horizontal lagering tanks at Brauerei Mittenwald, keep otherwise forward-thinking modern brewers anchored to certain older technologies.

Nestled in the foothills of the Alps, Brauerei Mittenwald is an example of the type of hybridization that is common to many older German breweries. The well-worked open fermentation and lagering tanks are nestled under a beauti-fully displayed new stainless steel brewhouse. Almost all breweries that practice the traditional methods we catalog here have done so alongside extensive mod-ernization of their breweries. Some of the traditional equipment and processes that remain are simply practicalities. Digging out centuries-old cellars to replace equipment is an expensive endeavor, so there is a strong incentive for brewers to apply their knowledge and experience using the tools at hand.

These surviving technologies have left us a connection to historical lager. All the improvements in efficiency and consistency wrought by moderniza-tion have changed the character of lager considerably over time, encouraging a kind of stylistic homogeneity. Some of the supplanted methods, like open fermentation and direct-fired kettles, lend distinct sensory characteristics to finished beer that some brewers of traditional lager still feel are important. They result in unique, characterful beers that defy easy categorization but delight consumers just the same.

There are common themes among all these practices: they add time, they are complicated, and they often come with a greater risk of microbial contamination. But there is an associated romance, too, that seems perfectly suited for craft beer culture. A growing number of craft breweries, Jack's Abby included, continue to experiment with the sensory impact of many of these techniques. Understanding their history can help brewers adapt these practices with sensory impact in mind. In a sense, some of the world's most forward-thinking lager brewers are looking to the past for inspiration.

Kellerbier

The story of Kellerbier is particularly relevant to traditional lager production techniques. Kellerbier is often described as "lager beer like it used to be," and, as one might expect, these beers are often produced using a variety of traditional lagering methods.

Kellerbier translates literally to "cellar beer." It is known by a variety of other names in the lager-producing world. Where you are will dictate whether you order an *ungespundetes Bier*, a *Zwickelbier*, or a *Zoiglbier*: all of these refer generally to an unfiltered, rustic lager, though each name has its own interesting story. For simplicity's sake, we'll generally use Kellerbier to refer to this category of beer.

Whatever you call Kellerbier, it is best understood as a process rather than a singular category. These are usually unfiltered, unpasteurized beers that can be brewed to any style. They are generally packaged with considerable haze and have yeast flavor as a main component of the flavor profile. Many are produced in small older breweries and packaged on ancient bottling and kegging lines. As a result of these factors, the shelf life of Kellerbier is considerably shortened. Exported versions are relatively rare, and those that do make the trip should probably be treated like hazy IPAs from a cold-storage and freshness perspective. Warm-stored, months-old Kellerbier is unlikely to impress.

The cold conditioning cellars of early lager breweries give Kellerbier its name. Sometimes these *Kellers* are right under the brewery, as is the case at Brauhaus Riegele and Müllerbräu. Some breweries grew beyond the capacity of their own cellars and pooled their resources in large communal cellar systems. One such cellar network, dug into the side of a mountain in Erlangen, still exists and celebrates its brewing history by throwing an annual party, Bergkirchweih, in the adjacent beer gardens that rivals Munich's Oktoberfest. The scale of the cellars in Erlangen allowed for this city to be the largest exporter of Bavarian beer before the advent of artificial refrigeration.

Figure 6.1. The old entrance to the Drei Kronen brewery cellars in Memmelsdorf, Germany.

In Memmelsdorf, outside of Bamberg, we met with now retired owner and brewer of Drei Kronen, Halu Straub. He explained that Kellerbier harkens to a time before electricity and a technical understanding of brewing. The former cellar of the Drei Kronen brewery is located about a half mile up the road, with an unassuming entrance in a suburban neighborhood (fig. 6.1). The brewery's cellar is no longer used, but in many ways it paved the way for the success of the brewery: the north-facing entrance to the cellar ensured that their beers stayed the coldest even during the summer. While four degrees Celsius may not seem to be a dramatic difference in temperature, Straub compared the rise in cellar temp from 50°C (10°C) to 57°F (14°C) as the difference between heaven and hell.

Beers lagered in these cellars were traditionally served fresh and unfiltered either at the brewery itself or within a small radius. We can imagine that the fresh, vibrant character of these lagers would resemble some of the unfiltered lager served as Kellerbier today. Many of these modern Kellerbiers express yeast and ester characteristics atypical of most modern lager. Most are unfiltered, though the intensity of the haze is quite variable due to the brightening effect of cold maturation. Most are bottled and kegged with normal carbonation, but those served from wooden barrels in beer halls have noticeably less. Served *vom Fass* ("from the barrel"), Kellerbier's lower carbonation gives it a reputation for being less filling, and thus drinkable in greater quantities.

Some Franconian brewers that produce Kellerbier use other traditional methods in search of more rustic characteristics. Though Bamberg's Brauerei Greifenklau was recently outfitted with an efficient new brewhouse, the modern design included a secondary heating source that can be used to mimic the intense heat of a direct-fired kettle. The brewery believes the flavor impact of direct heating is important in its standard Zwickelbier. The brewery relies on the more efficient heating system for its Helles, which requires a cleaner and less intense heating process.

One of Kellerbier's many names, Zwickelbier, provides some hints as to how freshly the beer was once consumed. German brewers refer to the sample port of their tanks as a *Zwickel*, and consider Zwickelbier to be their standard lager poured directly from the conditioning tank into whatever vessel is at hand. Breweries like Klosterbrauerei Ettal honor this tradition by offering occasional events for the public to get tank fills into bottles and growlers. Beer sampled this way often has an intense, yeasty, sulfury character that older beer drinkers may correlate with freshness. They are vibrant, full bodied, and quite flavorful, especially as compared to drier, more "refined" modern lagers.

In the east of Bavaria, a truly old-school style of beer production results in Zoiglbier, or simply *Zoigl*. Again, rather than a style of beer, true Zoigl beers are individual house recipes brewed in a communal village brewhouse and brought back to each individual brewery for serving. In the small village of Windischeschenbach, the handful of *Zoiglstuben* alternate their opening days, advertising they are open with the six-sided brewer's star. Each family has a different recipe, and a few days a year the village organizes an open house with all the breweries serving their versions. Though each Zoigl is unique, some commonalities can be found, including being lightly carbonated and full-bodied with a somewhat yeast-driven character.

In the beautiful rolling hills of the Mühlviertel region of northern Austria, Brauerei Hofstetten brings a regional tradition to life with its *Kübelbier*, or "bucket beer." Owner and brewmaster Peter Krammer grew up working in the brewery, which he inherited from his father Franz Krammer. It was Franz who brought back the idea of serving freshly fermented lager in pails filled directly from the conditioning tank. For local old-timers, this would have been reminiscent of the communal stoneware vessels passed around after a day at work in the fields. Today a packaged version of Kübelbier is available, but visitors to Hofstetten are rewarded with samples poured in the old way (fig. 6.2).

Figure 6.2. Owner and brewmaster Peter Krammer topping off a sampling bucket in the Hofstetten cellar.

Whatever you call them, these rustic lagers are throwbacks to preindustrial lager production. As an open-ended style, Kellerbier lends itself to exploration by interested craft brewers and consumers alike. While it may not be possible to serve samples in your cellar from a bucket, an emphasis on the unique qualities of freshly fermented beer can provide considerable consumer interest.

Serving from Wooden Barrels

Though *vom Fass* is today used to refer to kegged beer, its original meaning referred to the wooden barrels once used exclusively for beer service. While most wooden barrels were replaced with steel kegs at some point in the middle of the twentieth century, Bavarian brewers held onto the tradition a bit longer. Though most were retired in the 1970s and '80s, a handful of German and Czech brewers have kept alive the tradition of serving lager from wooden barrels.

It's not surprising that steel has all but completely replaced wood as the medium of choice for beer service. We take for granted the many conveniences offered by stainless steel kegs. Barrels suitable for beer service are uniquely challenging to produce and maintain, and require the attention of master craftsmen throughout their lifetime. They have to be lined and treated to preserve the flavor profile of the beer during storage.

Beer barrels must be sturdy enough to withstand up to 29 psi (2 bar) of pressure, with little tolerance for oxygen ingress. That means 30- and 50-liter (7.9–13.2 gal.) barrels require 5 cm thick wood (about 2 inches), much thicker than what is required for wine or spirit barrels. The fact that beer barrels must be filled, transported, emptied, and cleaned regularly means they are moved far more often and thus require a cooper's frequent attention.

Constant maintenance and ideal conditions are required for barrels to stay in working condition. Barrels need wet and humid conditions to maintain internal and external integrity. A steady routine of filling, emptying, cleaning, and refilling is required. This ensures that the barrels stay in good condition and the beer in the barrels remains consistent. Left empty, barrels will begin to dry out and become leaky within two weeks.

Wooden barrels used for beer service are intended to be flavor neutral, necessitating a lining to prevent contact with the wood. This was usually accomplished by pitching barrels, as in, to smear the insides with pitch. Pitch is a resin derived from the tree sap of larch, fir, and pine. The resin is a mixture of pinic and abietic acids, turpentine, and resin. When hot, good pitch should have an agreeable incense-like smell, a bitter taste, and a shiny appearance (Thausing 1882, 660). When pitch is first added to barrels, a water soak is used to help dissolve most of the aromatic compounds from the pitch. Once it hardens and cools into a glossy black surface, the pitch prevents beer from coming into contact with the oak, which might otherwise transfer significant flavor compounds to the beer.

There are limited options available to clean pitched barrels between uses. Hot water rinses are the best option, but water hotter than 140°F (60°C) should not be used; at 149°F (65°C) the pitch will begin to melt. Barrels need to be visually inspected before every fill for cleanliness and to ensure the pitch is still intact and covering the entire barrel. For barrels that smell sour or moldy, older texts suggest that the barrels should be rinsed with boiling water and caustic soda (Thausing 1882, 665). This might have made more sense when reapplying pitch to barrels was a common process, unlike today.

The flavor neutrality of beer served out of pitched barrels is a matter of debate. For one thing, as beer writer Evan Rail notes, breweries typically reapply pitch to their barrels every year, as the pitch dissolves slowly into the beer over that time. Some feel that the pitch lends a round mouthfeel and a fullness to the finished beer. Some breweries even have historical records suggesting the pitch flavor was prized in their finished beer, as is the case at Pilsner Urquell.

Though Pilsner Urquell no longer ferments in its famous wooden vats, the brewery retains a staff of coopers who raise and pitch barrels for special tappings and demonstrations. In the past, the brewery was noted for reapplying pitch to lagering vessels after every use, bunging the tanks immediately afterward to retain the strong pitch aroma. The flavor contribution was so significant that in a 1901 meeting of the American Brewing Institute there were accusations that the brewery added pitch directly to the brewing kettle (Fischer 1902, 30). Other breweries purposely reapplied pitch to serving casks after every use to add the bitterness and aroma of pitch into their beer (Rühl 1910, 550), perhaps as a substitute for increased hopping.

For modern tastes, however, pitch is likely only desired as a very minor part of the sensory experience, if at all. The large beer hall at Augustiner Bräu in Salzburg only serves beer from wooden barrels, but steps are taken to make sure that the beer does not stay in the barrel long: brewmaster Hansjörg Höplinger ensures that the beer is not left in the barrel longer than ten days. Over time, not only does the carbonation begin to dissipate, but the flavor of pitch from the barrel will slowly become more and more noticeable.

Modern coopers are also able to replace pitch entirely with a new plastic coating. This option lasts five to eight years before needing replacement, but the replacement process is complicated, requiring the barrels to be disassembled and planed before being reassembled and the pitch reapplied. This can only be done a few times before the wood staves become too thin to support the barrel (Peter Schmid, pers. comm.)

The few breweries that still bother with all this hassle do so at least in part for the customer experience. Watching an experienced tapster juggle handfuls of stone mugs, slinging liter after perfectly frothy liter by gravity alone is simply impressive. It harkens back to a bygone era, evoking the traditions of centuries of brewing culture. To the knowing eye, serving delicious beer this way is also perhaps a subtle boast of the brewer's care and attention to detail.

An inquisitive palate will also notice that beer served *vom Fass* is distinct from traditional kegged beer. By relying on gravity for dispensing rather than gas pressure, beer served this way is similar to English-style cask ale. The quickly poured steins have less carbonation, a robust frothy head, and preeminent drinkability. They are, perhaps, a taste back in time.

Open Fermentation

Open fermentation is certainly one of the more photogenic brewing processes. Huge crowns of foam and yeast rise from open-top, unpressurized vessels, seemingly completely exposed to the atmosphere. In addition to being visually compelling, this brewhouse arrangement provides an environment for lager yeast distinct from the typical cylindroconical tanks. Yeast in these conditions behave differently and can be coaxed to produce unique flavor compounds, like the yeast-driven fruit characteristics of *Hefeweizen*. While relatively rare, some lager brewers still ferment their beer this way.

Of course, open fermentors are inherently risky, which accounts in part for their rapid disappearance from most lager breweries—it is rare to see a modern brewery buildout that includes open fermentors. Breweries that continue to use open fermentation must take special measures to ensure the beer's quality. As we will explore below, great care must be taken to prevent contamination, monitor fermentation, and effectively harvest yeast. But these are surmountable obstacles, and the considerations required can be helpful to anyone wanting to brew world-class lager.

Sanitation is perhaps the biggest concern with open fermentors. Water, bugs, birds, and dust can easily fall in and contaminate the fermenting wort. In some larger open-fermenting breweries, HEPA-filtered, positive-pressure rooms are used to minimize contamination risks. A simpler, cheaper solution is a stainless-steel cover to protect the fermenting wort. Both solutions mitigate the risk of contamination without completely preventing it. In fact, some traditional brewers believe that a small amount of contamination is preferable to the stresses their yeast would endure in a cylindroconical tank.

Fermentation in open vessels necessitates moving the beer to a secondary vessel for conditioning. Once the strong primary fermentation has ended, the beer needs to be moved to protect the beer from the atmosphere and ensure that the beer does not oxygenate. This extra step is one that carries on even in breweries that have moved away from open fermentation. While the open fermentation cellars at Klosterbrauerei Andechs have been dormant for years, they still move their beer from their modern cylindroconical tanks to conditioning tanks after primary fermentation is complete.

Open tops mean that venting of carbon dioxide (CO_2) is continuous, which can create a hazard for brewers in close confinement with the tanks. Proper ventilation of fermentation rooms is a must. Cleaning can also be challenging for open tanks in close proximity as care must be taken to avoid contaminating any fermenting beer nearby with cleaning chemicals.

Potentially the most challenging part of using open fermentors is harvesting yeast. While contamination is an obvious concern, the simple logistics of physically removing the yeast presents a unique challenge. It's uncommon to top-crop lager yeast, as lager yeast strains don't generally create enough kräusen (i.e., the rocky, or "cauliflower," yeast head; borrowed from the German *Kräusen*, "wrinkled" or "curled") to provide yeast for a repitch. In addition, most lager brewers purposefully skim and destroy yeast and accompanying protein from the kräusen. Yeast is usually collected from the bottom of the empty tank after racking the beer to secondary. Squeegees or scoops are then used to harvest this yeast. This needs to be done very carefully to ensure that trub is not collected.

Brewers at Augustiner Bräu in Salzburg use a unique apparatus to help harvest yeast and separate it from trub. A table set on a quickly vibrating slope separates yeast from larger particles with a screen, depositing trub down a drain. Before this was installed, the process was completely manual, which meant that brewers had to shake pans of yeast as if they were prospectors hunting for gold.

At Schlossbrauerei Eichhofen in southern Germany, brand new open fermentors with conical bottoms were installed to make it easier to harvest yeast. This new tank style attempts to combine some of the advantages of cylindroconical tanks with the fermentation characteristics of open fermentation. These newer tanks also have design features to improve cleaning, including vacuums built within a ring along the top of the tank. These features address both CO_2 and clean-in-place (CIP) challenges. With CIP, the cleaning solution gently flows up to this ring and cascades down the sidewalls of the open tank. The ring has a vacuum applied to it during fermentation, which helps to displace the CO_2 emitted from the fermentation.

Even with all these risks and challenges, open fermentation is unique in its ability to optimize yeast health and metabolism. This is the reason cited most often by brewers to explain their decision to ferment this way. Open fermentors reduce hydrostatic pressure and minimize CO_2 concentrations within the fermenting wort. This environment is dissimilar from the pressurized environments of cylindroconical tanks, and yeast behaves very differently when allowed to ferment this way.

Most designs for open fermentors are short and wide to encourage lower pressure on yeast during fermentation. In general, low-pressure fermentations increase production of esters, fusel alcohols, and sulfur compounds while decreasing the production of acetaldehyde. The open design of the tanks allows for volatile compounds to dissipate so that they do not end up at perceptible levels in the finished beer.

Horizontal and dish-style tanks can yield similar results as open fermentors, with less risk for contamination. While not exactly traditional for primary fermentation, the long, shallow nature of these tanks offer many of the same advantages as an open fermentor design because they result in lower hydrostatic pressures. Austin's Live Oak Brewing Company in Texas goes a step further by only filling the brewery's horizontal primary fermentors two-thirds of the way up to ensure that the yeast has as friendly a fermenting environment as possible. Since the main downsides to this sort of tank are poor circulation and yeast flow, Live Oak uses a slightly higher cell count when pitching to ensure a strong fermentation.

The Weihenstephan brewery in Freising uses both traditional cylindroconical tanks and long horizontal tanks for primary fermentation. Brewmaster Tobias Zollo explains that the horizontal tanks are ideal for wheat beer due to the increased ester production of the brewery's yeast in that environment. For Weihenstephaner lagers, the brewery relies on the usual cylindroconical tanks for their limited ester production.

One of the few ways in which open fermentors are more practical than closed systems is that brewers can use visual cues to understand a fermentation's progression. The brewers at Únětický pivovar in Czechia track fermentations by their appearance, from the early "white rings" phase, during which the crown forms large, looping curls (*see* fig. 3.2), to the later "brown circles" phase, which signals that it will soon be time to rack to conditioning tanks. Any deviation from these patterns is a clue that something is amiss.

Coolships and other Wort Cooling Devices

Coolships were once a standard part of every brewery, being the primary technology available for cooling wort prior to fermentation. Coolships are generally associated with brewing *lambic* and other Belgian-style beers; their use for "clean" lager production is less common. Most have been replaced by heat exchangers, but a handful of breweries around the world still employ coolships to brew lager.

Coolships cool wort by increasing the surface area exposed to cooler air, allowing for heat transfer over a large area. Cooling to fermentation temperatures can take many hours, and the exact timing is dependent on the ambient air temperature. During this time the cooling wort is susceptible to contamination.

Contamination is not the only reason coolships have fallen out of favor. The extra time, extravagant space required, and the fact that coolships can cost more than heat exchangers have all but eliminated them from breweries around the world. But coolships still occupy spaces in a select few lager breweries throughout the world.

Figure 6.3. A typical Franconian coolship at Brauerei Hölzlein in Lohndorf.

Brauerei Drei Kronen in Memmelsdorf still uses a coolship for its 20-hectoliter brewhouse. Halu Straub is proud that the centuries-old brewery preserves this dying tradition. Straub believes that this is one of fewer than a hundred operating coolships in Germany and Belgium.

At Drei Kronen, the wort is allowed to cool to 149°F (65°C) in the coolship before it is cooled the remainder of the way with a more modern plate heat exchanger. When pumping the wort into the coolship, the brewers do their best to create a circular motion with the wort in an attempt to replicate the effect of a whirlpool. Doing this results in most of the trub collecting in the middle of the coolship, making it easier to separate the wort from the trub.

The 100-hectoliter coolship at Augustiner Bräu in Salzburg receives wort twice a day. When the 100-year-old iron vessel first receives the hot wort, the quickly expanding metal makes its presence known with a series of pops and bangs. The entire coolship was covered in a black film, which de Clerck describes as a coating of iron tannate that is deposited on the surface from the tannins in wort (de Clerck 1957, 340). Unlike most other lager breweries that still use coolships, Augustiner Bräu finishes the cooling of wort in a Baudelot cooler (German: *Berieselungskühler*). This is a series of horizontal copper tubes filled with cool water set at offset angles, down which wort flows over the rounded edges. This invention was intended as a time-saving improvement upon the coolship, with the added bonus of aerating the wort as it flowed down the apparatus. Brewmaster Hansjörg Höplinger believes that the coolship and Baudelot cooler are essential for the character of Augustiner Bräu's fine *Märzen* lager. While some elements of the operation have been updated and automated, trial brews run at the brewery with a heat exchanger convinced Höplinger that the impact of the traditional pieces of equipment on the finished beer was worth the extra effort. He believes that both the coolship and Baudelot cooler have positive impacts on the mouthfeel of Augustiner Bräu's beer, and that the aeration enhances the color of the beer by darkening it slightly.

In a way, Augustiner Bräu Salzburg's process is similar to other lager breweries with coolships, where the cooling process is typically split between the coolship and another device. Many brewers choose to do this to avoid the threat of microbial contamination, only allowing wort in the coolship to cool to a specific threshold; generally, this means no lower than 140°F (60°C), just above pasteurization temperatures. This means the coolship won't be a source of contamination while still getting many of the benefits that can be obtained from using one. Hot-side aeration of the wort with a coolship also darkens the beer slightly through oxidation. Enough oxygen will dissolve into the wort that additional aeration prior to yeast pitching is not necessary.

Brewers can expect up to 10% evaporation with a coolship, which needs to be factored into the brewing and recipe development process. Seasonal shifts in weather will affect how much evaporation occurs, with time, temperature, and humidity all playing a factor.

In addition to losses from evaporation, a significant amount of wort will be left over with the trub in a coolship. In former times, this trub-laden wort would have been filtered or pressed to preserve as much extract as possible (de Clerck 1957, 340). At Augustiner Bräu Salzburg, the brewers used to collect this liquid and allow the trub to settle before blending back the separated wort. These wort reclamation practices have fallen out of use, presumably due to the microbial contamination risk they present.

Coolships Old and New

There's little else in the world like the U Flekŭ restaurant, nestled in the heart of Prague's fifteenth-century "New Town." While its reputation as one of the oldest brewpubs in Europe may be up for debate, there is no doubt that little has changed over the years at this grand, rambling establishment that encompasses a variety of great rooms and courtyards.

Servers roam the pub with glasses of the brewery's staple black lager, replenishing empty glasses and keeping tabs tallied on coasters. This 13° Plato black lager was for centuries the only beer available at U Flekŭ, until a pale lager was recently added as a second option. The brewery claims the recipe for the dark lager has not changed, though notably it is no longer produced with house-smoked malt as it once would have been.

Nestled in a city block surrounded by streets named for its former brewmasters, U Flekŭ's coolship may be a historical relic, but it is one that still sees regular use. Considerable imagination would be required to remove it or otherwise change the workflow of the brewery to replace it. Having done the job with aplomb for so long, there is little pressure to change this part of their operation.

Across the Atlantic, tucked into a green hillside in Oxford, Connecticut, OEC Brewing was founded in 2014. This relatively young brewery's coolship and Baudelot chiller are far from technological necessities. They were built alongside the rest of the custom Kaspar Schulz brewhouse on a site shared with B. United International. It is a family affair, B. United being owned by Matthias Neidhart and OEC by his son, Ben Neidhart. The complex is a must-see for all epicureans, boasting not only the brewery's fermentation program but a coffee roaster, some underground fermentation pits, and various food-bearing greenhouses. Ben was inspired by the wild beers of Belgium his father had been importing for years.

Though the inclusion of the coolship was initially with spontaneous fermentation in mind, OEC has adapted to produce quite a lot of lager, ranging from classically refreshing pale lagers to complex, malt-focused, and wood-aged lagers of all colors and strengths. The coolship and Baudelot chiller are used for all OEC's lagers, a feature dictated by the brewery's design. Though this design was not necessarily intentional, it has proven to be an ideal setup for exploring many traditional and historical lager styles and techniques. There are precious few modern breweries in the world attempting such classic lager styles with coolships and open fermentation. Any limitations this system presents are used by the brewery as a launchpad for curiosity and creativity. The lengthy list of beers brewed at OEC is even more impressive with all this in mind.

U Fleků and OEC may be separated by oceans and centuries, but they share a few things at their core. Where one brewery is adhering to generations of tradition, the other is using the past as a launchpad for modern sensory exploration. Both are producing characterful, interesting lagers that offer the drinker windows into the past and future of lager brewing. May they continue to do so for generations to come.

Cold Break: Sedimentation and Flotation Tanks

After the boiling process begins, there are two types of "break" that occur in the wort at the end of the boil: hot and cold. These are the processes in which proteins, tannins, polyphenols, hop material, and other compounds are allowed to precipitate out of solution. Some compounds are easily precipitated on the hot side in the brewhouse, whereas other compounds won't precipitate until the wort is cooled. The amount of break is determined by a few variables. Poorly modified malts will leave more hot and cold break than well-modified malts. Decoction mashing will decrease the total amount of hot and cold break by coagulating proteins during mash boiling, which will then be removed with the spent grain instead at the end of the boil. Aeration both on the hot side and cold side will also increase trub precipitation (Gloetzl 1967, 185–187).

In historical brewhouses, both the hot and cold breaks would have occurred in the coolship, which was also referred to as a settling tank. Most contemporary brewers utilize a whirlpool to eliminate hot break; the cold break that forms is generally less of a concern for modern brewers. Advanced brewing equipment and the availability of highly modified malts with less nitrogenous material have all but eliminated the need for brewers to worry about cold break. Even so, a reduction in the cold break can still lead to a more rounded beer flavor, reduced bitterness, improved beer foam, and a stronger fermentation (Kunze 2014, 367).

We may take for granted that the whirlpool is a part of every brewhouse, but it was only introduced into breweries at the end of the 1950s. To this day in Germany, the whirlpool is considered additional technology rather than part of the brew-house itself. German brewers will thus refer to a brewery with a mash tun, lauter tun, boil kettle, and whirlpool as a three-vessel system—what American brewers would call a four-vessel brewhouse. This transition from coolships to whirlpools has inspired some consideration for cold break and its effect on fermenting lager. Cold break consists of about 50% protein and 25% polyphenols, with the remainder being carbohydrates and lipids (Ockert 2006a, 63). Removing the cold break improves the wort, promotes yeast health, and changes the fermentation profile of the finished beer. The process is likely responsible for less ester formation in finished beer. The quantity of esters lowers as more unsaturated fatty acids are removed with the trub (Basařová et al. 2017, 348).

There are two methods that can be employed to eliminate cold break material from the wort. The first is a sedimentation tank: cold wort is sent to the sedimentation tank without oxygen or yeast and allowed to sit undisturbed until the cold break drops to the bottom of the tank. A cone or a tank standpipe can then be used when pumping the clear wort off the trub into a fermentation tank with yeast and aerated. Though straightforward, this process does add considerable time. The height of the sedimentation tank will determine exactly how long it takes the particulates to drop out of solution, so a tank with a fill level no higher than 4–5 ft. (1.2–1.5 m) is recommended.

The second cold break separation method is the flotation tank. Cold wort is sent to a flotation tank with yeast and is heavily aerated. During aeration, cold break and dead yeast cells are transported by the air bubbles to the top of the liquid, creating a foam cap. The beer is then pumped out of the tank, leaving behind the foam. Because so much yeast is left behind in this process, it's important to overpitch by 10%–15% to ensure the correct yeast counts in primary fermentation. The foam created in a flotation tank is slimy, gray, and smelly, and was referred to as "cooler grounds" or "grey [sic] matter" by nineteenth-century English brewing texts (Moritz and Morris 1891, 273). This substance is fairly unpleasant, so it is logical to assume that skipping this process means including these unpleasant compounds in the finished beer.

There are other tangible benefits to using a sedimentation tank. Brewer and owner Ashleigh Carter of Bierstadt Lagerhaus in Denver, Colorado, uses a flotation tank for her lagers. By aerating and pitching yeast in the flotation tank, she finds that overall bitterness/grassiness is reduced, while hop aroma is highlighted. Because so much hop particulate is removed during the cold break, she can use more kettle hops without driving perceived bitterness as high.

Performing a cold break is particularly important when non-conical fermentors are used for primary fermentation, especially when yeast needs to be harvested from those vessels. By co-sedimenting with any remaining trub, cold breaks can improve the quality of yeast that will be harvested from an open fermentor. Flotation tanks also reduce overfoaming during fermentation, allowing the fermentation vessel to be fully filled.

The choice to use a sedimentation or flotation tank often comes down to what style of beer is being produced and the desired flavor profile. At Wagner-Bräu Kemmern, owner and brewmaster Toby Wagner believes that sedimentation and flotation tanks are preferred for brewing Pilsners because they help remove bitterness while preserving hop aromatics. This process doesn't offer as much advantage for darker or maltier beers for which hop character is less of a focus.

Lager brewers have also used centrifuges or *kieselguhr* (diatomaceous earth) filtration to separate cold break. These methods were usually used by the largest brewers, and so have fallen out of favor as breweries have deprioritized cold break separation. We have yet to encounter any brewers still using these methods.

Biological Acidification

Mash pH is a key variable to control when brewing lager. The pH of wort can affect the enzymatic reactions of malt as well as hop flavor, bitterness, and absorption. For any brewery not under the jurisdiction of the Reinheitsgebot, adjusting mash pH is conveniently done with salts and acids; it is significantly more challenging if a brewery has to, or chooses to, adhere to the purity law. Historically, the use of an acid rest during the mash would have provided a brewer with some help in lowering the pH. Today, the use of acidulated malts is acceptable under the Reinheitsgebot, but this malt is expensive and may not otherwise match the grist recipe.

An alternative means of adjusting pH is using bacterial fermentations to produce *Sauergut*. This biologically acidified liquid is made by fermenting wort with specific bacterial strains that are naturally found on barley. *Lactobacillus delbrueckii* is often used for this fermentation due to its ability to ferment at very high temperatures around 122°F (50°C). The effect of these fermentations can be rapid, the wort acidifying down to pH 2.9 within 48 hours with limited diacetyl production (Back et al. 2020, 119).

There are a few pros and cons to using biological acidification instead of direct acid additions. One advantage of biological acidification of wort is that it induces a more extensive precipitation of proteins and ultimately results in improved chemical and physical stability. It also improves flavor stability, head retention, and microbiological stability. Sauergut is added at the end of a boil to improve hop utilization, reduce DMS, and increase the supply of yeast nutrients in the wort (Back et al. 2020, 261). Adding Sauergut before the boil can result in lower hop utilization rates, lower bitterness, and increased DMS.

Creating Sauergut on a small or batch scale is fairly straightforward. The biggest challenge is maintaining the proper temperature in the fermentor. Temperatures that drop too far below 119°F (48°C) are prone to infection from other microbes, which will also slow down the fermentation. Limiting oxygen is another challenge. Carbon dioxide flushing or scrubbing of fresh wort will help to reduce oxygen.

Larger breweries who use this method often have completely automated systems that monitor the Sauergut fermentations, control how they are dosed in the brewhouse, and feed fresh wort to the next ones. Due to the high temperature fermentations involved, these systems have been known to continuously run for years, in one instance for two decades (Hutzler et al. 2018).

Steinbier

Steinbier is a method of brewing that employs the use of superheated stones as a heat source for mashing and boiling. Though it is a very old method of brewing, there is little documentation pertaining to its original methods or practitioners. Beer writer Lars Marius Garshol believes that the modern understanding of Steinbier doesn't match its actual history. Steinbier likely originated in small farmhouse breweries that couldn't afford proper brewing kettles (Garshol 2020, 169). In these primitive breweries, wooden vessels would have been the norm, making it difficult for the brewer to use any external heat source. While the first Steinbier was likely an ale rather than a lager, the tradition has been carried on by a number of modern lager brewers who have resurrected this process.

The use of superheated stones in the brewing process creates intense caramelization of the wort. As we discovered during two test brews conducted while researching this book, rocks can hold an amazing amount of energy: enough to destroy a slow-roasting box, for example, and to bring many barrels of beer to a boil in a very short period of time. Fewer rocks are needed to do this than you might think.

Brewing Steinbier is not for the faint of heart, and safety is an obvious concern. First off, the right rocks need to be used. Granite is the first choice,

Figure 6.4. One of the authors (Joe) heating stones over a fire for a Steinbier collaboration brew at Wibby Brewing in Longmont, Colorado.

but other rocks can be used. It is important that the rock selected can withstand rapid cooling in the wort without exploding. Heating the rocks over wood fires can take many hours and consume many cords of firewood. The vessel used for this must be able to sustain temperatures up to 800°F (427°C) for several hours. Once superheated, transporting the rocks to the brewing vessel is a challenge and requires fire-proof gloves and/or tongs.

At Wibby Brewing in Longmont, Colorado, owner and brewer Ryan Wibby has become a veteran brewer of Steinbier. He transports the superheated stones in a few old stainless steel kegs (with tops removed) that are chained to the forks of a forklift, and uses this arrangement to lower the superheated stones into a receiving vessel full of wort. The cloud of steam produced is impressive, as is the speed with which the wort reaches a boil.

At Brauerei Hofstetten in Austria, owner Peter Krammer regularly brews Granitbock, an interesting version of Steinbier using superheated granite stones to caramelize the wort prior to pitching the house yeast strain. With a nod to the historical nature of this style, Krammer forgoes his modern automated brewhouse in favor of using the 1929 brewhouse that is still on site and fully operational (*see* fig. 4.9). He also takes the extra step of fermenting Granitbock in granite vats in this older brewhouse, some of which were used to ferment sauerkraut centuries ago. The resulting beer has an intensely deep, rich malt character that suggests a far more complex malt bill.

7

THE FUTURE OF LAGER BREWING

*A*S INDUSTRIAL LAGER CONTINUES ITS DOMINANCE OF THE MODERN BEER WORLD, "THE YEAR OF THE CRAFT LAGER" IS ALWAYS AROUND THE CORNER. There certainly have been plenty of positive trends in craft lager in recent years, inspiring genuine confidence among craft lager brewers. These brewers find themselves in good company, as more and more lager-focused breweries continue to open. Lager in its various forms has held onto its share of the craft beer market, despite the struggles of the industry overall in recent years (Bart Watson, pers. comm.). Since we enjoy access to lots of this great lager, as well as the healthy imaginations of plenty of other brewers, we're just foolish enough to try and answer the question: where does lager go from here?

Lager has been on a wild ride over the last century and a half, being probably the most researched and studied type of beer over that time. Given how quickly lager attained its huge market share, this should come as no surprise.

The proliferation of American craft breweries has created no shortage of inter-esting ways in which brewers approach lager production. As connected to the past as some of these techniques may be, they are continuously being shaped by the modern world. Raw materials are changing, in ways both intentional and not; they are shaped by economic conditions, consumer preferences, and our changing climate. It all makes for a richly diverse mosaic of techniques and philosophies surrounding lager beer production.

One philosophy of American brewers is a desire to temporarily transport their consumers to Europe with the beer in their glass. These experiences are rooted to the sensory memory of the brewer—a desire to not only cross a spa-tial boundary but one that reaches back in time as well. And so, we end up with modern American examples of full-bodied Helles and richly colored Märzen that are arguably more "traditional" than many equivalent European beers that have themselves dried out and lightened in color over time.

Not all lager exploration is so rooted in tradition. Brewers continue to broaden the scope of lager styles by exploring previously unexplored sensory spaces. New ingredients, new processes, and new techniques continue to shift and change existing styles. Novel styles continue to emerge, filling out lager's flavor spectrum along the way.

Of particular interest is how American craft brewers can make lager their own, using local ingredients and resources to mold their beers into singular expressions of place. Rather than looking to Europe for inspira-tion, this school of thought expresses an idea that American brewers can define beers to reflect their own identities, much like those original brewers who came to the New World used corn and rice to create the first American lagers. But rather than trying to shape their unsuitable raw materials towards some impossible ideal like their forebears, today's progressive lager brewers emphasize and embrace the very characteristics that make them unsuitable for brewing European-style lager.

The American craft beer spirit emphasizes exploration and rebellion, and so American brewers can choose to embrace tradition or eschew it altogether. While European lager brewers may seem more conservative, they are no less concerned with the progression of lager. This influence is generally more sub-tle and incremental than their American counterparts: while American craft consumers expect (or demand) new flavors and styles, European brewers are sensitive to unbroken generations of customer expectation. With that sensitiv-ity in mind, European brewers must creatively and progressively respond to changing raw materials.

As for how tradition will continue to influence American brewers, there is certainly no single answer. One particularly heartening and noteworthy trend is that of a subset of (mostly) newer American lager producers who choose to specialize their breweries around a limited product line. Rather than the endless experimentation and unlimited exploration American consumers may be conditioned to expect from craft brewers, these brewers challenge their customers to appreciate the specialty of their craft. This specialized approach is a healthy echo of the landscape of small, local breweries that dot the landscape in Franconia.

The future of lager will inevitably expand the boundaries of what we consider lager. Many craft breweries are already challenging the notions of lager as either a commodified, industrially produced beer or one that is all about traditional techniques. Through process changes, new raw materials, and hybridized styles, the humble lager will no doubt continue to evolve.

Hops for the Future

Perhaps one of the most noticeable changes to lager beer has been the growth of the hoppy lager category. Considering the prominence of hop-forward beers in the craft beer scene, it is no surprise that hop selection and treatment methods are opening new frontiers for lager. Current examples include India pale lager, cold IPA, Italian Pilsner, and West Coast-style Pilsner, among a number of other variations. Whatever you like to call them, these lager styles attempt to frame hops as the central component of the flavor and aroma profiles. As of 2022, the Great American Beer Festival® now boasts two new hoppy lager categories, the India Pale Lager or Cold IPA category and the Other Hoppy Lager category.

The original dark lager of Bavaria did not depend on hops for preservation, relying instead on the stabilization effect offered by cold maturation. Since few Bavarian lagers had to travel far to be consumed, hops remained mostly an accent in lager, rather than the featuring role they played in English pale ales of the same period. This changed with the introduction of Pilsner in the mid-nineteenth century. Pilsner's relatively high hop bitterness and aroma were given the perfect backdrop with lighter Pilsner malt. This tradition carries on today in Czechia, where Czech pale lager still exhibits impressive (and ever-increasing) IBU levels. Certainly in the nineteenth century there were probably few 4.5% ABV beers in the world that featured hops with such assertive aroma and bitterness as the original Pilsner.

All of which is to point out that pale lager has, historically, featured plenty of hops and hop character, even if those characteristics have mostly been associated with IPA. Modern lager brewers are carrying that tradition forward by experimenting with new hopping techniques and unusual varieties.

Brewer and founder of Birrificio Italiano in Lombardy, Italy, Agostino Arioli is admittedly not a fan of pigeon-holing beer into styles, so it is rather ironic that his Tipopils is considered by others as the benchmark for Italian Pilsner. This dry-hopped Pilsner was intended as an homage to northern Germany's Jever Pilsener (a task at which Arioli admits he failed) and stands as one of the first modern hop-forward lager styles to emerge into the craft beer scene, inspiring a wave of imitations in Italy, the US, and beyond. First brewed in 1996, Tipopils is nowadays dry hopped with Spalter Select. Some brewers of Italian Pilsner have taken to including Italian malt, while others have explored outside the noble hop lineage favored by the style's founders.

"I want craft brewers to brew more brave lagers like me," says Arioli when asked about his hopes for the future of craft lager. Judging by the proliferation of hoppy lager in the US, Arioli is indeed in good company.

Bob Kunz brews some of the finest hop-forward lager in the country at his Los Angeles brewery, Highland Park. Timbo Pils, the brewery's "West Coast Pilsner," is bright, clean, and wildly aromatic, bursting with New World hop character from Citra and Mosaic. Highland Park brews a variety of hop-forward lagers and coined the style "West Coast Pilsner," for which Bob and his team use IPA dry hopping regimens on lager. Highland Park also uses lager yeast in the production of their West Coast IPAs.

Ryan and Robin Wibby brew delightful hop-forward beers at Wibby Brewing in Longmont, Colorado. Ryan and Robin forgo dry hopping, instead relying on huge quantities of kettle hops. Some of these beers use 3.0–3.5 lb. of hops per barrel (1.16–1.35 kg/hL). Ryan estimates that their average utilization rate from these hops is 2%, a very low average contribution. The brewers did experiment with dry hopping but found that the aroma changed significantly over the lagering time in a horizontal tank. They achieved a more stable hop aroma with their kettle hopping practice.

In Portland, Oregon, Kevin Davey tapped into the Pacific Northwest region's love affair with the hop when he coined the Cold IPA style while working at Wayfinder Beer. Davey had noted how craft breweries were creating India pale lagers by either substituting lager yeast for ale yeast in an IPA or by dry hopping a Pilsner. He wanted to try something new at Wayfinder, releasing the brewery's first "Cold IPA" in 2018.

Davey's approach for Cold IPA is to use adjuncts to lighten the body and color of the beer and provide a lean platform for expressive hop character.

He also uses lager yeast at a warmer temperature to limit the final amount of sulfur compounds but still provide very subtle esters. In addition, the Cold IPA process makes use of yeast-driven biotransformation during natural carbonation. Biotransformation unlocks otherwise inert hop-derived compounds, with the potential for huge sensory impact. Controversy over naming conventions aside, Cold IPA is delicious and distinct enough to warrant the differentiation.

The selection of hops for their biotransformative properties is an exciting new frontier for hop-forward lagers, though not one without potential pitfalls. Jace Marti, formerly of Schell's in New Ulm, Minnesota, points out that interactions between hop character and yeast-derived sulfur compounds can have unintended effects. For example, there is potential for the creation of unpleasant thiols that can present as distracting off-flavors in the finished beer. Of course, positive interactions are also quite possible.

As a significant sensory compound in beer, thiols themselves have recently received much attention from researchers. Thiols are a class of organosulfur compounds with a molecular structure similar to alcohols and phenols but with a sulfur replacing the oxygen in the alcohol group. Thiols, also called mercaptans, are derived from both malt and hops. They are highly aromatic, with aromas ranging from rotten egg, onion-like, lightstruck, and catty, to pleasant tropical, fruity, and citrus aromas that are often highly prized.

Lager yeast's biotransformative properties, along with its propensity for higher hydrogen sulfide (H_2S) production, gives it the potential to create these flavor-active compounds during fermentation (Vermeulen et al. 2006). Hydrogen sulfide has been identified as a key catalyst for these reactions. Research has shown that certain lager strains are great at producing free thiols from molecules that normally bind them (these bound forms are known as thiol precursors and are not aroma active), and that colder fermentation temperatures along with reduced wort nitrogen levels strongly increases this effect (Chenot et al. 2022). This research is still in its early stages.

Brewers are experimenting with different lager yeast strains and hop varieties to discover which combinations yield noteworthy results through biotransformation. The qualities that make hops ideal for biotransformation are distinct from other brewhouse uses. Hops with a lower level of sulfur aroma compounds but high amounts of bound, or precursor, thiols like Saaz have been prized for biotransformation, while hops with a higher level of aroma sulfur compounds can produce distracting off-flavors. Some with the highest concentrations of bound thiols are the North American hop varieties Citra, Simcoe, Mosaic, and Cascade as well as some European varieties like Saaz, Perle, Tradition, and Hallertau Blanc. The release of these bound thiols will create many unique flavors that may be desirable in the finished beer.

Another challenge for creating heavily hopped lagers is the management of time during the cellaring process. Shawn Bainbridge of Halfway Crooks Beer in Atlanta, Georgia, notices the hop character of their hop-centric lagers noticeably diminishes after six weeks of cellaring. Biotransformation reactions by lager yeast will also begin to change the aroma profile during lagering, converting thiols into esters and other compounds. A calculation needs to be made to determine what hop aroma is expected in the finished beer. Dry hopped lagers tend to have shorter lagering times in order to achieve the desired aroma.

Our Hoppy Family

At Jack's Abby Craft Lagers, we have long celebrated the hop as a featured player in our progressive lagers. We may not have cracked the code on how to classify them, but we've enjoyed exploring the ever-expanding horizons of the hoppy lager. Here's just a snapshot of the hoppy delights we've shared over the years:

Jack's Abby brand	Style	ABV	IBUs	Grains	Hops	Dry hop quantity, lb./bbl. (kg/hL)
Hoponius	India Pale Lager	6.5%	50	US 2-row, Munich, Cara 10	Citra, Centennial	2.0 (0.77) at knockout
Kiwi Rising	Double India Pale Lager	8.5%	65	US 2-row, dextrose	Nelson Sauvin, Motueka	4.0 (1.55)
Bella Lago	Italian-Style Pilsner	4.7%	35	Pilsner malt	Hallertau Blanc	1.25 (0.48)
Chill Haze	N.E.-Style Hazy Lager	7.5%	30	US 2-row, oats, wheat	Citra, Mosaic, Galaxy	5.0 (1.93)
Bräu Series	West Coast-Style Pils	5.5%	40	Pilsner malt	Rotating	1.5 (0.58)

Future of Yeast

As lager yeast is such a defining feature of lager beer, one might think that *Saccharomyces pastorianus* has an unwavering hold over lager breweries. However, recent research and development has begun to alter our understanding of lager yeast and its traditional sensory impact. Research into expanding the genomes of lager yeast has honed our understanding of classic strains to the genetic level. This understanding has paved the way for novel strains as well as new approaches for working with classic strains.

There are three main approaches challenging the hegemony of *S. pastorianus*: the creation of new hybrid strains, forced mutations of existing strains, and genetic modification of lager yeast DNA. The development of new hybridized *S. cerevisiae* × *S. eubayanus* strains may help to generate a set of distinct lager yeasts that in some ways bridge the gap between existing ale and lager strains. Pilot-scale fermentations can confirm the suitability of new hybrids for commercial lager productionr, with some even producing distinct aromatic profiles (Mertens et al. 2015). In addition to *S. cerevisiae* and *S. eubayanus*, new hybrids from other *Saccharomyces* species might be able to combine cold tolerance with maltotriose fermentation. While this could happen accidentally in a brewery somewhere (as indeed it has in the past with the formation of *S. pastorianus*), hybridization studies to develop new commercial strains with these traits in mind are much more likely to produce novel "lager-type" yeast strains.

The selection and hybridization of individual *S. eubayanus* and *S. cerevisiae* strains that have desirable flavor profiles is a potentially useful way to create novel strains that can be used immediately in brewery applications, avoiding the difficulties of relying on genetic crosses between the limited pool of existing *S. pastorianus* strains (Gibson and Liti 2015). Using other cold-tolerant yeast strains like *S. uvarum*, or other strains capable of fermenting maltotriose like *S. mikatae*, opens up possibilities for completely novel non-*cerevisiae* strains (Gyurchev et al. 2022).

One such new development comes from Lallemand, whose LalBrew Novalager™ is a new *S. pastorianus* hybrid from *S. cerevisiae* and *S. eubayanus* parents. Lallemand have termed Novalager a "Group III" *S. pastorianus* lineage. Unlike the Saaz-type lager yeast family, which has two-thirds *S. eubayanus* DNA, and the Frohberg-type family, which has one-half *S. eubayanus* DNA, this new third lineage is only one-quarter *S. eubayanus* DNA. Novalager thus inherits the cold tolerance, low-ester production, and higher alcohol tolerance of its *S. eubayanus* parent, while possessing recognizable ale qualities. It produces less H_2S and diacetyl and is tolerant of a wider temperature range than most lager yeast. Novalager is designed to be more forgiving than other lager strains and to ferment a bit faster. This strain is intended to operate more like its *S. cerevisiae* parent, making it more accessible for ale brewers. As of this writing, Novalager is so new that its biotransformation performance is still being explored.

While genome editing technology allows for even greater potential creativity on the part of yeast scientists, the resulting lager yeast strains will be unavailable to brewers in parts of the world where genetically modified organisms in foods are banned. In some cases, the genetic modifications are to "switch on" (express) genes already existing in the yeast DNA but that are not normally expressed, essentially turning on traits that would otherwise be turned off. In other cases, novel DNA from other organisms is incorporated into the yeast strain's genome.

Omega Yeast Labs' Cosmic Punch® is a genetically modified yeast noted for its thiol production, expressing intense notes of passion fruit and grapefruit akin to New Zealand sauvignon blanc. These aromas are formed by the conversion of bound thiols from both malt and hops, taking advantage of a natural metabolic pathway in brewer's yeast that is normally dormant. The yeast has been genetically modified to turn on these fermentation traits.

Omega Yeast's founder Lance Shaner believes that genetically edited strains like Cosmic Punch are just the beginning. Using gene editing technology to turn on and off selective traits could result in strains that would produce any number of flavors, from vanilla to strawberry and beyond. The question will likely be not what flavors they can produce but what flavors brewers want and their commercial viability.

More commonly though, variations within lager strains come from natural gene mutations. These may be caused by new stresses, but are likely more specific to the processes and conditions found at various breweries. Many of the brewers we spoke to in Germany have been using the same exact lineage of yeast for decades. Each brewer believes these lineages impart unique attributes that make them ideal for their individual brewery. However, recent experiments have shown that genetic variations can be accelerated. In one experiment, lager yeast strains were submitted to heat-shock treatment and the resulting mutants were studied. While no determinations were made as to the commercial viability of the mutants, novel fermentation aromas were found (de la Cerda Garcia-Caro et al. 2022).

Potentially the simplest way to diversify lager fermentation character is to work with existing yeast strains. At Highland Park, Bob Kunz and his team take it a step further, brewing West Coast IPA with lager yeast at slightly warmer temperatures. This type of unconventional use of lager yeast is not new, as it is found in the history of cream ale, steam beer, and other in-between styles. It's an example of meeting customers where they are at, or, as Bob puts it, "adapting their process to the vision of the beer in the glass." When the vision calls for clean, bright hop character with minimal or neutral yeast character, lager yeast fits the bill.

Future of Malt

For Mike Schroth, founder and owner of Stone Path Malt in Wareham, Massachusetts, being a maltster in an IPA-obsessed world has been a challenge. Malt production is one part of the beer industry that has enthusiastically welcomed the rise of craft lager, and with good reason. Where malt has felt like a secondary concern for many craft IPA brewers, it becomes a much more prominent flavor component in lager. The opportunities are seemingly endless for small malting operations to produce characterful products that brewers can feature in their lagers.

The sheer amount of craft breweries in the world has created the demand for unique, small-batch raw materials. While hop farmers and processors have grown to meet this new worldwide demand, the nature of barley growing and malting means there has been more of a lag time built in for smaller maltsters to catch up. Much like brewing, the global malting industry underwent massive consolidation as it concerned itself with a handful of huge customers for whom efficiency and price were the most important variables. Brewers who wanted interesting and flavorful, but potentially inefficient, malt varieties had little in the way of options even as recently as 2010.

In the US, a new generation of smaller craft maltsters is seeking out heritage grains, novel barley varieties, and unique processing methods in order to meet the needs of the craft beer movement. Some of the efficiency-driven changes in modern malthouses have ironically helped to spawn a demand for small-batch, artisan malting that leaves a measure of modification control in the hands of the brewer. These operations eschew some of the efficiencies and consistency of larger maltsters for more variety and fine-tuned control of malt. The craft malting movement has taken to highlighting terroir in their malts, choosing locally grown grains over which they can assert significant control over the processes used to create them. For brewers interested in investing time and effort into working with these unusual ingredients, there's plenty of upside.

Sugar Creek Malt Co. in Boone County, Indiana, is a small craft maltster that is working with heritage grains, a standout being a Czech winter barley called Edelweiss. While not typical for North American malting varieties, winter barley works well in Indiana due to its early harvest in June, which protects the crop from the high heat of summer. When it comes to malting and brewing with Edelweiss, it's impossible to modify the grain to modern standards and the resulting malt requires decoction or step mashing. Caleb Michalke, Sugar Creek's owner and maltster, notes that even though he has tried extending the malting process he cannot get the grains to fully modify. The grains only have 80% friability and incredibly high levels of β-glucans that create stuck mashes without proper mashing considerations. Yet Edelweiss is a favorite of several American decoction brewers, who appreciate its character of fresh hay and bread crust.

Montana Craft Malt, based just outside Butte, began growing and malting Steffi barley in the US based on its emerging reputation in Germany. Head maltster Bryan Taylor is the first to admit that, from a modern efficiency perspective, US-grown Steffi malt is not competitive. Being adapted to the wetter climes of Continental Europe, Steffi requires irrigation to grow in the arid conditions of the Great Plains. The barley is also a challenge to malt, requiring extra steps in the malthouse that amount to an extra full day of processing. The resulting malt is high in β-glucans that in turn necessitate extra modification in the brewhouse, ideally with a decoction mash.

Taylor believes that all this extra effort is worth the results. While high β-glucan levels may cause problems with lautering, there are some significant sensory benefits that come from decreased malt modification. The lower degree of modification and higher β-glucan levels allow the kernels to be dried at higher temperatures while still keeping the very pale color that typifies Pilsner malt; this high heat also enhances malt intensity, leading to a highly aromatic, lightly colored malt. Higher kilning temperatures also help mitigate some of the dimethyl sulfide (DMS) typical of pale colored malts. Taylor describes Steffi as imparting clean, soft, grassy flavors to the finished beer.

Traditionally, US-grown malt has been designed and bred with adjunct brewing in mind. The future of barley breeding for brewing is currently in limbo in the US. Much of the progress of the previous century has been driven by the interests of the largest American brewers, but the growing craft segment clearly has different needs.

Jari Zitzewitz, a plant geneticist at Rahr Malting Co., sees a future shift toward barley varieties that are better suited to all-malt beers. He believes that the influence of technically minded craft brewers will win out. The American Malting Barley Association (AMBA) seems to agree and added new guidelines in 2021 for barley breeding for all-malt beers, though they are still significantly different from the standards in Germany (*see* table 2.3). More interest from craft brewers will continue to help direct the breeding objectives of North American barley growers.

Unlike the dramatic shifts seen with the flavor profiles of hops, it seems unlikely that there will be huge changes in flavor profiles of barley varieties. Dr. Patrick Hayes of Oregon State University has been involved in barley breeding, malting, and brewing trials involving hundreds of new varieties of barley without seeing any evidence that a completely novel barley cultivar will enter the market. As Dr. Hayes put it, there will be no equivalent to basmati rice in the barley world—no single barley cultivar for brewing that will stand out as a complete outlier to the rest.

One study using Maris Otter barley as the parent showed that while the hybrid varieties were dramatically different in certain genetic areas there was not a significant sensory difference between them (Morrissy et al. 2022, 204–208). There is evidence supporting the notion that barley malt flavor affects beer flavor due to certain morphological and physiological traits arising from barley cultivar genetics, but scientists are still working to determine what genetic components cause these effects (Sayre-Chavez et al. 2022). While different barley varieties have different flavor profiles, even the same varieties can have different flavor profiles depending on where and how they are grown.

A New Type of *Landbier*

There is a growing desire among American brewers to carve their own identity in lager beer. Brewers that are well-versed in European techniques and styles are applying these skills to beers made with local ingredients, leading to new and subtly distinct styles of lager in the process.

These present-day brewers have a surprising amount in common with the first generation of American lager brewers. Like that earlier generation, the new generation of brewers is attempting to apply old-world brewing techniques using novel ingredients. How these present-day brewers differ is in their desire to brew beer that expresses character that is totally divergent from classically refined European styles. Many of these brewers have instead gravitated to the "non-style" exemplified by the *Landbier* of Franconia. Landbier belongs in the class of the Kellerbier and Zwickelbier; rustic, characterful lagers with little in the way of official style guidelines.

As interpreted by the likes of John and Bonnie Branding at Wheatland Spring Farm and Brewery in Virginia, "land beer" becomes a totally unique expression of place. Located in the Virginia Piedmont region, John and Bonnie call Wheatland Spring an estate brewery, and actually grow most of the barley they use. Their plantings include new varietals being trialed by Virginia Tech, for which they provide valuable brewhouse feedback for the university's barley breeding program. In this way, Wheatland Spring helps close the loop on the development cycle of new barley cultivars. Although still in its early stages, the program aims to shrink a decade-long cycle into a theoretical three-year cycle.

The Brandings' approach to lager is to keep processing to a minimum, and to allow their ingredients to speak loudly. They invite their customers to appreciate and celebrate the differences between batches of beer, rather than striving for rigid sensory consistency. After all, consumers are accustomed to treating vintages of wine that way. The Brandings hope that their "land beer" becomes a blueprint for similar beer appellations across the country.

Surrounded by quickly disappearing warehouses deep in a formerly industrial part of Brooklyn, Wild East Brewery's relationship with the land is different. No gentle rolling hills and quiet farmland here, though the brewery would be in the shadow of Prospect Hill were it large enough to cast one. In this rapidly changing neighborhood, head brewer Brett Taylor brews delightful European-style beers, including a line of Czech-inspired lagers of a variety of colors and strengths. "I'm a cover band when it comes to brewing European styles," he says. But, ultimately, Taylor thinks that the future of his lager is in land beer. He is excited to expand his own land beer series, in which he uses raw materials from New York State. Our conversation continued over a bright, expressive lager called Seneca that prominently features New York-grown wheat. Pointing out that shipping raw materials around the globe is costly in more ways than one, Taylor says, "We are going to have to make agronomically sound decisions going forward." By learning about and brewing classic European styles, Taylor hopes to learn lager well enough to brew delightful land beer with locally grown and processed raw materials.

Lager Aged on Wood

While pitch lined wooden barrels to serve lager were once commonplace, the labor and care required for this type of service has seen stainless steel vessels all but completely replace wood. Distinct from these "neutral" serving vessels, the practice of using unpitched wood to age and condition lager is becoming more popular among some craft lager brewers. Lager is now being fermented and aged in *foeders*, puncheons, and other wooden barrels that help to impart unique flavors to the finished beer. Lager aged this way can range from delicate expressions to over-the-top, intense oak-forward flavors. The vision of the brewer is important, as is the age and treatment of the wood. Learning how to present oak as an accent rather than a feature takes time and experience.

Another Brooklyn brewery, Threes Brewing, pioneered the foeder-aged lager, albeit unintentionally. The brewery's everyday Pilsner brand, Vliet, was initially used to fill a foeder as a way of taming the wood's fresh flavor, but the results were surprising enough to warrant further exploration. Head brewer Matt Levy and his team developed recipes and learned to use the wood of the foeder as part of the recipe and it is a significant flavor contributor. Levy describes how the foeder influences the beer, softening its bitterness, drying out the body, and adding a creaminess to the mouthfeel.

Many factors such as the size and age of the foeder will dictate how long a beer needs to sit on the wood to create the right flavor profile. New foeders might only need a few weeks' contact with the beer, whereas older foeders may need a few months. Levy suggests a slow ramp up in the amount of time beer sits on wood. The first few batches may not need much time in the wood, but as the wood ages more time will start to be required for a similar flavor impact. When only using a foeder for lagering, the cold aging slows the process and allows for a mellow wood character that isn't overpowering, especially after the first few aging cycles.

In Denver, Colorado, Cerebral Brewing uses foeders to ferment most of its lager beer. While owner and brewer Sean Buchan cites a few other American brewers as inspiration for initially trying this technique, he and his team have invested time and attention in the process to make it their own. Buchan employs steam sterilization to moderate the oak flavor imparted by the lightly toasted wood of the vessels used by Cerebral, prizing instead the soft, round character that oak contact imparts on the finished lager. Glycol-filled fins help moderate the temperature inside the foeders, and the beer is racked to a pressure-rated steel vessel for natural carbonation prior to packaging.

At Modist Brewing in Minneapolis, Minnesota, head brewer Jackson Greer believes that foeders are a key component of the brewery's lager program. Producing upward of 600 bbl. (roughly 700 hL) a year of wood-treated lager for sale in Modist's taproom and beyond requires active quality control. Beers aged in foeders are regularly tested to monitor the contribution of wood flavor. When the foeders were first used at Modist, that first lager only aged for one week before the wood character became very noticeable. After many uses, most of Modist's lagers spend four to five weeks in the foeders to achieve the right amount of wood character.

As Benjamin Neidhart of OEC Brewing in Connecticut puts it, to brew great lager with oak vessels "you have to knock the oak out of them." Neidhart makes sure to bump up the IBUs for foeder lagers to account for the extra time on wood. The result is a softened bitterness that lets the malt body shine.

For all brewers working with oak, and perhaps especially lager brewers, the use of wood presents some obvious risks. Contamination is a constant threat. Cleaning wood vessels is difficult and can usually only be accomplished with steam and hot water. Some mild chemicals may be used, particularly if there is a long period between fills. Temperature control is also difficult in wooden vessels, even those that are built with cooling jackets. Wood does possess natural insulating qualities, but oak vessels are not truly insulated, and it is challenging, if not impossible, to quickly and efficiently cool down beer.

With care and attention, wood contact presents an opportunity for brewers to explore new horizons. Lager may not be an obvious choice for oak character, but it can be a perfect medium for the simple expression of the subtleties of wood.

Serving Lager

Brewers are putting more and more thought into how their lager is presented to customers. Increasingly, there's a desire to apply as much care to the serving of lager as goes into the production of it. Some of these methods are rooted in European lager culture, while others forgo tradition completely.

The side-pull faucet, also known by its most common brand name, Lukr, has seen a surge in popularity in American lager breweries and taprooms. Czech tapsters partially open this graduated faucet to build pints with dense, wet foam before fully opening it to finish the pint quickly. Done properly, the tip is submerged for the second portion of the pour, and the entire motion is completed in seconds.

Side-pull faucets can also be used to pour beer with varying levels of foam, something of a specialty of Czech beer culture. Some American breweries offer these with their original Czech names, from the little *šnyt* to the everyday *hladinka*. In particular, the all-foam *mlíko*, or "milk pour," a pour that presents a creamy, sweet foam that fills most of the glass, has inspired many US breweries. In Philadelphia, the folks at Human Robot offer rod-shaped *Kölsch* glasses filled with foam as "milk tubes," little slurps of foam meant to be downed quickly.

Besides riffing on these established pours, the side-pull faucet does present beer service as an extension of the labor involved in making beer. The side-pull faucet is a fast-pouring device that can even be used to pour beer at stadiums, though it is often conflated with the concept of a slow pour.

Slow pouring beer is not a new concept, but it is exemplified by one beer in particular. Bierstadt Lagerhaus in Denver has served the delightful Slow Pour Pils the same way since the brewpub opened in 2016: poured over the course of five minutes into a paper-skirted, tubular stemmed glass, topped with a distinctly rocky and robust cap of foam. Founder and brewer Ashleigh Carter built this beer around the slow and intermittent pour she preferred for a hop-forward lager. The care and attention to detail in the presentation of Slow Pour Pils is an intentional echo of the thought that Ashleigh and her partner and husband Bill Eye put into their brewing process. The time built into the pour invites the consumer to ponder the beer's origins as it is methodically poured. That it has inspired so many copycats is evidence that the idea of applying precious time to the final step of a beer's preparation resonates with lager brewers.

Bierstadt Lagerhaus has another unusual quality, one from which an increasing number of US breweries are also taking inspiration: a limited product line. Surrounded by over a dozen breweries in a single square mile, Bierstadt's lineup of three year-round beers and up to three other lines is a perfect fit for the location. Ashleigh and Bill do not have to be everything to every customer, which gives them the freedom to focus on what they love to make.

It's not hard to view the emergence of small breweries serving limited selections as a positive trend, especially for the world of craft lager. A brewery with only a few offerings issues a challenge to its customers, inviting them to appreciate what the brewery does best without any compromise. By setting this kind of expectation, a brewery can focus on the quality of its beers without constantly trying to find the answer to "What's new?"

Daniel Suarez took a leap in 2022 when he reopened his Suarez Family Brewery taproom in Hudson, New York, with just a single draft beer available on site. It was as much an adaptation to the post-pandemic world as it was a devotion to the idea that focus requires limits by definition. In Suarez's bucolic taproom, overlooking farm fields that border onto low-slung mountains, the experience of savoring a single beer can be a transcendent one.

In some sense, one vision of craft lager's future in America can be seen in the form of many small breweries, each focusing on fewer high-quality choices. This is a challenge to the idea of unlimited choice, a gauntlet thrown down by breweries willing to be specialists rather than generalists.

Lager, and Beyond

We may well be awaiting the age of craft lager dominance for some time. Where lager will go, how it will taste, and who will be brewing it is anyone's guess, of course. Yet we believe that craft lager will continue to gain footholds in breweries, restaurants, and store shelves in the years to come. Looking at how we've come this far is instructive. We can certainly expect craft brewers to continue pushing the envelope, but the evolution of classic styles reveals some interesting hints too.

Perhaps the best example of how classic styles have evolved is *Münchner Helles*, or Munich Helles. The modern Munich Helles is a great example of how subtle changes over generations can add up over time. Fans of the style note that it has gradually lightened in body over generations, resulting in some modern iterations that bear a passing resemblance to the industrial pale lagers of the world. Yet on our travels around Germany, many brewers we spoke to were quick to point out that Helles is the fastest growing beer style in Germany, growing at the expense of even Pilsner and wheat beer. Once contained mainly to Munich and the surrounding areas, Helles is gaining ground even in Franconia, where previously its Bavarian origins had worked against it. That such a subtle, light beer as Helles is the fastest growing style in Germany is, in a way, the inverse to the story of craft beer in the US. The American craft beer market exploded as consumers increasingly sought bigger, hoppier, oftentimes darker brews, eschewing the trend of macrobreweries offering lighter, less bitter, and less filling beer.

The rebound and growth of lager in the American craft market is understood by some brewers as a particular reaction to the explosive growth of hazy IPA. The proliferation of this style resulted in a host of new brands all competing for consumers, a dangerous proposition for a beer with such a short shelf life. A growing number of consumers are retreating from these myriad options to the more familiar grounds of pale lager beer. This shift in consumer preference can only be a benefit to brewers of high-quality lager.

We may not recognize the lager of the next century, but we can be sure it will have a home wherever beer does. From traditional dark lagers, subtle pale lagers, and hop-focused craft lagers, the horizon for lager grows wider every day.

8

RECIPES

LAGER BEER SPANS A WIDE SENSORY SPECTRUM, FROM THE PALE AND SLIGHT TO THE HEFTY AND INTENSE. Within this range, the philosophies, opinions, and techniques of the brewers help shape these beers into their final forms. For any brewer, home or professional, brewing better lager means brewing lager consistently. Many a professional brewer will advise acolytes to brew and re-brew a recipe until the end beer matches the initial vision.

The contributors named within this chapter have kindly shared their recipes and processes. Where information on aspects such as specific mash regimens, acid additions, water profiles, or yeast strains was provided, we have included it here; just know that some recipes will be more detailed than others. Assume that hops are in T-90 pellet form unless otherwise stated.

A note about the most famous lager strain in the world, known colloquially as 34/70. Most yeast providers sell this strain under one name or another, though often by describing it as the "most commonly used lager strain in the world" to aid in its identification. Some of the most common options are given in table 8.1.

Table 8.1
Selected commercial yeast strains for use as "34/70" lager yeast

Commercial Strain ID	Manufacturer/Yeast Bank
"Frisinga" – TUM 34/70®	Technical University of Munich, Weihenstephan (the original yeast from TUM)
3470 German Lager	Brewing Science Institute (BSI)
W34/70	Hefebank Weihenstephan
SafLager™ W-34/70	Fermentis
L13 Global	Imperial Yeast
OYL-106 German Lager I	Omega Yeast Labs
WLP830 German Lager Yeast	White Labs

What follows are recipes from some of the world's oldest, best, and most interesting lager breweries. We hope something here inspires your own exploration.

Adjunct Pale Lagers

RIGGS BEER COMPANY AMERICAN LAGER

American Corn Lager

Contributed by Matt Riggs of Riggs Beer Company, Urbana, Illinois

Riggs Beer Company is the family business of Darin, Gail, Matt, and Caroline Riggs in Urbana, Illinois. They grow their own grains and supervise the malting, going on to use them to make lovely German-inspired beers. Their low-oil white corn (maize) was developed in a long-running experiment at the University of Illinois and thought to have no commercial use until the Riggs realized its unique potential in the brewhouse.

American Lager is a Midwestern American classic, brewed with six-row barley and low-oil white corn for a distinctly American flavor and unbeatable drinkability.

Batch volume:	5 US gallons (19 L)
Original gravity:	1.046 (11.5°P)
Final gravity:	1.008 (2.1°P)
Color:	3 SRM (5.9 EBC)
Bitterness:	17 IBU
Alcohol:	5.0% by volume

GRAIN BILL
Adjunct Mash

1 lb. 5 oz. (595 g)	six-row base malt
2 lb. (907 g)	corn (maize) – use a low-oil variety, if possible

Main Mash

5 lb. 12 oz. (2.6 kg)	six-row base malt

HOPS

0.3 oz. (9 g)	Magnum 14.0% AA @ 60 min.
0.2 oz. (6 g)	Crystal 3.5% AA @ 10 min.

WATER

When using water with high alkalinity, you can reduce total alkalinity to ≤150 ppm as $CaCO_3$ by adding distilled water. Add calcium salts to reach total Ca^{2+} levels of 100–150 ppm. Sulfate-to-chloride ratio should be close to 1:1.

YEAST
German lager yeast, 34/70 strain (see table 8.1, p. 243)

ADDITIONAL ITEMS
Lactic acid or sour wort should be used in the mash and toward the end of the boil to target pH 5.40 and pH 5.20, respectively.

BREWING INSTRUCTIONS
Adjunct mash: Mill the grains. Mix 1.25 gal. (4.7 L) of 167°F (75°C) strike water with 1 lb. 5 oz. (595 g) of the six-row and all the corn. That should bring the mash to about 154°F (68°C). Rest 15 minutes. Boil for 15 minutes to gelatinize the corn starch. (If using a direct fire kettle, continuously stir the adjunct mash to prevent scorching.)

Main mash: As the adjunct mash approaches 200°F (93°C), start the protein rest by mashing in (in a separate vessel) the remaining 5 lb. 12 oz. (2.6 kg) of six-row malt to hit a mash temp of 120°F (49°C). Once the adjunct mash has finished boiling for 15 minutes, combine the two mashes. Once combined, the total mash should reach about 149°F (65°C) (if needed, apply heat to hit this temperature). Rest 30 minutes. Then raise the temperature to 155°F (68°C) and rest 30 minutes. Raise to 168°F (76°C) and mash out.

Boil: Boil for 70 minutes, following the hops schedule.

Fermentation: Chill to 50°F (10°C), aerate the wort, and pitch the yeast. Ferment at 50°F (10°C) until gravity reaches 1.024 (6.1°P), then raise the temperature to 54°F (12°C) for 7 days. Chill beer and rack off the yeast.

Conditioning: Lager at 31°F (−0.5°C) for 1 month.

Carbonation: Carbonate to 2.8 volumes (5.5 g/L) CO_2.

ADDITIONAL NOTES
If using whole-kernel corn, you must grind it finely with a mill that can handle corn's hardness. Don't try milling corn with a malt mill. Feel free to substitute flaked corn for whole kernel. It just might not taste quite as good!

F.X. MATT UTICA CLUB 1933 PILSENER

Prohibition-Era Pilsner

Contributed by F.X. Matt Brewing Co. and Scott Grenier of Utica, New York.

F.X. Matt Brewing Co. is one of the oldest family-owned breweries in the US. Their Utica Club brand has had a storied past and has recently been growing for the brewery. This recipe is based on the 1933 recipe for Utica Club Pilsener, the first beer legally sold after Prohibition. The brewery still uses the same drum cooker for cereal grains, which almost mimics a decoction step.

Batch volume:	5 US gallons (19 L)
Original gravity:	1.047 (11.7°P)
Final gravity:	1.009 (2.2°P)
Color:	5 SRM (10 EBC)
Bitterness:	26 IBU
Alcohol:	5.0% by volume

GRAIN BILL

6.0 lb. (2.7 kg)	six-row pale malt
2.0 lb. (907 g)	flaked corn
1.0 lb. (454 g)	flaked rice
4 oz. (113 g)	Briess Caramel Malt 60L
Rice hulls	(optional lautering aid)

HOPS

0.50 oz. (14 g)	Saaz 3.5% AA @ first wort hop
0.75 oz. (21 g)	Cluster 6.5% AA @ 60 min.
0.50 oz. (14 g)	Saaz 3.5% AA @ 30 min.
0.50 oz. (14 g)	Saaz 3.5% AA @ 10 min.

WATER

Very soft water is treated with lactic or phosphoric acid to obtain a mash pH of 5.4 and a sparge pH <5.8. Calcium chloride is added to the mash and boil to achieve 60 ppm Ca^{2+}. Burton Salt was originally used for water adjustment at a rate of 3.5 g/gal. (0.9 g/L) for all water included in the mash and sparge.

YEAST

German lager yeast, 34/70 strain (see table 8.1, p. 243),
or
Wyeast 2035-PC American Lager

ADDITIONAL ITEMS

½× Whirlfloc tablet @ 10 min.

BREWING INSTRUCTIONS

Mash: Single-infusion mash for 60 minutes at 151°F (66°C), then 10 minutes at 168°F (76°C). Add first wort hops to the kettle as wort from the mash is transferred following mashout.

Cereal mash option: A 90-minute cereal mash can also be used, substituting corn grits/polenta and non-enriched white rice in place of the flaked grains. Remember to add first wort hops to the kettle following mashout.

0 min:	In a separate vessel, mash in corn, rice, and one-third of malt at 153°F (67°C).
20 min:	In the main mash tun, mash in remaining six-row and caramel malt at 104°F (40°C).
25 min:	Bring the cereal mash to a boil.
35 min:	Increase main mash to 145°F (63°C).
65 min:	Add cereal mash to main mash and adjust temperature to 158°F (70°C).
85 min:	Increase combined mash temperature to 168°F (76°C) and mash out.

Boil: 90 minutes.

Fermentation: Pitch at 48°F (9°C), hold at 50°F (10°C) for 5 days, then raise to 60°F (16°C) for a three-day diacetyl rest. Chill and rack off the yeast.

Conditioning: Lager 4–6 weeks at 34°F (1°C).

Carbonation: Carbonate to 2.6 volumes (5.1 g/L) CO_2.

PFRIEM JAPANESE LAGER
Rice Lager
Contributed by Josh Pfriem

Nestled along the spectacular Columbia River in the town of Hood River, Oregon, pFriem Family Brewers is surely one of the most scenic places to enjoy craft lager in the US. Melding an appreciation for European tradition and technique with a Pacific Northwest flair, pFriem's exploration of lager beer has stretched beyond its classic Central European origins. This award-winning Japanese-style lager combines delicate floral aromatics with a snappy, satisfying finish.

Batch volume:	5 US gallons (19 L)
Original gravity:	1.044 (11°P)
Final gravity:	1.007 (1.7°P)
Color:	2 SRM (3.7 EBC)
Bitterness:	17 IBU
Alcohol:	4.9% by volume

GRAIN BILL
Adjunct Mash

1 lb. 5 oz. (595 g)	rice grits
5 oz. (142 g)	US Pilsner malt

Main Mash

2 lb. 14.5 oz. (1.32 kg)	German Pilsner malt
2 lb. 2.5 oz. (978 g)	US Pilsner malt

HOPS

0.21 oz. (6 g)	German Magnum 15% AA @ 10 min.
0.21 oz. (6 g)	Willamette 4.5% AA @ 10 min.
0.29 oz. (8 g)	Hersbrucker 2.5% AA @ whirlpool
0.08 oz. (2 g)	Hersbrucker 2.5% AA @ whirlpool

YEAST
German lager yeast, 34/70 strain (see table 8.1, p. 243)

BREWING INSTRUCTIONS

Adjunct mash: Using a boil kettle as a mash-lauter tun, combine rice grits and 5 oz. of Pilsner malt at a liquor-to-grist ratio of 3.5 L/kg. Heat to 195°F (91°C) and cook for 20 minutes to gelatinize starch.

Main mash: Mash in the remaining malt into the same vessel with a cold strike temperature (Josh says they use a strike temperature of 128°F, or 53°C). When combined, the total mash should be 144°F (62°C); rest for 21 minutes. Step up the mash temperature to 154°F (68°C) and rest for 27 minutes. Mash out at 174°F (79°C).

Boil: 80 minutes

Fermentation: Ferment at 54°F (12°C); raise to 62°F (17°C) for a diacetyl rest once the gravity reaches 1.018 (4.5°P).

Conditioning: Lager for 6 weeks at 35°F (2°C).

Carbonation: Carbonate to 2.7 volumes (5.3 g/L) CO_2.

German-Inspired Pale Lagers

GOLDFINGER ORIGINAL LAGER

Helles-Style Lager

Contributed by Thomas Beckmann of Goldfinger Brewing Company, Downers Grove, Illinois

Goldfinger Brewing Company gets its name from Thomas Beckmann's ancestor Markus Goldfinger, who operated a brewery and brewery manufacturing company in Poland and Czechia in the nineteenth century. Today, Beckmann and his team brew a concise list of delicious lagers that evoke the best lagers from central Europe. Goldfinger uses an assortment of mash regimens for its beers, using a single decoction step on the brewery's Original Lager. In this recipe, Beckmann provides a simpler mash regimen for the homebrewer.

Batch Volume:	5 US gallons (19 L)
Original Gravity:	1.048 (12°P)
Final Gravity:	1.009 (2.3°P)
Color:	2.9 SRM (5.7 EBC)
Bitterness:	18 IBU
Alcohol:	5.2% by volume

GRAIN BILL

8 lb. 5oz. (3.77 kg)	Weyermann Pilsner Malt
5.5 oz. (156 g)	Weyermann Acidulated Malt (adjust depending on mash pH)

HOPS

0.50 oz. (14 g)	Hallertauer Mittelfrüh 5% AA @ 60 min.
0.75 oz. (21 g)	Hallertauer Mittelfrüh 5% AA @ 15 min.
0.75 oz. (21 g)	Hallertauer Mittelfrüh 5% AA @ 5 min.

WATER

Ca^{2+} 60 ppm, Mg^{2+} 5 ppm, Na^+ 10 ppm, Cl^- 95 ppm, SO_4^{2-} 55 ppm, HCO_3^- 0 ppm

YEAST

German lager yeast, 34/70 strain (see table 8.1, p. 243)

ADDITIONAL ITEMS

1× Whirlfloc tablet @ 10 min.

BREWING INSTRUCTIONS

Multistep mash option: First rest 45 minutes at 143°F (62°C); second rest 15 minutes at 152°F (67°C); third rest 20 minutes at 161°F (72°C). Mash out.

Infusion option: Single-infusion mash for 80 minutes at 150°F (66°C).

Boil: 90 minutes

Fermentation: Ferment 10 days at 48°F (9°C), then raise to 60°F (16°C) for a three-day diacetyl rest. Transfer to secondary vessel.

Conditioning: Lager 5 weeks at 34°F (1°C).

Carbonation: Carbonate to 2.6 volumes (5.1 g/L) CO_2.

RIEGELE FEINES URHELL

Helles Lager

Contributed by Frank Müller and Sebastian Priller-Riegele,
Brauhaus Riegele, Augsburg, Germany

Augsburg's Brauhaus Riegele is in its 28th generation of family ownership, being run today by Sebastian Benedikt Priller-Riegele. In a long history dating back to the fourteenth century, Brauhaus Riegele has won much acclaim, and today operates a beautiful 235-hectoliter copper-clad brewhouse. Riegele still uses many traditional brewing practices, at least one of which is completely their own—the brewers ensure happy yeast by playing Beethoven in the lager cellar. Riegele also has an enormous catalog of 206 yeast strains that are unique to the brewery. Some of its beers use up to three strains at once.

Batch volume:	5 US gallons (19 L)
Original gravity:	1.047 (11.6°P)
Final gravity:	1.007 (1.8°P)
Color:	3 SRM (6 EBC)
Bitterness:	25 IBU
Alcohol:	4.8% by volume

GRAIN BILL

4 lb. 10 oz. (2.10 kg)	Pilsner malt
4 lb. 10 oz. (2.10 kg)	Steffi Pilsner malt

HOPS

0.25 oz. (7 g)	Opal 8.9% AA @ 70 min.
0.38 oz. (11 g)	Hersbrucker 3% AA @ 30 min.
0.50 oz. (14 g)	Hallertauer Mittelfrüh 7% AA @ 5 min.
0.50 oz. (14 g)	Saaz 8% AA @ 5 min.
0.50 oz. (14 g)	Spalter Select 8% AA @ 5 min.

YEAST

Riegele UY House Yeast
(The Riegele house strain is a Frohberg yeast strain, so substitute your favorite 34/70 German lager yeast—see table 8.1, p. 243.)

WATER

Ca^{2+} 150 ppm, Mg^{2+} 10 ppm, Na^+ 12 ppm, SO_4^{2-} 224 ppm, Cl^- 15 ppm, HCO_3^- 10 ppm.

BREWING INSTRUCTIONS

Decoction mash: Use a double-decoction mash method. Mash in at 122°F (50°C), then raise the mash temperature of the entire mash to 149°F (65°C). Take the first decoction portion and raise it to 162°F (72°C), then raise to 208°F (98°C) for a short time (don't boil). Return the first decoction back to the mash tun, which should raise the entire mash temperature to 153°F (67°C). Take the second decoction and raise it to 162°F (72°C), then to 208°F (98°C) for a short time (don't boil). Return the second decoction back to the mash, which should raise the entire mash to 162°F (72°C).

Rest for 15 minutes and then raise the temperature to 167°F (75°C) for 10 minutes. Raise the mash temperature the final time to 172°F (78°C).

Boil: 70 minutes.

Fermentation: Ferment for around 7 days at 46°F (8°C). When gravity hits 1.011 (2.8°P), cool down to 41°F (5°C) and add a spunding valve.

Conditioning: Once terminal gravity has been reached, lager for about 4 weeks at 32–35°F (0–2°C).

SEITZ-BRAU HALLERTAUER HOF-BIER HELL

Landbier

Contributed by Georg Seitz, Seitzfarm, Wolnzach, Germany

This is a house beer recipe from an upcoming brewery in the hop growing region of the Hallertau. The Seitz family are multi-generational hop farmers (*see* pp. 72–73) who have designs on opening a small brewery on their property. They've already added a private taproom with a lovely collection of beer coasters from around the globe and have been steadily collecting equipment for the brewery.

Batch volume:	5 US gallons (19 L)
Original gravity:	1.048 (12.0°P)
Final gravity:	1.011 (2.8°P)
Color:	6 SRM (12 EBC)
Bitterness:	25 IBU
Alcohol:	5.1% by volume

GRAIN BILL

7 lb. 11 oz. (3.49 kg)	Pilsner malt
0.67 oz. (19 g)	acidulated malt (depending on mash pH)

HOPS

0.90 oz. (26 g)	Hersbrucker 2.7% AA @ 70 min.
0.40 oz. (11 g)	Hersbrucker 2.7% AA @ 35 min.
0.23 oz. (7 g)	Hallertauer Mittelfrüh 3.6% AA @ 35 min.
0.47 oz. (13 g)	Hallertauer Mittelfrüh 3.6% AA @ 5 min.
0.67 oz. (19 g)	Hallertauer Mittelfrüh (whole cones) 3.6% AA, added in the hop back while knocking out into the coolship. If you don't have a hop back or coolship, hops can be added at the end of boil—proceed immediately to alternative cooling instructions.

YEAST

German lager yeast, 34/70 strain (see table 8.1, p. 243)

BREWING INSTRUCTIONS

Mash: Mash in at 126°F (52°C) and immediately heat up to 144°F (62°C) and rest for 30 minutes. Heat up to 162°F (72°C) and rest for 20 minutes. Remove a portion of the mash for decoction and boil it for 5 minutes, then return it to the main mash.

Boil: 70 minutes.

Cooling: After 2-hour coolship rest, cool wort to 8°C (46.5°F).

Alternatively, if you don't have a coolship setup, chill the wort to 180°F (82°C), rest for 2 hours or until temperature falls to 150°F (65.5°C), whichever is slower, and then chill and transfer to the fermentor.

Fermentation: Pitch yeast at 46–47°F (8°C) and set the fermentation temperature to 49°F (9.5°C). Ferment for 5–6 days until gravity falls to 4.5–5.0°P (1.018–1.020 SG).

Conditioning: Transfer to secondary lagering tank and slowly cool down via indirect cooling to 36°F (2°C). Lager for about 3–4 weeks.

Carbonation: Adjust spunding valve on the secondary lagering tank to reach approx. 2.5 volumes (4.9 g/L) CO_2.

JACK'S ABBY POST SHIFT

Bavarian-Style Pilsner

Contributed by Jack Hendler and Joe Connolly, Jack's Abby Craft Lagers, Framingham, Massachusetts

When we founded Jack's Abby there was no Pilsner in our lineup. Post Shift was born after a few years of selling lager in New York City, where Pilsner still reigns supreme. It's grown to be a core part of our portfolio, and one of a handful of Pilsners we brew. This beer was developed with inspiration from a trip to the Seitz hop farm (pp. 72–73), where we fell in love with Hallertau Blanc.

Batch volume:	5 US gallons (19 L)
Original gravity:	1.045 (11.2°P)
Final gravity:	1.008 (2.2°P)
Color:	2 SRM (4 EBC)
Bitterness:	38 IBU
Alcohol:	4.7% by volume

GRAIN BILL

7 lb. 8 oz. (3.4 kg)	Pilsner malt

HOPS

0.18 oz. (5 g)	Hersbrucker 5.5% AA @ first wort hop
0.27 oz. (8 g)	Hallertau Blanc 11.5% AA @ first wort hop
0.15 oz. (4 g)	Hallertau Blanc 11.5% AA @ 60 min.
0.16 oz. (4.5 g)	Hallertau Blanc 11.5% AA @ whirlpool
0.37 oz. (10.5 g)	Hersbrucker 5.5% AA @ whirlpool

For an Italian Pils version, also add:

1.0 oz. (28 g)	Hersbrucker 5.5% AA @ dry hop
1.0 oz. (28 g)	Hallertau Blanc 11.5% AA @ dry hop

YEAST

German lager yeast, 34/70 strain (see table 8.1, p. 243)

WATER

Add calcium sulfate to 50 ppm SO_4^{2-}. Add lactic acid to hit mash pH 5.4. Add lactic acid to the whirlpool to hit wort pH 5.1.

BREWING INSTRUCTIONS

Step mash option: Use a step mash to maximize saccharification rests for high attenuation (p.154). Mash in at 148°F (64.5°C) with a water-to-grist ratio of 3 L/kg. This is the β-amylase rest. Rest for 45 minutes, then add 1 part boiling water to raise the temperature to 158°F (70°C) for 30 minutes. This is the α-amylase rest.

Decoction option: Use same rest temperatures as in step-mash option but employ a single-decoction method. Pull approximately 25% of the mash for a decoction portion and boil for 15 minutes. Then add back to main mash to raise temperature to the next step. Decoct either from (a) the β- to α-amylase rest or (b) α-amylase to mashout temperature. Have each rest be 30 minutes.

Infusion mash option: A single-infusion mash can be used. Mash in at 149°F (65°C) for 60 minutes.

Boil: 60 minutes.

Fermentation: Pitch yeast at 46°F (8°C), set fermentation temperature to 48°F (9°C). When the beer reaches terminal gravity, rack to a secondary tank and cool to 40°F (4°C) for about 10 days. Then cool to 33°F (1°C) for two weeks before packaging.

Carbonation: Carbonate to 2.7 volumes (5.3 g/L) CO_2.

WEIHENSTEPHANER HELLES

Helles Lager

Contributors: *Tobias Zollo, Brewmaster and Head Brewer, Bavarian State Brewery Weihenstephan; Matthias Ebner, Brewing Engineer and Brand Ambassador International, Bavarian State Brewery Weihenstephan*

From the "oldest brewery in the world," this bright Helles takes inspiration from the late Prof. Dr. Ludwig Narziß. Dr. Narziß was a Bavarian brewing legend who taught at the Technical University of Munich and advised generation after generation of brewers at Weihenstephan. He was a world-renowned beer scholar whose works are frequently cited, including in these pages. The current generation of Weihenstephan brewers created a unique Helles recipe that incorporates the teachings and philosophy of Dr. Narziß.

Batch volume:	5 US gallons (19 L)
Original gravity:	1.048 (11.8°P)
Final gravity:	1.011 (2.75°P)
Color:	pale
Bitterness:	25 IBU
Alcohol:	5.1% by volume

GRAIN BILL

7 lb. 14 oz. (3.57 kg)	Pilsner malt (two-row summer barley)

HOPS

0.22 oz. (6 g)	Perle 8.0% AA @ 70 min.
0.35 oz. (10 g)	Hallertauer Tradition 5.0% AA @ 35 min.
0.27 oz. (8 g)	Hersbrucker 5.5% AA @ 5 min.

YEAST

German lager yeast, 34/70 strain (see table 8.1, p. 243)
(The brewers at Weihenstephan use "Frisinga" – TUM 34/70)

BREWING INSTRUCTIONS

Decoction mash: Use a double-decoction mash method.

1. Mash in at 140°F (60°C). Raise mash temperature to 147°F (64°C) and rest for 10 minutes. Keep main mash at 147°F (64°C) for duration of first decoction.
2. Take first decoction (30% of volume).
3. Heat up decoction from 147°F (64°C) to 162°F (72°C) and rest it for 30 minutes.
4. Heat up from 162°F (72°C) to 203°F (95°C) and rest it for 10 minutes.
5. Return the 203°F (95°C) decocted portion back to main mash to target 154.5°F (68°C).
6. Rest main mash at 154.5°F (68°C) for 30 minutes. Keep main mash at 154.5°F (68°C) for duration of second decoction.
7. Take second decoction (30% of volume).
8. Heat up second decoction from 154.5°F (68°C) to 162°F (72°C) and rest it for 30 minutes.
9. Heat up from 162°F (72°C) to 203°F (95°C) and rest it for 10 minutes.
10. Return the 203°F (95°C) decocted portion back to main mash to target 167°F (75°C).
11. Rest main mash at 167°F (75°C) for 10 minutes. Vorlauf and then run off. The first wort runnings should be around 16°P.

Boil: 70 minutes.

Fermentation: Ferment at 50°F (10°C) for 5–7 days. Fermentation is done when gravity falls below 1.012 (3°P)—target a terminal gravity of 1.011 (2.75°P). Once fermentation is finished, transfer beer directly to a secondary for conditioning/maturation.

Conditioning: Keep at 45°F (7°C) for a diacetyl rest (typically, diacetyl should be gone after 10 days). Cool from 45°F (7°C) to 32°F (0°C) over 48 hours. Keep at 32°F (0°C) within ±2°F (±1°C) for 30 days in horizontal maturation tanks.

Carbonation: Spund beer after racking to a secondary lagering tank and set for approx. 7.25 psig (0.5 bar gauge) to target 2.53 volumes (5 g/L) CO_2.

Czech-Inspired Pale Lagers

BŘEVNOV MONASTIC BREWERY BENEDICT PALE LAGER

Pilsner-Style Pale Lager (Světlý Ležák)

Contributed by Aleš Potěšil, Břevnovský klášterní pivovar, Prague

Though the current Břevnovský klášterní pivovar was founded in 2011, it resides on the site of the Břevnov monastery in Prague where there has been a history of brewing since the monastery's founding back in 993, making it one of the oldest brewery traditions in the world. The brewery performs decoctions and some open fermentations, but also produces American-inspired craft beer for its network of pubs. The Benedict Pale Lager (Světlý Ležák Benedict) is round, spicy, and demanding of second and third sips.

Batch volume:	5 US gallons (19 L)
Original gravity:	1.050 (12.5°P)
Final gravity:	1.012 (3.15°P)
Color:	5.6 SRM (11 EBC)
Bitterness:	34 IBU
Alcohol:	5.0% by volume

GRAIN BILL

7 lb. 12 oz. (3.52 kg)	two-row Pilsner malt
0.05 oz (1.5 g)	black malt, 500° Lovibond (1,300 EBC)

HOPS

0.25 oz. (7.1 g)	Saaz 4.7% AA @ first wort hops
0.35 oz. (10 g)	Saaz 3.5% AA @ first wort hops
0.26 oz. (7.5 g)	Saaz 4.7% AA @ 90 min.
0.26 oz. (7.5 g)	Saaz 4.7% AA @ 80 min.
0.36 oz. (10.2 g)	Saaz 3.5% AA @ 80 min.
0.40 oz. (11.5 g)	Saaz 3.5% AA @ 75 min.
0.21 oz. (6.0 g)	Saaz 3.5% AA @ whirlpool

WATER
Ca^{2+} 31.5 mg/L, Mg^{2+} 8 mg/L, SO_4^{2-} 43.5 mg/L, Cl^- 23.3 mg/L, Hardness 112 mg/L as $CaCO_3$.
Acidify sparge water to pH of 6.6.

YEAST
Pilsner yeast H7, or homebrewers may consider WY2001 or OYL-101.

BREWING INSTRUCTIONS
Decoction mash: Use a double-decoction method. Mash in at 99°F (37°C) and rest for 10 minutes. Heat mash to 126°F (53°C) and immediately take a decoction portion, approximately 1.5 gal. (5.7 L). Raise the decoction portion to 145°F (63°C) for 15 minutes, then to 162°F (72°C) for 15 minutes, then boil for 15 minutes. Return the decoction to the main mash, which should bring the temperature of the combined mash to 145°F (63°C).

Take the second decoction, approximately 1.75 gal. (6.6 L), and raise to 162°F (72°C) for 15 minutes, then bring to a boil for 15 minutes. Return the second decoction to the main mash. Vorlauf the combined mash and start the runoff.

Boil: 90 minutes.
Fermentation: Ferment 10 days at 50°F (10°C).
Conditioning: Lager for 4 weeks at 37°F (3°C).
Carbonation: Carbonate to 2.5 volumes (4.9 g/L) CO_2.

LIVE OAK PILZ

Czech-Style Pilsner

Contributed by Dusan Kwiatkowski , Head Brewer, Live Oak Brewing Company, Austin, Texas

Live Oak Brewing Company has long been a stalwart of the American craft lager scene. Chip McElroy had to work to get Moravian malt imported in the 1990s to brew his Czech-style Pilsner, inadvertently creating an export market for Czech maltsters in the process. For a modern-built brewery, Live Oak exhibits a dedication to process and tradition that is remarkable. The brewhouse installed in 2015 is custom built for mash and decoction flexibility. The brewery's flagship Pilz is a classic, endlessly drinkable but with enough complexity to capture a drinker's attention. A traditional decocted Czech Pilsner recipe with Czech malt, hops, and yeast. (The malt and hop quantities were estimated based on the recipe specifications supplied by Live Oak.)

Batch Volume:	5 US gallons (19 L)
Original Gravity:	1.046 (11.5°P)
Final Gravity:	1.010 (2.6°P)
Color:	4.5 SRM (9 EBC)
Bitterness:	40 IBU
Alcohol:	4.7% by volume

GRAIN BILL (BASED ON 75% EXTRACT EFFICIENCY)

8 lb. 4 oz. (3.74 kg)	Moravian Pilsner malt, undermodified

HOPS

1.25 oz. (35 g)	Sladek / Saaz 3.5% AA @ 60 min. for 20 IBU
0.62 oz. (18 g)	Sladek / Saaz 3.5% AA @ 15 min. for 10 IBU
0.62 oz. (18 g)	Sladek / Saaz 3.5% AA @ 5 min. for 10 IBU
0.25–1.00 oz. (7–28 g)	Sladek / Saaz 3.5% AA @ flameout – add qty. to reach your desired aroma level

YEAST

Wyeast 2278 Czech Pils or other Czech lager yeast strain.

WATER

Austin water, carbon filtered. Use lactic acid for pH adjustments.
At the end of the boil adjust wort pH to 5.1–5.2.

BREWING INSTRUCTIONS

Decoction mash: Use a double-decoction method. The volume of mash to split off may vary slightly based on the ability of your cooker to hold the temperature of the resting portion.

1. Mash in and rest at 122°F (50°C) for 15 minutes. Heat to 144°F (62°C). Adjust mash pH to 5.4–5.5.
2. For the first decoction, decoct 20% of the mash.
3. Heat decoction portion to 158°F (70°C) and rest for 10 minutes.
4. Heat decoction portion to boiling and boil for 30 minutes.
5. Return the boiled decocted portion back to the main mash to target 154.5°F (68°C).
6. Rest main mash at 154.5°F (68°C) for 20 minutes. Heat to 162°F (72°C) and rest for 10 minutes.
7. For the second decoction, decoct 15% of the mash.
8. Heat decoction portion to boiling and boil for 30 minutes.
9. Return boiled decocted portion back to main mash to target 172°F (78°C).
10. Begin vorlauf. Lauter first wort to kettle. Adjust sparge water pH to maintain 4.4–4.5 wort pH as you fill the kettle. When full, adjust wort pH to 5.3–5.4.

Boil: 80 minutes. Follow hops schedule.

Chill: When boil is finished, chill wort to 46°F (8°C) and aerate before pitching.

Fermentation: Pitch lager yeast, 2.5×10^6 cells per ml, and raise temperature to 48°F (9°C). When gravity hits 1.024 (6°P) conduct a diacetyl rest, warming to as much as 57°F (14°C). At about gravity 1.014 (~3.5°P), begin cooling to 39°F (4°C).

Conditioning: Transfer to a horizontal conditioning tank and lager at 39°F (4°C) for 2 weeks, then lager at 34°F (1°C) for 4 weeks.

Carbonation: Carbonate to 2.7 volumes (5.3 g/L) CO_2. Serve in a dimple mug poured with a lot of foam.

COHESION 12° – PALE CZECH LAGER

Czech-Style Pilsner

Contributed by Eric Larkin, Cohesion Brewing Company, Denver, Colorado

Cohesion Brewing Company's beers exhibit the rustic, hand-hewn quality of smaller Czech breweries, but from an American perspective. Not only does the Denver-based brewery use locally-grown malt made to its specifications, it employs triple decoctions, open and horizontal fermentation tanks, and natural carbonation in the production of its lagers. Cohesion's brewers apply this philosophy to the production of all manner of Czech styles, including many pale lagers with varying degrees of strength. The differences between these subtly distinct beers is impressive, especially when appreciated with varying degrees of custom foam in the tradition of Czech draft beer service.

Says owner and brewer Eric Larkin about this světlý ležák (pale lager), "This was a pale lager recipe that played into some of the more traditional elements we've found in Czech pale lagers."

Batch volume:	5 US gallons (19 L)
Original gravity:	1.048 (12°P)
Final gravity:	1.013 (3.25°P)
Color:	5 SRM (10 EBC)
Bitterness:	43 IBU
Alcohol:	4.8% by volume

GRAIN BILL

9 lb. (4.08 kg)	floor-malted Pilsner malt
8 oz. (227 g)	caramel malt 20L

HOPS

0.5 oz. (14 g)	Premiant 7.0% AA @ 90 min.
0.5 oz. (14 g)	Premiant 5.5% AA @ 60 min.
1.0 oz. (28 g)	Saaz, whole cone, 3.5% AA @ whirlpool

WATER

Ca^{2+} 7 ppm, Mg^{2+} 3 ppm, Na^+ 2 ppm, SO_4^{2-} 5 ppm, Cl^- 5 ppm, HCO_3^- 25 ppm.

YEAST

Inland Island INIS-760 Czech Lager, Wyeast 2278 Czech Pils, or other favorite Czech lager yeast

BREWING INSTRUCTIONS

Decoction mash: Use a triple-decoction mash method.

1. Mash in at 105°F (40.5°C) and rest 30 minutes.
2. Take first decoction, roughly one-third of mash, and transfer to the kettle.
3. Heat up decoction to 145°F (63°C) and rest 10 minutes.
4. Heat up decoction to boiling and boil for 20 minutes.
5. Return boiled decocted portion to main mash to target a rest temperature of 125°F (52°C).
6. Rest main mash at 125°F (52°C) for 20 minutes.
7. Take second decoction, roughly one-third of mash, and transfer to the kettle.
8. Heat second decoction to 145°F (63°C) and rest 10 minutes.
9. Heat up decoction to boiling and boil for 20 minutes.
10. Return boiled decocted portion to main mash to target a rest temperature of 145°F (63°C).
11. Rest the whole mash at 145°F (63°C) for 30 minutes.
12. Take third and final decoction, roughly one-third of mash, and transfer to the kettle.
13. Heat the third decoction to boiling and let boil for 20 minutes.
14. Return boiled decocted portion to main mash to target a mashout temperature of 168°F (76°C).

Boil: 90 minutes.

Fermentation: Ferment 7 days at 48°F (9°C). When gravity is within roughly 4–8 degrees specific gravity (1°–2° Plato) of final gravity, spund the fermentation vessel to capture natural carbonation at 2.3 volumes CO_2. During the spunded stage raise the temperature to 51°F (10.6°C) for diacetyl rest.

Conditioning: Lager 4 weeks at 34°F (1°C).

Carbonation: Adjust spunding valve to target 2.3 volumes (4.5 g/L) CO_2.

Copper to Brown Lagers

RITTMAYER KELLERBIER
Kellerbier
Contributed by Georg Rittmayer and Kevin Düsel,
Brauerei Rittmayer, Hallerndorf

Claiming a history beginning in 1422, the Rittmayer brewery is located just south of Bamberg in Franconia. Owner Georg Rittmayer not only leads the brewery but is also the president of Private Brauereien, a trade organization representing Bavarian brewers. Rittmayer and his brewmaster, Kevin Düsel, operate a regional brewery that also runs a contract filling operation that allows many smaller breweries in the area to bottle their beer. This Franconian Kellerbier is full-bodied, with light fruity esters and a malty sweet finish.

Batch volume:	5 US gallons (19 L)
Original gravity:	1.051 (12.7°P)
Final gravity:	1.010 (2.6°P)
Color:	16–17 SRM (31.5–33.5 EBC)
Bitterness:	12.6 IBU
Alcohol:	5.1% by volume

GRAIN BILL
5 lb. 12 oz. (2.6 kg)	Munich malt
1 lb. 8 oz. (670 g)	Pilsner malt
4.2 oz. (120 g)	IREKS Crystal Rosewood (or Weyermann CaraMunich Type 2)
4.2 oz. (120 g)	IREKS Crystal Mahogany (or Weyermann CaraMunich Type 1)

HOPS
0.32 oz. (9 g)	Perle 8% AA @ 60 min.
0.15 oz. (4 g)	Tettnanger 6% AA @ 30 min.

YEAST
German lager yeast, 34/70 strain (see table 8.1, p. 243)

BREWING INSTRUCTIONS

Decoction mash: Use a double-decoction mash method. Using a boil kettle as a mash tun, mash in at 126°F (52°C) and rest for 10 minutes. Heat up the mash to 144°F (62°C) and rest for 5 minutes. Transfer two-thirds of the mash to a lauter tun. Bring the remaining one-third of the mash to the boil and add it slowly back to the rest of the mash in the lauter tun. Rest the main mash at 163°F (73°C) for 25 minutes. Transfer one-fifth of the mash back to the kettle and bring it to the boil. Then add the boiling portion slowly back to the rest of the mash. Rest at mashout temperature for 10 minutes, then start lautering.

Fermentation: Ferment 7 days at 48°F (9°C); once it hits terminal gravity leave the beer for a three-day diacetyl rest.

Conditioning: Lager 4 weeks at 34°F (1°C).

Carbonation: Carbonate to 2.6 volumes (5.2 g/L) CO_2.

BRANDHOLZ BRAUEREI GOLDEN BROWN

Franconian Märzen Lager

Contributed by Christian Grasser, Brandholz Brauerei, Melkendorf, Litzendorf

Brandholz Brauerei, in the small Franconian town of Melkendorf, operates as a hobby brewery by some moonlighting brewery manufacturers. The friends who operate Brandholz use the site of the old brewery at the center of the village, which had fallen into disrepair. Now refurbished by the Brandholz brewers, it is typically opened to visitors a few times a month. Golden Brown, Brandholz's amber lager, is one of those Franconian beers that is hard to classify. Brewing it involves a 12-hour coolship rest. It may be hard to classify, but it is easy to drink.

Batch volume:	5 US gallons (19 L)
Original gravity:	1.055 (13.5°P)
Final gravity:	1.014 (3.5°P)
Color:	9 SRM (17.7 EBC)
Bitterness:	28 IBU
Alcohol:	5.8% by volume

GRAIN BILL

5 lb. 8 oz. (2.5 kg)	Vienna malt
4 lb. 7 oz. (2.0 kg)	Pilsner malt
2 lb. 3 oz. (1.0 kg)	Munich malt

HOPS

0.18 oz. (5 g)	Hallertauer Tradition 8% AA @ first wort hop
0.18 oz. (5 g)	Perle 8% AA @ first wort hop
0.18 oz. (5 g)	Hallertauer Tradition 8% AA @ 60 min.
0.18 oz. (5 g)	Perle 8% AA @ 60 min.
0.18 oz. (5 g)	Hallertauer Tradition 8% AA @ 30 min.
0.18 oz. (5 g)	Perle 8% AA @ 30 min.
0.35 oz. (10 g)	Spalter Select 6% AA @ whirlpool

YEAST

German lager yeast, 34/70 strain (see table 8.1, p. 243)

BREWING INSTRUCTIONS

Decoction mash: Use a single-decoction method. Mash in at 126°F (52°C), no rest; raise mash temperature to 144°F (62°C) and rest for 10 minutes. Remove one-third of the mash for the decoction. Raise the decoction portion to 153°F (67°C) and hold for 10 minutes, then raise to 162°F (72°C) and hold for 15 minutes, then raise to 208°F (98°C) and hold for 10 minutes. Return the decocted portion back to the main mash—the total mash should hit 162°F (72°C). Immediately heat to a final mash temperature of 169°F (76°C).

Boil: 60 minutes.

Cooling: Transfer for 12-hour coolship rest.

Alternatively, if you don't have a coolship setup, chill the wort to 180°F (82°C), rest for 2 hours or until temperature falls to 150°F (65.5°C), whichever is slower, then chill and transfer to the fermentor.

Fermentation: Pitch yeast at 46–47°F (8°C); set the temperature during fermentation to 54°F (12°C).

UTEPILS BREWING BROOMSTACKER

Red Lager

Contributed by Eric Harper, Utepils Brewing, Minneapolis, Minnesota

Utepils Brewing in Minneapolis, Minnesota, gets its name from a Norwegian word (pronounced "OOH-ta-pilz") describing something familiar to all who live in colder climes: the first beer enjoyed outside after a long winter. If that beer is an Utepils, consider yourself lucky. The brewery's broad range of European-inspired lagers and ales explore many delightful and delicious corners of beer culture. Broomstacker is named for the curling tradition of laying down your brooms and sharing a drink with your opponent after the game.

Batch volume:	5 US gallons (19 L)
Original gravity:	1.055 (13.6°P)
Final gravity:	1.010 (2.6°P)
Color:	21 SRM (41.4 EBC)
Bitterness:	41 IBU
Alcohol:	5.9% by volume

GRAIN BILL

8 lb. 2 oz. (3.69 kg)	Weyermann Pilsner Malt
14.4 oz. (408 g)	Weyermann CaraRed
14.4 oz. (408 g)	Simpsons Crystal Medium
14.4 oz. (408 g)	Briess Victory Malt

HOPS

0.75 oz. (21 g)	Cascade 6.5% AA @ 70 min.
0.30 oz. (9 g)	Cascade 6.5% AA @ 30 min.
0.30 oz. (9 g)	Hallertauer Mittelfrüh 4.0% AA @ 30 min.
0.40 oz. (11 g)	Cascade 6.5% AA @ 15 min.
0.40 oz. (11 g)	Hallertauer Mittelfrüh 4.0% AA @ 15 min.
0.75 oz. (21 g)	Hallertauer Mittelfrüh 4.0% AA @ 0 min.

WATER

Ca^{2+} 90 ppm, Mg^{2+} 12 ppm, Na^+ 45 ppm, Cl^- 82 ppm, SO_4^{2-} 65 ppm, HCO_3^- 223 ppm.

YEAST

German lager yeast, 34/70 strain (see table 8.1, p. 243)

ADDITIONAL ITEMS

Yeast nutrient
1× Whirlfloc tablet @ 10 min.

BREWING INSTRUCTIONS

Multistep mash: Use a multistep mash with three rests and a mashout step.

20 minutes @ 147°F (64°C)
20 minutes @ 154°F (68°C)
20 minutes @ 161°F (72°C)
5 minutes @ 169°F (76°C)

Boil: 70 minutes.

Fermentation: Ferment at 52°F (11°C) until specific gravity reaches 1.016 (4.0°P), then raise temperature to 55°F (13°C) until beer reaches terminal gravity. Hold at 55°F (13°C) for an additional three days for diacetyl rest.

Conditioning: Lager 4 weeks at 34°F (1°C).

Carbonation: Carbonate to 2.6 volumes (5.1 g/L) CO_2.

JACK'S ABBY RED TAPE AMBER LAGER

Munich-Style Dunkel

Contributed by Jack Hendler and Joe Connolly, Jack's Abby Craft Lagers, Framingham, Massachusetts

This is the style that started it all for us. We've christened every new brewery with a batch of Red Tape and are still chasing perfection with it.

Batch volume:	5 US gallons (19 L)
Original gravity:	1.050 (12.4°P)
Final gravity:	1.013 (3.2°P)
Color:	24 SRM (47.3 EBC)
Bitterness:	24 IBU
Alcohol:	5% by volume

GRAIN BILL

5 lb. 10 oz (2.55 kg)	dark Munich malt
3 lb. 6 oz. (1.53 kg)	Pilsner malt
1.5 oz. (43 g)	black malt—do not mill; add to mash post-decoction

HOPS

Add 24 IBUs @ 60 min.   Perle or Magnum are two good options.

YEAST

German lager yeast, 34/70 strain (see table 8.1, p. 243)

WATER

Add lactic acid to hit mash pH 5.4. Use a water-to-grist ratio of 3.5 L/kg. Add lactic to the whirlpool to hit wort pH 5.1.

BREWING INSTRUCTIONS

Double-decoction mash option: Mash in only the Pilsner and Munich malts at 149°F (65°C) for 15 minutes. Pull the first decoction, boil for 15 minutes, and return to the main mash to raise the mash temperature to 158°F (70°C) for 30 minutes. Pull the second decoction, boil for 15 minutes, and return to the main mash. Add the black malt at this time and begin the vorlauf (recirculation).

Single decoction mash option: Mash in only the Pilsner and Munich malts at 149°F (65°C) for 30 minutes. Raise the entire mash temperature to 158°F (70°C) and rest for 30 minutes. Pull 25% of the mash for the decoction and boil it for 15 minutes. Return the decocted portion to the mash and add the black malt. Begin the vorlauf.

Infusion option: Perform a single-infusion mash at 154°F (68°C) for 60 minutes. The black malt can be added directly to the beginning of the mash.

Boil: 60 minutes. Add your chosen hops at the start and aim for 24 IBUs.

Fermentation: Pitch yeast at 46°F (8°C), set the fermentation temperature to 48°F (9°C). When it reaches terminal gravity, rack beer to a secondary tank and cool to 40°F (4°C) for a diacetyl rest, which should take about 10 days. Then cool to 33°F (0.5°C).

HEATER ALLEN DUNKEL

Munich-Style Dunkel

Contributed by Lisa Allen, Head Brewer/Owner of Heater Allen Brewing & Gold Dot Beer in McMinnville, Oregon

Heater Allen was founded by Lisa's father Rick Allen in 2007, making Heater Allen one of the first American craft breweries to specialize in lager beer. Firmly ensconced in Oregon's wine country, Heater Allen's beers have earned much acclaim for their quality, and rightfully so. In 2023, Lisa announced a new venture at the same site as Heater Allen with her partner Kevin Davey, formerly of Wayfinder Beer. Gold Dot Beer will be taking the reins of the future of lager beer as of this writing. This beer is that rare thing: a Dunkel from an American brewery that is available year-round.

Batch volume:	5.0 US gallons (19 L)
Original gravity:	1.050 (12.5°P)
Final gravity:	1.012 (3°P)
Color:	12.5 SRM (23.6 EBC)
Bitterness:	23 IBU
Alcohol:	5% by volume

GRAIN BILL

6 lb. 10 oz. (3.0 kg)	Weyermann Munich Malt Type 1
3 lb. 1 oz. (1.4 kg)	Weyermann Munich Malt Type 2
2.6 oz. (75 g)	Weyermann CaraAroma
2.6 oz (75 g)	Weyermann Carafa Special Type 2

HOPS

0.18 oz. (5 g)	German Magnum 15% AA @ first wort hop
0.36 oz. (10 g)	Willamette 4.5% AA @ first wort hop
0.48 oz. (14 g)	Hersbrucker 2.5% AA @ 15 min.
0.96 oz. (27 g)	Hersbrucker 2.5% AA @ whirlpool

WATER

Use filtered water and adjust Ca^{2+} levels with calcium sulfate and calcium chloride. Add directly to the mash when mashing in.

YEAST
German lager yeast, 34/70 strain (see table 8.1, p. 243)

BREWING INSTRUCTIONS
Multistep mash: Use a multistep mash schedule with three rests.
1. Mash in at 122–124°F (50–51°C).
2. Raise mash temperature to 142°F (61°C). Rest for 60 minutes.
3. Raise mash temp to 155°F (68°C). Rest for 30 minutes.
4. Raise mash temp to 161°F (72°C). Rest for 15 minutes, check with iodine for conversion.
5. Raise mash temp to 168°F (76°C). Move into lauter tun.

Boil: 80 minutes.
Fermentation: Ferment 14 days at 51°F (10.5°C); slowly chill over three days to 39°F (4°C) and move into lagering tank.
Conditioning: Lager 6 weeks at 35°F (2°C).
Carbonation: Carbonate to 2.6 volumes (5.1 g/L) CO_2.

Strong Pale Lagers

PRIVATBRAUEREI STÖTTNER EXPORT "HELL"

Export-Style Lager

Contributed by Andreas, Birgit, and Kilian Stöttner, Privatbrauerei Stöttner, Pfaffenberg, Germany

Privatbrauerei Stöttner is a medium-sized, family owned and operated brewery in Pfaffenberg, Bavaria. After WWII, the brewery was limited in how much malt it could use and was forced to only make weak beer. Once these limitations were removed, Stöttner brewed its first high-gravity beer as an export lager, which has been a standard bearer for the brewery ever since. This beer is full-bodied and has sweet malt notes, but is perfectly balanced for drinkability. This export style of beer should not be confused with Helles.

Batch Volume:	5 US gallons (19 L)
Original Gravity:	1.052 (12.8°P)
Final Gravity:	1.006–1.007 (1.6–1.8°P)
Color:	3 SRM (6 EBC)
Bitterness:	25 IBU
Alcohol:	5.5% by volume

GRAIN BILL

13 lb. 1.5 oz. (5.94 kg)	Pilsner malt
2.10 oz. (60 g)	Weyermann CaraHell
0.24 oz. (7 g)	caramel Munich

HOPS

0.08 oz. (2.4 g)	Herkules 17.3% AA @ 65 min.
0.24 oz. (6.7 g)	Perle 8.0% AA @ 30 min.
0.06 oz. (1.6 g)	Diamant or Spalter Select 5.9% AA @ 10 min.

YEAST

German lager yeast, 34/70 strain (see table 8.1, p. 243)

WATER

Hardness of brewing water is 5°dH (degrees German hardness), which converts to 89 ppm as $CaCO_3$.

BREWING INSTRUCTIONS

Mash: Mash in to target 126°F (52°C). Raise mash to 143°F (62°C) for 15 minutes, then heat to 145°F (63°C). Take a decoction portion, raise it 162°F (72°C) for 25 minutes, then heat to 167°F (75°C), then heat to boiling temperature. Return to mash to hit mashout temperature.

Boil: 65 minutes.

Fermentation: Ferment 7 days at 49°F (9.5°C).

Conditioning: Lager 5 days at 38°F (3.5°C). Use indirect cooling in a cold room or cellar to go from 38°F (3.5°C) to an end temperature of 33°F (0.5°C). Leave for 6 weeks.

Carbonation: Carbonate to 2.7 volumes (5.3 g/L) CO_2.

JACK'S ABBY AND WEIHENSTEPHAN FEST OF BOTH WORLDS

Festbier

Contributors: Tobias Zollo, Brewmaster, and Matthias Ebner, Brewing Engineer and Brand Ambassador International, both of Bavarian State Brewery Weihenstephan; Jack Hendler and Joe Connolly, Jack's Abby Craft Lagers, Framingham, Massachusetts

This collaboration was born out of our admiration for Bayerische Staatsbrauerei Weihenstephan and its steadfast commitment to brewing progressive lager. As such an old brewery, Weihenstephan could be forgiven for resting on its laurels, but that is not its way. Touring the state-of-the-art brewery and laboratory space, it is clear that Weihenstephan intends to be a proactive participant in the future of lager. This collaborative recipe was designed to balance an Old World malt profile with American hops, and it incorporates SMARTBEV® frozen liquid yeast developed by the Technical University of Munich (TUM).

Batch volume:	5 US gallons (19 L)
Original gravity:	1.057 (14°P)
Final gravity:	1.011 (2.8°P)
Color:	4 SRM (8 EBC)
Bitterness:	28 IBU
Alcohol:	6.0% by volume

GRAIN BILL

7 lb. 8 oz. (3.40 kg)	Pilsner malt
12 oz. (340 g)	Munich malt

HOPS

0.35 oz. (10 g)	Sterling 9.5% AA @ first wort hops
0.35 oz. (10 g)	Sterling 9.5% AA @ whirlpool
0.60 oz. (17 g)	aromatic European hop @ whirlpool (choose your favorite—aim for ~5% AA)

YEAST

German lager yeast, 34/70 strain (see table 8.1, p. 243)
(We used the SMARTBEV® Lager – TUM 34/70)

BREWING INSTRUCTIONS

Decoction mash: Use a single-decoction method.

1. Mash in and rest at 149°F (65°C) for 45 minutes.
2. Raise temperature of the mash to 158°F (70°C) and rest for 45 minutes.
3. For the decoction, transfer two-thirds of the mash to the lauter tun.
4. Heat remaining portion to boiling and boil for 15 minutes.
5. Add the boiled portion back to the main mash to target 172°F (78°C). Start the vorlauf and the add first wort hops once the runoff has begun.

Boil: 75 minutes.

Fermentation: Pitch yeast at 46°F (8°C), and set the fermentation temperature to 48°F (9°C). Primary fermentation should last 7–10 days.

Conditioning: Once primary fermentation is done, transfer to secondary and lager 4–6 weeks.

ENEGREN BREWING COMPANY MAIBOCK

Maibock

Contributed by Chris Enegren, Enegren Brewing Co., Moorpark, California

Enegren Brewing Co. is a lager-inspired brewery just north of Los Angeles. The brewery's airy courtyard is a small slice of German-inspired beer culture, complete with *Biergarten* tables and plenty of Bavarian flare. The impressively automated modern brewery shows off the brewery's engineering chops and is reminiscent of many modern German breweries. Enegren's range of lagers includes plenty of special event beers like this Maibock, a style traditionally made to be drunk after Lent to celebrate the coming of spring.

Batch Volume:	5 US gallons (19 L)
Original Gravity:	1.068 (16.6°P)
Final Gravity:	1.013 (3.3°P)
Color:	6.1 SRM (12 EBC)
Bitterness:	35 IBU
Alcohol:	7.2% by volume

GRAIN BILL

8 lb. 10.5 oz. (3.93 kg)	Weyermann Barke Pilsner Malt
2 lb. (907 g)	Weyermann Barke Vienna Malt
4.5 oz. (128 g)	Weyermann CaraMunich Type 3

HOPS

0.75 oz. (21 g)	Hallertauer Mittelfrüh 3.6% AA @ 60 min.
0.70 oz. (20 g)	Czech Saaz 3.1% AA @ 20 min.
0.80 oz. (23 g)	Hallertauer Mittelfrüh 3.6% AA @ 20 min.

YEAST

White Labs WLP833 German Bock Lager Yeast

BREWING INSTRUCTIONS

Decoction mash: Use a single-decoction mash method.

1. Mash in at 135°F (57°C) and rest 15 minutes.
2. Raise mash temperature to 140°F (60°C) and rest 50 minutes.
3. Raise mash temperature to 158°F (70°C) for conversion rest.
4. Immediately remove roughly one-third of the mash for the decoction. Heat this portion to boiling and boil for 20 minutes.
5. Return the boiled decoction portion to the main mash to bring the temperature of the total mash to 168°F (76°C) for mashout.

Boil: 90 minutes.

Fermentation: Ferment at 52°F (11°C) and spund the fermentor when gravity reaches 1.020 (5.1°P). After terminal gravity is reached, conduct a diacetyl rest for 7–10 days. Step down fermentation temperature by 3°F (~1.5°C) per day until lagering temperature of 33°F (0.5°C) is reached.

Conditioning: Lager 6 weeks at 33°F (0.5°C).

Carbonation: Set spunding valve for 2.7 volumes (5.3 g/L) CO_2 (or adjust carbonation if needed).

Dark and/or Strong Lagers

BRAUEREI HOFSTETTEN GRANITBOCK

Historical Stone Beer (Steinbier)
Contributed by Peter Krammer, Brauerei Hofstetten,
St. Martin im Mühlkreis, Austria

The Brauerei Hofstetten is located on an estate overlooking the rolling hills of the Mühlviertel in Austria. The family-owned and operated farmhouse brewery is proud to source all its raw materials locally, and brewer and owner Peter Krammer is working to grow even more on the property. The local history of stone masonry and the unique geological nature of the region inspired Hofstetten's Granitbock, an amber Steinbier. Blocks of local granite are superheated and used to caramelize the beer. Fermentation occurs in seventeenth-century stone vessels once used to ferment sauerkraut at a local restaurant.

Batch volume:	5 US gallons (19 L)
Original gravity:	1.073 (17.8°P)
Final gravity:	1.013 (3.2°P)
Color:	51 SRM (100 EBC)
Bitterness:	23 IBU
Alcohol:	7.3% by volume

GRAIN BILL

7 lb. 13 oz. (3.55 kg)	Weyermann Pilsner Malt
1 lb. 13 oz. (0.83 kg)	Weyermann Melanoidin Malt
1 lb. 6 oz. (0.62 kg)	Weyermann CaraMunich Type 2
14.5 oz. (410 g)	Weyermann CaraWheat
7.5 oz. (210 g)	Weyermann CaraAroma
0.7 oz. (20 g)	Weyermann Carafa Type 1

HOPS

0.28 oz (8 g)	Taurus 18.2% AA @ 90 min.
0.88 oz (25 g)	Golding 5.6% AA @ 5 min.

YEAST

German lager yeast, 34/70 strain (see table 8.1, p. 243)

WATER
Ca^{2+} 140.6 ppm; Mg^{2+} 23.1 ppm; Na^+ 9.1 ppm; SO_4^{2-} 12.4 ppm; Cl^- 4.5 ppm; HCO_3^- 99.1 ppm

ADDITIONAL ITEMS
Hofstetten uses granite vats that are unique to the brewery. Granite vessels or stone pieces could be used as a substitute.

BREWING INSTRUCTIONS
Decoction mash: Start mash temperature at 122°F (50°C) for 5 minutes, then raise to 131°F (55°C) for 30 minutes. Raise the mash to 144°F (62°C) and separate a portion of the mash for decoction. Heat the decoction to 162°F (72°C) and rest for 10 minutes, then raise it to 212°F (100°C). Return the decoction to the main mash and rest for 30 minutes at 162°F (72°C). Raise entire mash to 172°F (78°C).

Boil: 100 minutes.

Caramelization: Before pitching the yeast, the Hoftstetten brewers take up to 120 blazing hot granite cubes and hold them into the wort, caramelizing the sugars and imparting many of the characteristic flavors of the beer.

Homebrewers wanting to experiment with this method should be mindful of the surface area of the rocks chosen, as well as their heat tolerances. Medium-sized rocks are easier to handle and will offer plenty of surface area for flavor interaction with the beer. As an igneous rock, granite tolerates temperature well, and its ready availability makes it a reliable choice.

Fermentation: At Hoftstetten, after 10 days in the brewery's granite vats in the cellar at 45–54°F (7–12°C) and only cooled by the outside temperature, the beer is moved to a storage tank, where it is kept for six months at 36°F (2°C) to become smooth and mellow.

Carbonation: Carbonate to 2.53 volumes (5.0 g/L) CO_2.

JACK'S ABBY FRAMINGHAMMER

Baltic Porter

Contributed by Jack Hendler and Joe Connolly, Jack's Abby Craft Lagers, Framingham, Massachusetts

Over the years, we've used our Baltic Porter as a vehicle for exploring the biggest, darkest flavors in lager. This beer has been a bed for adjuncts, additives, and barrel conditioning. Some experiments have never seen the light of day, like the strangely compelling gin barrel–aged Framinghammer. We find that this Baltic Porter recipe is versatile enough for presentation with or without oak contact and additives.

Batch Volume:	5 US gallons (19 L)
Original Gravity:	1.094 (22.5°P)
Final Gravity:	1.020 (5°P)
Color:	105 SRM (207 EBC)
Bitterness:	30 IBU
Alcohol:	10% by volume

GRAIN BILL

14 lb. (6.35 kg)	pale malt
2 lb. 4oz. (1.02 kg)	Munich malt
10 oz. (280 g)	chocolate malt
10 oz. (280 g)	roasted barley
10 oz. (280 g)	caramel Munich
8 oz. (230 g)	brown sugar

HOPS

0.2 oz. (6 g)	Magnum 14.0% AA @ 60 min
0.2 oz. (6 g)	Magnum 14.0% AA @ 30 min.
0.2 oz. (6 g)	Magnum 14.0% AA @ 10 min.

YEAST

German lager yeast, 34/70 strain (see table 8.1, p. 243)

WATER

Add lactic acid to hit mash pH 5.2.

BREWING INSTRUCTIONS

Multistep mash: Mash in at 148°F (64°C) and rest 60 minutes. Raise the temperature of the mash to 158°F (70°C) and rest for 60 minutes. Raise the mash temperature to 172°F (78°C) for mashout.

Boil: 90 minutes.

Fermentation: Ferment for 7 days at 50°F (10°C), then set fermentation temperature to 53°F (12°C) for one week.

Conditioning: Lager two weeks at 40°F (4°C) then cool to near freezing for 4 weeks.

Carbonation: 2.43 volumes (4.8 g/L) CO_2.

EAST ROCK BLACK LAGER
German-Style Schwarzbier

*Contributed by Tim Wilson, East Rock Brewing Company,
New Haven, Connecticut*

East Rock Brewing Company is a family-owned, Bavarian-inspired brewery in New Haven, Connecticut. Owner and head brewer Tim Wilson says this about the Black Lager: "It is our winter seasonal lager. At 6.2% ABV it's not exactly brewed to style, but it really seems to hit the spot on a cold New England night."

Batch volume:	5 US gallons (19 L)
Brewhouse efficiency:	65%
Original gravity:	1.059 (14.5°P)
Final gravity:	1.010 (2.6°P)
Color:	41 SRM (81 EBC)
Bitterness:	20 IBU
Alcohol:	6.2% by volume

GRAIN BILL

5 lb. 4 oz. (2.38 kg)	IREKS Pilsner Malt
5 lb. (2.27 kg)	IREKS Munich Malt
12 oz. (340 g)	IREKS Aroma Malt
12 oz. (340 g)	Weyermann Carafa Special Type 2 (dehusked)
12 oz. (340 g)	flaked oats

HOPS

0.3 oz. (9 g)	German Magnum 16.7% AA @ 60 min.

WATER

Tim Wilson explains: "Our water is soft, and we typically use it as is for this beer, without any salt adjustments. We target a mash pH of 5.2–5.4 and a knockout pH of 5.2. We typically adjust pH with food-grade lactic acid when needed."

YEAST

Fermentis SafLager™ W-34/70

ADDITIONAL ITEMS

0.50 g Whirlfloc G @ 15 min. (granulated Whirlfloc)

0.75 g Yeastex 82 @ 15 min.

BREWING INSTRUCTIONS

Mash: Single-infusion mash for 15 minutes at 148°F (64.5°C). Yes, it is a very short time! Target a liquor-to-grist ratio of 1.8–1.9 qt./lb. (3.7–4.0 L/kg).

Boil: 90 minutes.

Fermentation: Ferment 14 days at 48°F (9°C), then drop to 30–31°F (between −1.0°C and −0.5°C).

Conditioning: Lager 3–4 weeks at 30–31°F (between −1.0°C and −0.5°C).

Carbonation: Carbonate to between 2.50 and 2.55 volumes (4.9–5.0 g/L) CO_2.

HUMAN ROBOT TMAVY 13°

Czech-Style Dark Lager

Contributed by Andrew Foss, Human Robot, Philadelphia, Pennsylvania

Located in Philadelphia, Pennsylvania, Human Robot focuses on brewing Czech- and German-inspired lagers. Head brewer Andrew Foss inherited a unique decoction-capable brewhouse that allows him to implement old-school mashing programs to brew Human Robot's beers. Ordering a "milk tube" of delicious foam is a must for any visit!

Batch volume:	5 US gallons (19 L)
Original gravity:	1.053 (13°P)
Final gravity:	1.012 (3°P)
Color:	dark
Bitterness:	30 IBU
Alcohol:	5.3 % by volume

GRAIN BILL

6 lb. (2.72 kg)	Czech Pilsner malt
3 lb. (1.36 kg)	Czech Munich malt
1 lb. (454 g)	Weyermann Carafa Type 3

– See Additional Notes below.

HOPS

2 oz. (57 g)	Czech Saaz 8% AA @ first wort hops
3 oz. (85 g)	Czech Saaz 8% AA @ 10 min.

– See Additional Notes below.

YEAST

German lager yeast, 34/70 strain (see table 8.1, p. 243)

BREWING INSTRUCTIONS

Decoction mash: Use a hybrid double-decoction method that involves pulling the entire decoction portion at once but returning it to the main mash in two stages.

1. Mash in with approximately 13 qt. (12.3 L) strike water to target a mash temperature of 140°F (60°C). Hold at 140°F (60°C) for 20 minutes.

2. Pull half of the thick mash for the decoction. Transfer to a heated kettle pot and raise the temperature to 158°F (70°C). Stir constantly while heating.

3. Hold heated decoction at 158°F (70°C) for 15 minutes.

4. Turn the heat back on or up and raise to a boil. Once boiling, you should not have to stir anymore. Boil the thick mash for 20 minutes.

5. Begin folding the boiled mash into the main mash until the main mash temperature is 154–161°F (68–72°C). This does not have to be exact, and it is better not to overstir the mash. You should not have to use all the boiling decocted portion to hit this temperature range.

6. Begin boiling the remaining decocted portion in the kettle again for an additional 20 minutes.

7. Begin slowly mixing the twice-boiled decoction back into the main mash until the temperature hits 169°F (76°F). You may not need to use all the boiling decoction to hit this temperature.

8. If you have thick mash left in the kettle, allow it to cool for a few minutes and then add it back to the mash (this prevents overheating the main mash). There is no need to over stir the main mash at this point, the temperature will stabilize during recirculation.

Boil: 75 minutes.

Fermentation: Cool the wort in the fermentor to 43°F (6°C) and oxygenate, then pitch a starter of 34/70 or your favorite lager yeast (Human Robot uses a 34/70 strain for all its lagers.) Hold at 43°F (6°C) for 24 hours. Allow the temperature to rise to between 48°F and 50°F (9–10°C) as fermentation progresses.

Keg conditioning: If you can keg your beer, transfer it to keg when the specific gravity has reached about 1.020 (around 5°P) and store the keg at serving temperature as it finishes fermenting. Use a spunding valve and do not let the head pressure exceed 12 psig (0.8 bar). The beer should mature in about two to three weeks. Serve as is or add finings and serve when bright.

Bottle conditioning: If you are bottling the beer, hold fermentor at 48°F (9°C) until the beer has passed a forced diacetyl test. Homebrewers can use a microwave and water bath to hold a sample of the beer between 170–190°F (77–88°C)

➤

for approximately half an hour. This mimics the natural aging process; once cooled, the sample can be tested for the classic buttery character of diacetyl. Once the beer passes the diacetyl test, prime/re-yeast and bottle as usual. Allow about a month at 50°F (10°C) for the beer to fully referment and carbonate.

ADDITIONAL NOTES

Andrew Foss offers up some useful advice on malts and hops:

Carafa Type 3: "Color obtained from a Carafa malt is largely determined by how finely it is crushed. This recipe has a higher proportion of Carafa Type 3 than our commercial recipe. It is a good idea to buy a little extra and reserve some of the Carafa until vorlauf. If the color looks too light, just add some more in at that point until the wort is sufficiently dark."

Malt flavor: "For more malt flavor, you can adjust the proportions of Pilsner to Munich, or add some melanoidin malt. Avoid the temptation to use crystal/caramel malts, or at least keep them below 2% of total grain bill. Crystal malts tend to make dark lagers taste like British ale styles, even at very low proportions."

Hops: "We tend to use all low-alpha acid hops in all our European-style beers. If desired, you can substitute a higher-alpha acid hop such as Magnum for bittering or first wort additions, but the utilization will be much higher than if you match the given AA%.

BIERSTADT LAGERHAUS SNÜPINATOR DOPPELBOCK

Doppelbock Dunkel

Contributed by Ashleigh Carter, Head Brewer/Co-Owner of Bierstadt Lagerhaus, Denver, Colorado

Much has and will be written about Bierstadt Lagerhaus's Slow Pour Pils, and rightfully so. But that conversation can overshadow the uniquely singular vision and philosophy of Ashleigh Carter and Bill Eye. At Bierstadt Lagerhaus, Ashleigh and Bill make three year-round beers, all on an imported 1930s German brewhouse that has been retrofitted for modern use. Their bold specialization rewards considered consumption, as each of the three beers occupies a well-thought-out flavor profile. Here they share their recipe for a classic strong seasonal bock.

Batch volume:	5 US gallons (19 L)
Original gravity:	1.076 (18.4° P)
Final gravity:	1.014 (3.5° P)
Color:	20 SRM (39.4 EBC)
Bitterness:	24 IBU
Alcohol:	8% by volume

GRAIN BILL

9 lb. 12 oz. (4.42 kg)	Weyermann Barke Munich Malt – Or use 50:50 Weyermann Munich Malt Type 1 and Munich Malt Type 2
2 lb. 7oz. (1.1 kg)	Weyermann Floor-Malted Bohemian Pilsner Malt
1.25 oz. (35 g)	Weyermann Carafa Special Type 3 (a dehusked malt) – **Keep separate** – do not add until sparge

HOPS

0.65 oz. (18 g)   Hallertauer Tradition 6.4% AA @ 60 min.

YEAST

German lager yeast, 34/70 strain (see table 8.1, p. 243)

➤

291

BREWING INSTRUCTIONS

Decoction mash: Use a double-decoction mash method.

1. Set aside Carafa Special Type 3 malt.
2. Mash in the Munich and Pilsner malts at 131°F (55°C) and rest 10 minutes.
3. Increase mash temperature slowly to 144°F (62°C) and rest 30 minutes.
4. Pull one-third of mash for the first decoction and transfer to a separate heating vessel.
5. Heat decoction gently to 160°F (71°C) and rest it for 10 minutes.
6. Bring decoction to the boil and boil it for 20 minutes.
7. Return the boiled decocted portion back to main mash and mix well. The recombined mash should be 160°F (71°C).
8. Rest entire mash at 160°F (71°C) for 40 minutes.
9. Pull one-third of mash for the second decoction and transfer to a separate heating vessel.
10. Bring second decoction to the boil and boil for 20 minutes.
11. Return the boiled decoction back to main mash to hit mashout temperature of 169°F (76°C).
12. After mashout, vorlauf (recirculate) until clear and then begin running off wort.
13. Add the Carafa Special Type 3 to the top of the mash before beginning the sparge.

Boil: 90 minutes.

Fermentation: Ferment 14 days at 48°F (9°C). Reduce the temperature by 2°F (1°C) per day to 40°F (4.5°C). Leave at 40°F (4.5°C) for 5 days or until beer passes a forced diacetyl test. Homebrewers can use a microwave and water bath to hold a sample of the beer between 170–190°F (77–88°C) for approximately half an hour. This mimics the natural aging process; once cooled, the sample can be tested for the classic buttery character of diacetyl. Once the beer passes the diacetyl test, reduce temperature again by 2°F (1°C) per day to at least 34°F (1°C), if not a couple of degrees colder.

Conditioning: Lager for at least 4 weeks at 34°F (1°C) or colder.

Carbonation: Carbonate to 2.6 volumes (5.2 g/L) CO_2.

Nouveau Lagers

HIGHLAND PARK BREWERY TIMBO PILS

West Coast-Style Pilsner

Contributed by Bob Kunz, Highland Park Brewery, Los Angeles, California

Highland Park Brewery in Los Angeles, California, brews wildly progressive lager beer, with a focus on hop-forward styles. Timbo Pils was the first beer to be labeled a West Coast Pilsner, and has inspired many other brewers to follow suit. It bridges the divide between the Old and New Worlds by using Continental hops for the bittering backbone and decidedly American hops for dry hopping. Fine bitterness and a refreshingly dry character make way for huge hop-driven aromatics.

Batch volume:	5 US gallons (19 L)
Original gravity:	1.055 (13.5°P)
Final gravity:	1.011 (2.75°P)
Bitterness:	40 IBU
Dry hop rate:	1.5 oz./gal. (11.23 g/L)
Alcohol:	5.8% by volume

GRAIN BILL

5 lb. 8 oz. (2.5 kg)	Weyermann Floor-Malted Bohemian Pilsner Malt
5 lb. 8 oz. (2.5 kg)	Rahr Standard 2-Row
1 lb. (454 g)	Weyermann Carafoam[1]

EXTRACT & STEEPING GRAIN ALTERNATIVE

7 lb. (3.18 kg)	Pilsner liquid malt extract (LME)
2.5 lb. (1.13 kg)	pale ale LME
1 lb. (454 g)	Weyermann Carafoam – steep for 30 min.

➤

---

[1] Note that Weyermann Carafoam® is sold as Weyermann Carapils® outside of North America. It is not equivalent to "carapils" malts marketed by other maltsters.

HOPS

1.65 oz. (47 g)	Sterling or German Saphir (aim for 4% AA) @ 60 min. (aim for 30 IBU)
0.55 oz. (16 g)	Sterling or German Saphir (aim for 4% AA) @ 30 min. (aim for 10 IBU)
1 oz./gal. (7.5 g/L)	Sterling or German Saphir (aim for 6% AA) @ whirlpool
2.5 oz. (70 g)	Mosaic 12.6% AA @ dry hop – day 6 (see notes)
1.25 oz. (35 g)	Citra 13% AA @ dry hop – day 6
2.5 oz. (70 g)	Mosaic 12.6% AA @ dry hop – day 7
1.25 oz. (35 g)	Citra 13% AA @ dry hop – day 7

Dry hop notes: The total dry hop rate should work out to 1.5 oz./gal. (11.23 g/L). Dry hop on day 6 or when the beer is near terminal gravity at 65°F (18°C). Dry hop 50% of your total dry hops on the first day of dry hopping and the other 50% the day after that. Leave the beer on dry hops for 6–8 days. If your fementor allows it, drop settled hops once a day.

WATER

Ca^{2+} 68 ppm; Mg^{2+} 13 ppm; Na^+ 45 ppm; SO_4^{2-} 42 ppm; Cl^- 105 ppm
Aim for a 2:1 chloride-to-sulfate ratio.

YEAST

Fermentis SafLager™ W-34/70
25–30 g dry yeast per 5 gal. (1.3–1.6 g/L) pitched directly into cooled wort

ADDITIONAL INGREDIENTS

1 mL Fermcap S @ start of boil (to minimize boilovers)
½× Whirlfloc tablet per 5 gal. (19 L) @ 10 min.
3.2 mg/5 gal. zinc @ whirlpool (or use your yeast nutrient of choice, but make sure it has zinc in it)
250 mg/gal. (66 mg/L) ALDC (diacetyl-reducing enzyme) – add prior to cold crashing

BREWING INSTRUCTIONS

The aim is to have made a concentrated wort by the end of the boil that is then immediately diluted. Before starting to brew, prepare at least 1 gal. (3.8 L) filtered water (adjusted to pH 5.0) and store in the fridge so that it is very cold when used.

Infusion mash: Use a single-infusion mash. Mash pH 5.3–5.4. Target mash temperature of 153°F (67°C) and rest for 60 minutes. Raise mash temperature to 168°F (75.5°C) for runoff. Recirculate wort until clear.

Boil: 90 minutes.

Dilution at flameout: Mash and boil to produce a concentrated wort. You should have 4 gal. (15.1 L) of 1.070 SG (17°P) wort at the end of boil. Add 1 gal. (3.8 L) of fridge-cold, filtered water (adjusted to pH 5.0) once you turn off your heat source. This cold-water addition should drop the temperature of the wort down to around 180°F (82°C) and the gravity down to around 1.055 (13.5°P). This will allow you to immediately move your wort out of the range where DMS could be an issue. It will also minimize bitterness pickup from your whirlpool hops and allow you to retain more hop aroma and flavor.

Knockout pH: Wort at knockout should have a pH of 5.0.

Fermentation: Pitch yeast and ferment at 56°F (13°C), although going as high as 62°F (16.5°C) should be fine. Ferment 6–10 days, raising temperature to 65°F (18°C) for diacetyl rest on day 3. Dry hop at 65°F (18°C), following advice in Hops section.

Conditioning: Duration 3–4 weeks. No lagering. Crash beer once it passes a forced diacetyl test. If you have access to ALDC, add 250 mg/gallon 12–18 hours before you are going to crash or package the beer.

Carbonation: Carbonate to 2.7 volumes (5.33 g/L) CO_2.

JACK'S ABBY HOPONIUS UNION

India Pale Lager (a.k.a. Hoppy Lager)

Contributed by Jack Hendler and Joe Connolly, Jack's Abby Craft Lagers, Framingham, Massachusetts

This is a beer that has been part of our lineup since we opened, though the 2011 Hoponius Union might not be recognizable next to its present-day form. Over the years we have made iterative changes to the hop profile and intensity of this beer and stopped our resistance toward calling it an IPL. Today, we think of it as being one of the few representations of old-school, West Coast–style hoppy beer still available in the Northeast.

Batch volume:	5 US gallons (19 L)
Original gravity:	1.060 (14.8°P)
Final gravity:	1.012 (3.0°P)
Color:	6 SRM (11.8 EBC)
Bitterness:	55 IBU
Alcohol:	6.5% by volume

GRAIN BILL

10 lb. 8 oz. (4.76 kg)	US two-row pale malt
8 oz. (227 g)	Munich malt
2.5 oz. (71 g)	caramel malt 10° Lovibond

HOPS

0.20 oz. (6 g)	Centennial 10% AA @ 60 min.
1.00 oz. (28 g)	Centennial 10% AA @ whirlpool
0.60 oz. (17 g)	Citra 13% AA @ whirlpool
2.50 oz. (71 g)	Citra 13% AA @ dry hop – during knockout in fermentor
2.50 oz. (71 g)	Centennial 10% AA @ dry hop – during knockout in fermentor
1.25 oz. (35 g)	Chinook 13% AA @ dry hop – during knockout in fermentor

YEAST

German lager yeast, 34/70 strain (see table 8.1, p. 243)

WATER

Starting with soft water, add 0.1 oz (3 g) calcium sulfate to the mash, then add lactic acid to hit mash pH 5.2.

BREWING INSTRUCTIONS

Step mash option: Mash in at 149°F (65°C) and rest for 45 minutes. Raise mash temperature to 158°F (70°C) and rest for 45 minutes.

Infusion mash option: Mash in at 150°F (65.5°C) and rest for 60 minutes.

Boil: 60 minutes.

Hopping: Add the dry hops to the fermentor before knocking out the wort. Rack the beer to a secondary after the primary fermentation.

Fermentation: Pitch yeast at 51°F (10.5°C), set fermentation temperature to 53°F (11.5°C). Change set temperature to 55°F (13°C) after gravity reaches 1.030 (7.5°P). Slowly cool down to lagering temperature. Total time three weeks.

THREES KICKING AND SCREAMING FOEDER LAGER

Foeder-Aged Pilsner

Contributed by Matt Levy, Threes Brewing, Brooklyn, New York

The brewers at Threes Brewing in Brooklyn inadvertently created the foeder-aged lager style by using their Pilsner to absorb some of the oak character of a new foeder. This was meant as a treatment for the wood before brewing a farmhouse beer, but the results of the aging on the Pilsner led to a change of plan. A light touch with oak is essential for a wood-aged lager: Levy cautions that a heavy hand with oak will be distracting to the drinker and can move the lager out of "pint beer" territory. He recommends considering the oak as an ingredient and planning your recipe accordingly.

Batch Volume:	5 US gallons (19 L)
Original Gravity:	1.048 (12°P)
Final Gravity:	1.009 (2.2°P)
Bitterness:	35 IBU
Alcohol:	5.2% by volume

GRAIN BILL

8 lb. (3.63 kg)   Weyermann Pilsner Malt

Acidulated malt to adjust mash pH to 5.3 (if not using lactic acid)

HOPS

0.24 oz. (6.8 g)	Hallertauer Tradition 6.3% AA @ first wort hops
0.24 oz. (6.8 g)	Hallertauer Tradition 6.3% AA @ 70 min.
0.24 oz. (6.8 g)	Diamant or Spalter Select 5.9% AA @ 20 min.
0.24 oz. (6.8 g)	Hallertauer Tradition 6.3% AA @ 20 min.
0.56 oz. (16 g)	Diamant or Spalter Select 5.9% AA @ whirlpool at 205–210°F (96–99°C)
1.59 oz. (45 g)	Hersbrucker 4.2% AA @ whirlpool at 205–210°F (96–99°C)

WATER

Ca^{2+} 60 ppm; Mg^{2+} 2.5 ppm; Na^+ 17 ppm; SO_4^{2-} 60 ppm; Cl^- 60 ppm; HCO_3^- 35 ppm. Add lactic acid to sparge water to keep mash pH in range of 5.2–5.8 throughout runoff.

YEAST
Weihenstephan 34/70

ADDITIONAL ITEMS
Lactic acid to adjust mash pH to 5.3 (if not using acidulated malt)
1× Whirlfloc tablet @ 10 min.

BREWING INSTRUCTIONS
Infusion mash: Single-infusion mash at 148°F (64.5°C) for 90 minutes. Then raise mash temperature to 168°F (75.5°C) for 10 minutes. Vorlauf (recirculate) until clear, then run off.

Boil: 90 minutes.

Fermentation: Pitch 1.5 million cells/mL/°Plato of healthy, robust lager yeast. Equates to 57 grams of dry yeast. Ferment at 48°F (9°C) until within about 4° specific gravity (1°P) of target final gravity, then raise the temperature to 55°F (13°C) degrees for a diacetyl rest (typically, this is days 7–10). Around day 14, cool beer down to lagering temperatures.

Conditioning: Lager for 4 weeks at 34°F (1°C).

Oaking post-conditioning: If using a foeder, send to foeder at 34°F (1°C) with glycol coils chilling the foeder and allow the beer to undergo cold maturation on oak until it tastes done. Matt Levy continues: "The goal is for a subtle oak accent rather than a dominating note. This will vary depending on the intensity of the wood and the size of the vessel. At Threes, we cold condition for six weeks in our 30 bbl. (35.2 hL) foeder and three weeks in our 15 bbl. (17.6 hL) foeder."

If using oak chips, add them to your conditioning vessel after four weeks of lagering and cold condition on oak chips until it tastes done, again looking for a subtle oak accent. The time to reach this stage will vary greatly depending on the intensity of the wood and the amount of chips used.

The beer will need to be transferred out of or off the oak prior to packaging.

Carbonation: Carbonate to 2.6 volumes (5.2 g/L) CO_2.

Smoked Lagers

JACK'S ABBY FIRE IN THE HAM

Rauchbier Hell

Contributed by Jack Hendler and Joe Connolly, Jack's Abby Craft Lagers, Framingham, Massachusetts

We've been brewing this beer at Jack's Abby since 2012. This beer has devoted fans who wonder why we don't brew it year-round, but our annual cadence feels about right. In recent years we've taken to open fermenting this beer and have enjoyed the results.

Batch volume:	5 US gallons (19 L)
Original gravity:	1.053 (13°P)
Final gravity:	1.010 (2.6°P)
Color:	3 SRM (6 EBC)
Bitterness:	20 IBU
Alcohol:	5.4% by volume

GRAIN BILL

8 lb. 13 oz. (4.0 kg)	beechwood-smoked malt
1 lb. (454 g)	Munich malt
4 oz. (113 g)	foam/chit/dextrin malt

HOPS

Add 20 IBUS with noble-type hops added @ 60 min.

YEAST

German lager yeast, 34/70 strain (see table 8.1, p. 243)

WATER

Add lactic acid to hit mash pH 5.5.
Add lactic to the whirlpool to hit wort pH 5.2.

BREWING INSTRUCTIONS

Double-decoction mash option: In a secondary mash kettle, mash in 25% grist (this is the first decoction) at 152°F (67°C) for 15 minutes, then raise to boil for 15 minutes. Immediately following the decoction coming to a boil, mash in remaining 75% of the grist at 152°F (67°C) in your main vessel. After the 15 minute boil, add the first decoction portion to the main mash, which should raise the temperature of the combined mash to 162°F (72°C). Rest for 30 minutes, then remove 25% of the mash for a second decoction and boil it for 15 minutes. Combine the mashes, vorlauf, and start the runoff.

Single-decoction mash option: Mash in 100% of the grist at 152°F (67°C) for 30 minutes. Raise the temperature of the entire mash to 162°F (72°C) for 30 minutes. Remove 25% of the mash and boil for 15 minutes. Return the decoction to the mash, then vorlauf and start the runoff.

Step mash option: Mash in 100% of the grist at 152°F (67°C) using a water-to-grist ratio of 3 L/kg. After 45 minutes, add 1 part boiling water to raise temperature to 162°F (72°C) for 30 minutes.

Infusion mash option: A single-infusion can be used. Mash in at 154°F (68°C) for 60 minutes.

Boil: 60 minutes.

Fermentation: Pitch yeast at 46°F (8°C), and set fermentation temperature to 48°F (9°C). When the beer reaches terminal gravity, rack to a secondary tank and cool to 40°F (4°C) for diacetyl rest, which takes about 10 days. Then cool to 33°F (1°C) for two weeks before packaging.

COUNTER WEIGHT BREWING
DRUDENHAUS RAUCHBIER

Märzen Rauchbier

Contributed by Matt Westfall, Counter Weight Brewing Company, Cheshire, Connecticut

Matt Westfall and his team at Counter Weight Brewing have been invested in lager from the start. While the brewery may be better known for its IPA, the taproom makes clear Counter Weight's love and dedication to lager beer. The lager room overlooks a custom Kaspar Schulz lager brewing system, complete with open fermentation tanks. The team's particular soft spot for the smoky, intense flavors of Bamberg smoked beer gives us this recipe.

Batch Volume:	5 US gallons (19 L)
Original Gravity:	1.056 (13.8°P)
Final Gravity:	1.013 (3.4°P)
Color:	22 SRM
Bitterness:	25 IBU (43.3 EBC)
Alcohol:	5.6% by volume

GRAIN BILL

10 lb. (4.54 kg)	Weyermann Beech Smoked Barley Malt
10 oz. (284 g)	Weyermann Munich Malt Type 1
6.4 oz (182 g)	Carafa Special Type 2
	– added to mash during vorlauf

HOPS

0.4 oz (11 g)	German Magnum 14.5% AA @ 60 min.
0.6 oz (17 g)	Hallertauer Mittelfrüh 4% AA @ 10 min.

WATER

Ca^{2+} 55 ppm; Mg^{2+} 8 ppm; Na^+ 22 ppm; SO_4^{2-} 8 ppm; Cl^- 25 ppm; HCO_3^- 128 ppm.

YEAST

German lager yeast, 34/70 strain (see table 8.1, p. 243)

BREWING INSTRUCTIONS

Target a mash pH of 5.3–5.4. Acidify mash with 1 mL of lactic acid for a 5 gal. (19 L) batch.

Decoction mash option: Use a single-decoction mash method.

1. Set aside the Carafa malt. Mash in the beech-smoked and Munich malts at 122°F (50°C) and rest 10 minutes.
2. Raise mash temperature to 150°F (65.5 C) and rest for 45 minutes.
3. Remove one-third of the mash for the decoction.
4. Bring the decoction to the boil and boil for 10 minutes.
5. Return the decocted portion back to the main mash and stir to hit a temperature of 170°F (77°C).
6. Add the Carafa Special Type 2 malt and begin vorlauf (recirculation).
7. Sparge with 170°F (77°C) water.

Infusion mash option: Use a single-infusion mash.

1. Set aside the Carafa malt.
2. Mash in the beech-smoked and Munich malts at 149°F (65°C) for 60 minutes.
3. Add the Carafa Special Type 2 malt during vorlauf.
4. Sparge with 170°F (77°C) water.

Boil: 90 minutes.

Fermentation: Ferment at 50°F (10°C) for 10 days. When fermenting beer reaches 8° specific gravity (2°P) above expected terminal gravity, increase the temperature to 60°F (15.5°C) and hold for two days for diacetyl rest.

Conditioning: Lager 4 weeks at 34°F (1°C).

Carbonation: Carbonate to 2.6 volumes (5.14 g/L) CO_2.

BIBLIOGRAPHY

Alberts, Brian. 2021. "Name Your Poison — Americans' 19th-Century Quest for 'Pure' Beer." *Stories* (blog), Good Beer Hunting. August 26, 2021. https://www.goodbeerhunting.com/blog/2021/8/26/name-your-poison -americans-19th-century-quest-for-pure-beer.

Alberts, Leendert. 2019. "Zatec, cradle of Saaz hops and landmark of commercial hop cultivation." *Brewery History*, no. 181 (Winter): 43–50.

AMBA (American Malting Barley Association). 2023. *Malting Barley Breeding Guidelines: Ideal Commercial Malt Criteria; June 2021.* PDF available via news release "AMBA Guidelines for Malting Barley Breeders," January 26, 2023. https://ambainc.org/news-details.php?id=63d2780a0c948.

Annemüller, Gerolf, Hans-J. Manger, and Peter Lietz. 2011. *The Yeast in the Brewery: Management - Pure Yeast Cultures - Propagation.* 1st English edition. Berlin: VLB (Versuchs- und Lehranstalt für Brauerei).

Back, Werner, Martina Gastl, Martin Krottenthaler, Ludwig Narziß, and Martin Zarnkow. 2020. *Brewing Techniques in Practice: An In-Depth Review of Beer Production with Problem Solving Strategies.* Nuremberg: Fachverlag Hans Carl.

Bamforth, Charles W. 2012. *Foam.* Practical Guides for Beer Quality. St. Paul, MN: American Society of Brewing Chemists.

Bamforth, Charles. 2023. "Provocation: Prolonged Maturation of Beer Is of Unproven Benefit". *Journal of the Institute of Brewing* 129(1): 3–14. https://doi.org/10.58430/jib.v129i1.6.

Basařová, Gabriela, Jan Šavel, Petr Basař, Tomáš Lejsek, and Pavlína Basařová. 2017. *The Comprehensive Guide to Brewing: From Raw Material to Packaging.* Nuremberg: Fachverlag Hans Carl.

Benbow, Mark. 2018. "German Immigrants in the United States Brewing Industry: 1840–1895." Immigrant Entrepreneurship. Last updated August 22, 2018. German Historical Institute. http://www.immigrantentrepreneurship .org/entries/german-immigrants-in-the-united-states-brewing-industry/.

Bergin, Sean A., Stephen Allen, Conor Hession, Eoin Ó Cinnéide, Adam Ryan, Kevin P. Byrne, Tadhg Ó Cróinín, Kenneth H. Wolfe, and Geraldine Butler. "Identification of European isolates of the lager yeast parent *Saccharomyces eubayanus.*" *FEMS Yeast Research* 22(1): foac053. https://doi.org/10.1093 /femsyr/foac053.

Booth, David. 1829. *Art of Brewing.* London: Baldwin and Cradock.

Brewers Association. 2019. *Draught Beer Quality Manual.* Technical Committee of the Brewers Association. Boulder, CO: Brewers Publications.

Briggs, D.E., J.S. Hough, R. Stevens, and T.W. Young. 1981. *Malting and Brewing Science: Malt and Sweet Wort, Volume 1.* 2nd edition. London: Chapman and Hall.

Carpenter, Dave. 2017. *Lager: The Definitive Guide to Tasting and Brewing the World's Most Popular Beer Styles.* Minneapolis, MN: Voyageur Press.

Casey, G.P. 1996. "Practical applications of pulsed field electrophoresis and yeast chromosome fingerprinting in brewing QA and R&D." *Master Brewers Association of the Americas Technical Quarterly* 33(1): 1–10.

Chenot, Cécile, William Donck, Philippe Janssens, and Sonia Collin. 2022. "Malt and Hop as Sources of Thiol S-Conjugates: Thiol-Releasing Property of Lager Yeast during Fermentation." *Journal of Agricultural and Food Chemistry* 70(10): 3272–3279. https://doi.org/10.1021/acs.jafc.1c07272.

de Clerck, Jean. 1957. *A Textbook of Brewing*. London: Chapman & Hall.

de la Cerda Garcia-Caro, Roberto, Georgia Thompson, Penghan Zhang, Karsten Hokamp, Fiona Roche, Silvia Carlin, Urska Vrhovsek, and Ursula Bond. 2022. "Enhanced flavour profiles through radicicol induced genomic variation in *S. pastorianus* lager yeast." Preprint, submitted May 17, 2022. https://www.biorxiv.org/content/10.1101/2022.05.17.491830v1.

Dredge, Mark. 2019. *A Brief History of Lager: 500 Years of the World's Favourite Beer*. London: Kyle Books.

Dvořák, Josef, Pavel Dostálek, Vladimír Kellner, Pavel Čejka, Jiří Čulík, Tomáš Horák, and Marie Jurková. 2008. "Significance of SO_2 in beer. Part 3: Factors which effect on production of sulphur dioxide during brewing fermentation." [In English and Czech]. *Kvasny prumysl* 54(5): 142–148. https://doi.org/10.18832/kp2008008.

Engan, S., and O. Aubert. 1977. "Relations between fermentation temperature and the formation of some flavour components." In *European Brewery Convention: proceedings of the 16th Congress, Amsterdam 1977*, 591–607. Rotterdam: European Brewery Convention.

Enge, Jan, Pavel Šemík, Josef Korbel, Jiří Šrogl, and Miroslav Sekora. 2005. "Technological aspects of infusion and decoction mashing" [In English and Czech]. *Kvasny prumysl* 51(5): 158–165. https://doi.org/10.18832/kp2005008.

Evans, Evan. 2021. *Mashing*. St. Paul, MN: American Society of Brewing Chemists.

Federated Institutes of Brewing. 1897. "Modification and Shortening of Brewing Processes and their Importance in the Production of Rich, Full-mouthed Beers which retain a 'Head.' By W. Windisch (Wochensch. Brau., 1897, 14, 21—23)." *Journal of the Federated Institutes of Brewing* 3:146–148.

Fischer, G. 1902. "Some Notes on Hops." In *Transactions of the American Brewing Institute: Vol. 1; May 1901—September 1902*. New York.

Gallone, Brigida, Jan Steensels, Troels Prahl, Leah Soriaga, Veerle Saels, Beatriz Herrera-Malaver, Adriaan Merlevede, Miguel Roncoroni, Karin Voordeckers, and Loren Miraglia. 2016. "Domestication and Divergence of *Saccharomyces cerevisiae* Beer Yeasts." *Cell* 1397–1410.e16. https://doi.org/10.1016/j.cell.2016.08.020.

Gallone, Brigida, Jan Steensels, Stijn Mertens, Maria C. Dzialo, Jonathan L. Gordon, Ruben Wauters, Florian A. Theßeling, et al. 2019. "Interspecific hybridization facilitates niche adaptation in beer yeast." *Nature Ecology and Evolution* 3:1562–1575. https://doi.org/10.1038/s41559-019-0997-9.

Garshol, Lars Marius. 2020. *Historical Brewing Techniques: The Lost Art of Farmhouse Brewing*. Boulder, CO: Brewers Publications.

Gibson, Brian, and Gianni Liti. 2014. "*Saccharomyces pastorianus*: Genomic insights inspiring innovation for industry." *Yeast* 32(1): 17–27. https://doi.org/10.1002/yea.3033.

Gibson, Brian, Erna Storgårds, Kristoffer Krogerus, and Virve Vidgren. 2013. "Comparative physiology and fermentation performance of Saaz and Frohberg lager yeast strains and the parental species *Saccharomyces eubayanus*." *Yeast* 30(7): 255–266. https://doi.org/10.1002/yea.2960.

Gloetzl, J. 1967. "Principles of Wort Treatment." *Master Brewers Association of the Americas Technical Quarterly* 4(3): 185–191.

Gyurchev, N.Y., Á. Coral Medina, S.M. Weening, S. Almayouf, N.G.A. Kuijpers, E. Nevoigt, and E.J. Louis. 2022. "Beyond *Saccharomyces pastorianus* for modern lager brews: Exploring non-*cerevisiae Saccharomyces* hybrids with heterotic maltotriose consumption and novel aroma profile." *Frontiers in Microbiology* 13:1025132. https://doi.org/10.3389/fmicb.2022.1025132.

Herb, Dustin, Tanya Filichkin, Scott Fisk, Laura Helgerson, Patrick Hayes, Amanda Benson, Veronica Vega, et al. 2017. "Malt Modification and its Effects on the Contributions of Barley Genotype to Beer Flavor." *Journal of the American Society of Brewing Chemists* 75(4): 354–362. https://doi.org/10.1094/ASBCJ-2017-4976-01.

Hieronymus, Stan. 2012. *For the love of Hops: The Practical Guide to Aroma, Bitterness and the Culture of Hops.* Boulder, CO: Brewers Publications.

Hill, Annie E., and Graham G. Stewart. 2019. "Free Amino Nitrogen in Brewing." *Fermentation* 5(1): 22. https://doi.org/10.3390/fermentation5010022.

Holle, Stephen R. 2003. *A Handbook of Basic Brewing Calculations.* St. Paul, MN: Master Brewers Association of the Americas.

Hutzler, Mathias, Jana Čmielová, Tobias Frank, Andreas Brandl, Fritz Jacob, and Maximilian Michel. 2018. "Identification of Microflora in a Biological Brewer's Wort Acidification Process Run Continuously for 20 Years." *Fermentation* 4(3): 51. https://doi.org/10.3390/fermentation4030051.

Hutzler, M., L. Narziß, D. Stretz, K. Haslbeck, T. Meier-Dörnberg, H. Walter, M. Schäfer, T. Zollo, F. Jacob, and M. Michel. 2019. "Resurrection of the lager strain *Saccharomyces pastorianus* TUM 35." *BrewingScience* 72: 69–77. https://doi.org/10.23763/BrSc19-06hutzler.

Hutzler, Mathias, John P. Morrissey, Andreas Laus, Franz Meussdoerffer, and Martin Zarnkow. 2023. "A new hypothesis for the origin of the lager yeast *Saccharomyces pastorianus*." *FEMS Yeast Research* 23:foad023. https://doi.org/10.1093/femsyr/foad023.

Jenkins, Cheryl L., Alan I. Kennedy, Jeff A. Hodgson, Pat Thurston, and Katherine A. Smart. 2003. "Impact of Serial Repitching on Lager Brewing Yeast Quality." *Journal of the American Society of Brewing Chemists* 61(1): 1–9. https://doi.org/10.1094/ASBCJ-61-0001.

Kieninger, H. 1977. "Current lager beer technology in continental European breweries and especially in German breweries." *Journal of the Institute of Brewing* 83(2): 72–77. https://doi.org/10.1002/j.2050-0416.1977.tb06415.x.

Krofta, K. 2003. "Comparison of quality parameters of Czech and foreign hop varieties." *Plant, Soil and Environment* 49(6): 261–268. https://doi.org/10.17221/4123-PSE.

Krogerus, Kristoffer, Frederico Magalhães, Virve Vidgren, and Brian Gibson. 2015. "New lager yeast strains generated by interspecific hybridization." *Journal of Industrial Microbiology and Biotechnology* 42:769–778. https://doi.org/10.1007/s10295-015-1597-6.

Kucharczyk, Krzysztof, and Tadeusz Tuszyński. 2015. "The effect of wort aeration on fermentation, maturation and volatile components of beer produced on an industrial scale." *Journal of the Institute of Brewing* 121(3):349–355. https://doi.org/10.1002/jib.242.

Kunze, Wolfgang. 1999. *Technology Brewing and Malting*. International edition. Berlin: VLB (Versuchs- und Lehranstalt für Brauerei).

Kunze, Wolfgang. 2014. *Technology Brewing and Malting*. Translated by Sue Pratt. 5th English edition. Berlin: VLB (Versuchs- und Lehranstalt für Brauerei).

Lawrence, Stephen J., Sarah Nicholls, Wendy G. Box, Raffaele Sbuelz, Francis Bealin-Kelly, Barry Axcell, and Katherine A. Smart. 2013. "The Relationship Between Yeast Cell Age, Fermenter Cone Environment, and Petite Mutant Formation in Lager Fermentations." *Journal of the American Society of Brewing Chemists* 71(2): 90–96. https://doi.org/10.1094/ASBCJ-2013-0405-01.

Layfield, J. Blake, and John D. Sheppard. 2015. "What Brewers Should Know About Viability, Vitality, and Overall Brewing Fitness: A Mini Review." *Master Brewers Association of the Americas Technical Quarterly* 52(3): 132–140. http://doi.org/10.1094/TQ-52-3-0719-01.

Lewis, Michael J., and Tom W. Young. 2001. *Brewing*. 2nd edition. New York: Kluwer Academic / Plenum Publishers.

Masschelein, Charles. 1986. "The biochemistry of maturation." *Journal of the Institute of Brewing* 92(3): 213–219. https://doi.org/10.1002/j.2050-0416.1986.tb04403.x.

Mayer, Susanna, and Dirk W. Lachenmeier. 2015. "The trend of reduced hop-content in Pilsner-type beer in Germany. A change in taste?" *Journal of the Institute of Brewing* 121(1): 28–30. https://doi.org/10.1002/jib.188.

McCaig, Robert, and D.S. Bendiak. 1985. "Yeast Handling Studies. II. Temperature of Storage of Pitching Yeast." *Journal of the American Society of Brewing Chemists* 43(2): 119–122. https://doi.org/10.1094/ASBCJ-43-0119.

Meier-Dörnberg, Tim, Mathias Hutzler, Maximilian Michel, Frank-Jürgen Methner, and Fritz Jacob. 2017. "The Importance of a Comparative Characterization of *Saccharomyces Cerevisiae* and *Saccharomyces Pastorianus* Strains for Brewing." *Fermentation* 3(3): 41. https://doi.org/10.3390/fermentation3030041.

Mertens, Stijn, Jan Steensels, Veerle Saels, Gert De Rouck, Guido Aerts, and Kevin J. Verstrepen. 2015. "A Large Set of Newly Created Interspecific *Saccharomyces* Hybrids Increases Aromatic Diversity in Lager Beers." *Applied and Environmental Microbiology* 81(23): 8202–8214. https://doi.org/10.1128/AEM.02464-15.

Mikyška, Alexandr, Martin Dušek, and Pavel Čejka. 2019. "Influence of barley variety and growing locality on the profile of flavonoid polyphenols in malt." [In English and Czech]. *Kvasny prumysl* 65(5): 149–157. https://doi.org/10.18832/kp2019.65.149.

Mikyška, Alexandr, Vratislav Psota, Katarína Bojnanská, Miroslav Ondrejovič, Markéta Musilová, Alena Bezdíčková, and Marta Zavřelová. 2022. "Old but still good – Comparison of malting and brewing characteristics of current and historical malting barley varieties." [In English and Czech]. *Kvasny prumysl* 68(6): 663–673. https://doi.org/10.18832/kp2022.68.663.

Montanari, Luigi, Simona Floridi, Ombretta Marconi, Michela Tironzelli, and Paolo Fantozzi. 2005. "Effect of mashing procedures on brewing." *European Food Research and Technology* 221:175–179. https://doi.org/10.1007/s00217-005-1166-8.

Moritz, Edward Ralph, and George Harris Morris. 1891. *A Text-book of the Science of Brewing.* London: E. and F.N. Spon.

Morrissy, Campbell P., Michael Féchir, Harmonie M. Bettenhausen, Karli R. Van Simaeys, Scott Fisk, Javier Hernandez, Kyle Mathias, Amanda Benson, Thomas H. Shellhammer, and Patrick M. Hayes. 2022. "Continued Exploration of Barley Genotype Contribution to Base Malt and Beer Flavor Through the Evaluation of Lines Sharing Maris Otter® Parentage." *Journal of the American Society of Brewing Chemists* 80(3): 201-214. https://doi.org/10.1080/03610470.2021.1952509.

Müller-Auffermann, K., A. Caldera, F. Jacob, and M. Hutzler. 2015. "Characterization of different bottom fermenting *Saccharomyces pastorianus* brewing yeast strains." *BrewingScience* 68:46–57.

Narziß, L. 1966. "Developments in the Malting and Brewing Industries in Germany." *Journal of the Institute of Brewing* 72(1): 13–24. https://doi.org/10.1002/j.2050-0416.1966.tb02927.x.

Narziss, L. 1974. "New barley varieties in continental Europe." *Journal of the Institute of Brewing* 80(3): 259-270. https://doi.org/10.1002/j.2050-0416.1974.tb03615.x.

Narziss, L. 1984. "The German Beer Law." *Journal of the Institute of Brewing* 90(6): 351–358. https://doi.org/10.1002/j.2050-0416.1984.tb04288.x.

Nobis, Arndt, Benjamin Berg, Martina Gastl, and Thomas Becker. 2022. "Changes in bioavailability of zinc during malting process and wort production." *European Food Research and Technology* 249:157–165. https://doi.org/10.1007/s00217-022-04141-5.

Noonan, Gregory J. 2003. *New Brewing Lager Beer: The Most Comprehensive Book for Home and Microbrewers.* Boulder, CO: Brewers Publications.

Ockert, Karl, ed. 2006a. *Fermentation, Cellaring, and Packaging Operations.* Practical Handbook for the Specialty Brewer, vol. 2. St. Paul, MN: Master Brewers Association of the Americas.

Ockert, Karl, ed. 2006b. *Raw Materials and Brewhouse Operations.* Practical Handbook for the Specialty Brewer, vol. 1. St. Paul, MN: Master Brewers Association of the Americas.

Ogle, Maureen. 2006. *Ambitious Brew: The Story of American Beer.* Orlando: Harcourt.

Olšovská, Jana, Pavel Čejka, Karel Sigler, and Věra Hönigová. 2014. "The Phenomenon of Czech Beer: A Review." *Czech Journal of Food Sciences* 32(4): 309–313. https://doi.org/10.17221/455/2013-CJFS.

Palmer, John, and Colin Kaminski. 2013. *Water: A Comprehensive Guide for Brewers.* Boulder, CO: Brewers Publications.

Pattinson, Ronald. 2011. *Decoction!* Self-published, Lulu Press, Inc.

Pfisterer, Egbert, Ian Richardson, and Attila Soti. 2004. "Control of Hydrogen Sulfide in Beer with a Copper Electrolysis System." *Master Brewers Association of the Americas Technical Quarterly* 41(1): 50–52.

Pires, Eduardo, José A. Teixeira, Tomás Brányik, and António A. Vicente. 2014. "Yeast: The soul of beer's aroma—A review of flavour-active esters and higher alcohols produced by the brewing yeast." *Applied Microbiology and Biotechnology* 98:1938–1949. https://doi.org/10.1007/s00253-013-5470-0.

Poreda, Aleksander, Agata Czarnik, Marek Zdaniewicz, Marek Jakubowski, and Piotr Antkiewicz. 2014. "Corn grist adjunct – Application and influence on the brewing process and beer quality." *Journal of the Institute of Brewing* 120(1): 77–81. https://doi.org/10.1002/jib.115.

Praet, Tatiana, Filip van Opstaele, Brecht de Causmaecker, Giulia Bellaio, Gert de Rouck, Guido Aerts, and Luc de Cooman. 2015. "De novo Formation of Sesquiterpene Oxidation Products during Wort Boiling and Impact of the Kettle Hopping Regime on Sensory Characteristics of Pilot-Scale Lager Beers." *BrewingScience* 68:130–145.

Rühl, C. 1910. "Lager Beer. Part III.-Fermentation." *Journal of the Institute of Brewing* 16(6): 545–558. https://doi.org/10.1002/j.2050-0416.1910.tb02266.x.

Sayre-Chavez, Brooke, Harmonie Bettenhausen, Sarah Windes, Patricia Aron, Luis Cistué, Scott Fisk, Laura Helgerson, et al. 2022. "Genetic basis of barley contributions to beer flavor." *Journal of Cereal Science* 104:103430. https://doi.org/10.1016/j.jcs.2022.103430.

Schwarz, P.B., and R.E. Pyler. 1984. "Lipoxygenase and Hydroperoxide Isomerase Activity of Malting Barley." *Journal of the American Society of Brewing Chemists* 42(2): 47–53. https://doi.org/10.1094/ASBCJ-42-0047.

Somani, Abhishek, Francis Bealin-Kelly, Barry Axcell, and Katherine A. Smart. 2012. "Impact of Storage Temperature on Lager Brewing Yeast Viability, Glycogen, Trehalose, and Fatty Acid Content." *Journal of the American Society of Brewing Chemists* 70(2): 123–130. https://doi.org/10.1094/ASBCJ-2012-0427-01.

Southby, E.R. 1885. *A Systematic Handbook of Practical Brewing.* 2nd edition. Self-published, London.

Stewart, Graham G., Annie E. Hill, and Inge Russell. 2013. "125th Anniversary Review: Developments in brewing and distilling yeast strains." *Journal of the Institute of Brewing* 119(4): 202–220. https://doi.org/10.1002/jib.104.

Takoi, Kiyoshi, Koichiro Koie, Yutaka Itoga, Yuta Katayama, Masayuki Shimase, Yasuyuki Nakayama, and Junji Watari. 2010. "Biotransformation of Hop-Derived Monoterpene Alcohols by Lager Yeast and Their Contribution to the Flavor of Hopped Beer." *Journal of Agricultural and Food Chemistry* 58(8): 5050–5058. https://doi.org/10.1021/jf1000524.

Techakriengkrai, Ittipon, Alistair Paterson, and John Piggott. 2004. "Relationships of Sweetness in Lager to Selected Volatile Congeners." *Journal of the Institute of Brewing* 110(4): 360–366. https://doi.org/10.1002/j.2050-0416.2004.tb00633.x.

Thausing, Julius E. 1882. *The Theory and Practice of the Preparation of Malt and the Fabrication of Beer.* H.C. Baird & Company.

Thevenot, G. 1897. "The Formation and Consistency of Foam, with Special Reference to the Influence of Albuminoids." *American Brewers' Review* 10, no. 7 (January 20): 241–242.

Vermeulen, C., I. Lejeune, T.T.H. Tran, and S. Collin. 2006. "Occurrence of Polyfunctional Thiols in Fresh Lager Beers." *Journal of Agricultural and Food Chemistry* 54(14): 5061–5068. https://doi.org/10.1021/jf060669a.

Wahl, Arnold S., and Robert Wahl. (1937) 2014. *Wahl Handybook of the American Brewing Industry: Vol. 1; Beer: From the Expert's Viewpoint.* Chicago: Wahl Institute. Reprint, Cleveland: BeerBooks.com. Citations refer to the reprint edition.

Wahl, R. 1897. "Windisch on the Functions of the Albuminoids in the Preparation of Beer." *American Brewers' Review* 10, no. 8 (February 20): 281–284.

Wendland, Jürgen. 2014. "Lager Yeast Comes of Age." *Eukaryotic Cell* 13(10): 1256–1265. https://doi.org/10.1128/ec.00134-14.

White, Chris, and Jamil Zainasheff. 2010. *Yeast: The Practical Guide to Beer Fermentation.* Boulder, CO: Brewers Publications.

Windes, S., H.M. Bettenhausen, K.R. Van Simaeys, J. Clawson, S. Fisk, A.L. Heuberger, J. Lim, S.H. Queisser, T.H. Shellhammer, and P.M. Hayes. 2020. "Comprehensive Analysis of Different Contemporary Barley Genotypes Enhances and Expands the Scope of Barley Contributions to Beer Flavor." *Journal of the American Society of Brewing Chemists* 79(3): 281–305. https://doi.org/10.1080/03610470.2020.1843964.

Wurzbacher, M., O. Franz, and W. Back. 2005. "Control of sulphite formation of lager yeast." *BrewingScience* 59:10–17.

Yang, Dongsheng. 2019. "Influence of Top Pressure on the Flavor and Sensorial Characteristics of Lager Beer." *Journal of the American Society of Brewing Chemists* 77(3): 170–178. https://doi.org/10.1080/03610470.2019.1603023.

INDEX